Recording on the Go: The Definitive Guide to Live Recording

Gary Gottlieb and Paul Hennerich

Course Technology PTR
A part of Cengage Learning

COURSE TECHNOLOGY
CENGAGE Learning™

Australia • Brazil • Japan • Korea • Mexico • Singapore • Spain • United Kingdom • United States

COURSE TECHNOLOGY
CENGAGE Learning

Recording on the Go: The Definitive Guide to Live Recording
Gary Gottlieb and Paul Hennerich

Publisher and General Manager, Course Technology PTR: Stacy L. Hiquet

Associate Director of Marketing: Sarah Panella

Manager of Editorial Services: Heather Talbot

Marketing Manager: Mark Hughes

Acquisitions Editor: Orren Merton

Development Editor: Cathleen D. Small

Project Editor/Copy Editor: Cathleen D. Small

Technical Reviewer: Per Boysen

PTR Editorial Services Coordinator: Erin Johnson

Interior Layout Tech: ICC Macmillan Inc.

Cover Designer: Mike Tanamachi

Indexer: Sharon Shock

Proofreader: Gene Redding

For product information and technology assistance, contact us at **Cengage Learning Customer & Sales Support, 1-800-354-9706**

For permission to use material from this text or product, submit all requests online at **www.cengage.com/permissions** Further permissions questions can be emailed to **permissionrequest@cengage.com**

All trademarks are the property of their respective owners.

Library of Congress Control Number: 2008931029

ISBN-13: 978-1-59863-501-0

ISBN-10: 1-59863-501-8

Course Technology
25 Thomson Place
Boston, MA 02210
USA

Cengage Learning is a leading provider of customized learning solutions with office locations around the globe, including Singapore, the United Kingdom, Australia, Mexico, Brazil, and Japan. Locate your local office at: **international.cengage.com/region**

Cengage Learning products are represented in Canada by Nelson Education, Ltd.

For your lifelong learning solutions, visit **courseptr.com**

Visit our corporate website at **cengage.com**

Printed in the United States of America
1 2 3 4 5 6 7 11 10 09

This book is dedicated:

*To all my teachers, who made me the best student
I could be, and all my students, who forced me to be
the best teacher I could be. GG*

To my father, who looked out for everyone. PH

Acknowledgments

No book writes itself, and this book took more than just the two of us. While we slaved away at our end, a talented team assisted us and brought a greater level of quality to this book than we ever could have hoped for. That team included Orren Merton, acquisitions editor at Cengage Learning, who had the foresight to recognize the need in the market that this book fills; Mark Hughes, marketing manager at Cengage Learning, for his contributions to the look, feel, and cover of the book; Cathleen Small, our editor extraordinaire, who didn't let a little thing like the birth of her first child stand between her and the task at hand; our technical editor, Per Boysen, in Sweden, who kept us in line; and Ruchika Vij and the group in India, our layout coordinator and team, who rounded out our international and multi-coastal crew while giving the book that crisp, professional look that audio guys like us can only dream of.

We would also like to thank our clients, students, colleagues, coworkers, and anyone else whose toes we stepped on in the making of this book. Thanks for taking pictures for us, letting us take pictures of you, and being tolerant when we seemed distant or distracted.

And most of all, we would like to acknowledge the love and support of our families and our friends. We couldn't have done it without that most critical support.

About the Authors

Longtime music business professional **Gary Gottlieb** refers to himself as a music generalist. A professional musician since age 13, he worked in radio on and off for 25 years and was a music critic for 9 years. As a recording engineer, live recordist, and music producer in New York, Gottlieb's long and distinguished career includes work with numerous Grammy Award winners and Rock and Roll Hall of Fame inductees in a variety of venues. His credits as a sound designer include off-off-Broadway productions, along with community and college theatre productions throughout New England.

Along with his history as a music critic and entertainment writer for the *Deerfield Valley News* in West Dover, Vermont, and a disc jockey for WEQX, a major modern rock station in Manchester, Vermont, Gottlieb owned and operated a mobile DJ service and was a venue director for numerous X Games and Winter X Games for ESPN. In 2002, he accepted a position as Professor of Audio Production at Webster University in St. Louis, where he now runs the audio program. In 2007, Course Technology PTR released Gottlieb's *Shaping Sound in the Studio and Beyond*, the definitive introductory textbook in audio.

Paul Hennerich is the owner and chief engineer of PanGalactic Recordings, whose clients include the Saint Louis Symphony Orchestra. Hennerich has been the recording engineer for the symphony for more than 10 years. For five years, he was recording engineer and audio producer for a syndicated National Public Radio show of the symphony's live performances. In addition, his work as recording engineer and editor for the symphony CD *Messiaen: Turangalila-symphonie* helped earn the CD a mention as a "Record to Die For" by *Stereophile* and a Netherlands' Edison Classical Music award in the Special Historical Editions category in 2008.

Hennerich is a contributing location producer and recording engineer for another syndicated NPR show, *JazzSet*, producing recordings of concerts by the Dirty Dozen Brass Band and others. In addition to his experience working with live recordings for national programs, Hennerich also has been technical director and audio producer for live broadcasts for KMOX and KFUO.

Hennerich, a full adjunct professor of audio for Webster University, is also a partner in AAM Recordings, a small independent record label specializing in location recording.

His experience also includes location recording and work as a mastering engineer for music from indie heavy metal to blues and location recording for web streaming of a concert series produced by the symphony and the Pulitzer Arts Foundation. He started his career as a front-of-house engineer for venues, including the 12,000-seat Muny (St. Louis Municipal Opera) and the more than 10,000-person crowd at the St. Louis Blues Festival.

Contents

Chapter 4
Gig Psychology: Playing with Others   49

Chapter 5
Understanding and Respecting Power and Ground   59

PART II
GEAR   89

Chapter 6
Basic Gear   91

Chapter 7
Where We Keep Stuff: Data Storage   111

Chapter 8
Decisions, Decisions—To Wheel In or Not to Wheel In:
That Is the Question   123

PART III
THE GIG   131

Chapter 13
Surrounded!   177

Chapter 14
Harnessing Sound   191

Chapter 15
Finding Your Perch   195

Chapter 16
Work and Play Well with Others: Interfacing with the
Live Sound System   201

PART IV
THE DAY AFTER   211

Chapter 17
What Have We Got? Can We Fix It in the Mix?   213

Chapter 18
Editing and Sweetening   233

Chapter 19
Software and Such   241

Chapter 20
The Final Frontier   251

Introduction

We have to learn too many things to work in audio. We need to know physics to judge the acoustics of the room we are working in today and to simulate that room tomorrow. We need to understand philosophy—mostly that branch of philosophy that applies to aesthetics, which we will use every day. We need to know paperwork, so we can be consistent and so we can usually be right. We need to know accounting, because if we don't bill our clients correctly, we'll be out of business. We need to know gear. (Of course we need to know gear!) We need to know people and how to handle them, from the receptionist or the security guard right on up to the superstar or label executive.

To varying degrees, we need to know all these things to work in any field within audio. So what makes live recording different than studio recording or sound reinforcement? It's the way you apply this knowledge that distinguishes each field under the broad heading of audio. Perhaps you are working in only one field within audio. You are in the same studio every day or in the same Broadway theatre every night, doing pretty much the same thing. Or perhaps you have more varied audio experience: You record a film soundtrack one week, and then find yourself in a live venue doing the monitor mix the next. Every one of these pieces of the audio puzzle is a new experience, and the pieces fit together slightly differently than they did anywhere else.

Does some of the knowledge from the studio help in a concert hall? Does some of the knowledge from a film set help in a broadcast booth? Sure, but there are differences every time you step into a new situation. Every different situation is like opening a door into another room—a room that looks and feels familiar, yet has significant and noticeable differences.

In this book, we hope to help you open the door and recognize much of what awaits you in this new room called live recording. Yes, many things will appear familiar, and depending on your background in audio, some of the equipment and operations will be identical, but there will also be important differences. Failure to recognize these differences could have grave ramifications on your final product—the recording you create.

If you bring some basic audio knowledge to the table, we can help you sort out the details of live recording. We can help you identify the similarities and differences. We can help you relate everything you already know about audio to the specific application of live recording. And when you are finished reading and on your way to the gig, throw the book in your gig bag and bring us along. We'd like to be there to help—we take our coffee light and sweet.

As we proceed through the basics, the gear, the gig itself, and finally the day after, we hope to make you aware of the risks and rewards and give you some insight into the best practices of our profession. Armed with this knowledge, some good skills, and a little bit of luck, you should have no problem creating a world-class live recording. And hopefully you will even have some fun while doing it.

The Basics of Live Recording

 # Why Record Live?

People love reliving their experiences. It begins at an early age—toddlers and young children love to read the same book, hear the same stories, or see the same movie over and over. It continues as children age and become teenagers who seek out CDs and DVDs of performances from their favorite artists. As they attend more concerts and other live performances, they seek out visual and audio recordings of these same performances. They are frequently thrilled to find a recording of a performance they actually attended. It also explains why so many still cameras, video cameras, and DV cameras are sold every day. In middle age, many people relive their glory days as high school athletes or performers. Even as people become senior citizens, one of their favorite hobbies often involves retelling the stories of their youth—stories that may begin, "Cough, cough. Why, when I was your age...."

Maybe we can't help people relive every experience in their lives; frankly, there are many personal situations I would shy away from recording. Nonetheless, many of the strongest, longest-lasting memories we carry with us are of musical or theatrical performances—some recent, some in the distant past. We capture a moment in time and space and create a testament of witness. As audio professionals, we can have a profound effect on people by helping them relive their most pleasant memories. If we do a better job of capturing an event for reproduction, the memory will be clearer, and the emotion evoked from that memory will be greater. Maybe this is why we record.

Perhaps this emotion that creates the lasting memory is what we are after when we record live music. How many times have you felt the emotion and energy of your favorite band at the local pub, club, or concert hall, only to be disappointed by their studio release later? Something was missing. Was it just the booze? Was it the guy smoking to your left (back when people were allowed to smoke in public)? Was it the ambience that only your favorite venue could deliver? Was it the vibe the band got from performing in their favorite pub in front of their regulars—that unexplainable exchange of energy? Or did the pub have the magic acoustic elements that fit the band's style? Or was it some combination of the above?

There are other factors as well. Sometimes the history of a location creates the inspiration to make the emotions open up, causing the music to flow. Both the musicians and the audience can feel it. How many of the best jazz recordings are made at Iridium, Town Hall, or the Village Vanguard in New York City? How many would have been made if John Coltrane had never recorded at the Village Vanguard (see Figures 1.1 and 1.2)?

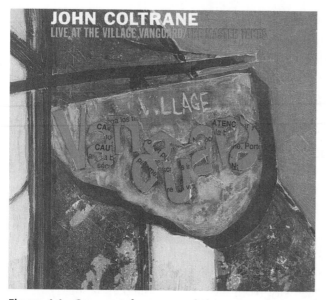

Figure 1.1 Cover art from one of the many albums John Coltrane recorded live at the Village Vanguard, New York, NY.

Another example of the power of a space is the concert series hosted by the Pulitzer Arts Foundation. Imagine modern chamber music set at the base of a large staircase in a beautiful modern gallery. At first glance, this would seem to be a less than ideal setting for capturing a performance, but the quality of the performance, played in a style that matches the photographs, paintings, and sculptures that surround the live audience and players, makes for a musical synergy that cannot be reproduced in a studio recording. When we record that event, we attempt to capture that energy and the enhanced performance that resulted from the musicians' comfort within that space.

A classic example in rock of a band that excelled in concert is the Grateful Dead. Their live recordings and performances are legendary; radio series and bootlegs abound, and their fans focus on the live body of work they created. Most agree that their studio work was solid but fell short of the magic created on stage in front of the audience. Thus, the Dead actively encouraged the taping of their live shows, which helped spread the mythos of the Dead live in concert.

coltrane
live at the
village
vanguard
again!

Figure 1.2 John Coltrane's live recordings from the Village Vanguard were so popular that they became a franchise.

As HD television and the Blu-ray HD-DVD wars rage, the need for quality location sound is growing. HD broadcast standards for audio specify the use of Dolby digital and have the capability for multichannel sound—the same quality that you would find on a typical DVD. TV has never sounded better, and thus a location production will need the audio to match the 1080-pixel progressive-scan image that is being transmitted. It is up to you, the engineer, to deliver that sound with the forest of microphones.

In a sporting event broadcast in HD, you see sharp, clear images—vivid greens, and you can see the sweat on the face of the quarterback as he faces the oncoming rush. If you don't hear the crack of the hit or the exasperation of the crowd, your experience is diminished. Good location recording is just as important. When it comes to a location recording for film or video, the engineer must remember the words of George Lucas: "Sound is 50 percent of the movie-going experience." With home-theater sale skyrocketing and computers being set up with 5.1 systems, it isn't just about the movie experience anymore.

Why Didn't We Listen to Our Mothers?

If we had listened to our mothers (see Figures 1.3 and 1.4), we would have become something other than audio professionals—maybe doctors, maybe plumbers, possibly even architects. Because we weren't listening, we have no idea what our mothers wanted

Figure 1.3   Dear Mother (Gary's).

Figure 1.4   Dear Mother (Paul's).

us to be. We do remember the acoustics in the rooms, though—they would have been great rooms in which to record. If we had only recorded our mothers in those rooms, we would know what they wanted us to be. Maybe that is why we record.

It's never too soon in a discussion of professional audio to suggest that you should consider going into the family business. As we move through the basics ideas we incorporate while recording live sound and then move on to an analysis of the gear needed to accomplish our goal, followed by some real-life scenarios and then the cleanup the day after the gig, we will be treading on some very messy terrain. This would be a good time to reconsider opening that restaurant or going into business with your brother-in-law. Of course, if you are like us and you have a feeling deep in the pit of your stomach that you will not be happy doing anything other than sound—live, studio, in the field, or otherwise—then read on. We believe this is the real reason we record sound—we have no choice.

You Know How This Stuff Works, Right?

"So I plugged the thing—you know, the thing with the things on the end—into the black thing, and, well, I'm pretty sure that always worked when we recorded our rehearsals, but it doesn't seem to be working now. What am I doing wrong?" asked the drummer in the club. The drummer was in the band I had been recording on nights when the studio was available (and studio time was free to employees). This was the drummer in the band who asked me to come to their live gig for moral support—the drummer who failed to mention that they really, really wanted to record the gig. Yes indeed, the same drummer who lacked the knowledge to make a good live recording. How fortunate for the band that I happened to be there. Yes, I *do* know how these things work, and yes, I can even make it sound pretty damn good with a few minutes to reposition a few microphones and reroute everything.

This is not fantasy; these are the types of favors audio professionals are expected to do every day. You read correctly: *favors*. Sometimes we get paid for helping; other times we do it for the love of our craft or for the experience. We always do our best work, regardless of whether we are working as a favor, working cheap, or getting paid well. You are always working for your reputation. This is more valuable than cash in hand because it will determine your future gigs as an engineer. This is what a true audio professional does. If that bothers you, reconsider the family business or listen to your mother next time.

If you are back home from college or visiting the town where you grew up, the phone call is inevitable. "We're doing this church production, and everyone wants it recorded so we'll have something to play for our grandkids someday. We have a really talented eleventh grader/soccer mom/beagle who we were sure could do this for us, but he/she/it has come down with mono/heartworms and had a kid throw up on her/got run over and is unavailable. Naturally we thought of you, and we are counting on you to come record us. You are our only hope!" Let's see, Aunt Helen's desiccated turkey, or record the high school choir? Easy choice—I'm recording (see Figure 1.5)!

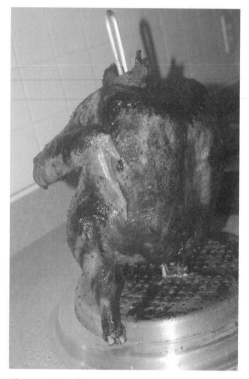

Figure 1.5   If Aunt Helen's turkey looked this good, I might reconsider.

If you hate light opera, the call will come from your old grade-school chum who you haven't spoken to in decades—the one who has now devoted his life to Gilbert and Sullivan. "We're doing *Pirates of Penzance*! I couldn't be more excited! And we're so lucky that you're here this week, because we'll never do anything this much fun again, and you simply *must* record it for us! We are *so* lucky to have a real professional like you doing this for us, and I told everyone you would do it since I let you cheat off my paper that time in third grade. You just *can't* say no!" So you do it. Why? Because recording is what we do, and sometimes we get paid for it.

Which One of These Is Different Than the Other?

All of the scenarios described previously are possible. Thousands of others are equally likely. Ultimately, how different will these gigs be? In each of these situations, in every gig, with or without pay, you will walk into a space; assess the acoustics and the available equipment; examine the area for anything unusual, such as safety hazards or a lack of electricity; and determine a plan of action. You will set up equipment in the best manner to be professional and unobtrusive and to maximize the quality of the recording. You will operate as a professional, moving confidently throughout the gig with few surprises, because you did such an excellent job of finding all the flaws in the space before they were able to interfere with your recording. Here are the things you will need to do to succeed in live recording:

- Make contacts.

- Talk to the client.

- Talk to the people at the site.

Figure 1.6 Powell Hall, home of the Saint Louis Symphony Orchestra.

Figure 1.7   Gentlemen Auction House at the Lot Festival at the Schlafly Tap Room, St. Louis, MO.

Figure 1.8   Gentlemen Auction House at Fair St. Louis, St. Louis, MO.

- Conduct a site survey:
    - Assess reflectivity and acoustics of space.
    - Assess available equipment.
    - Assess any unusual conditions.
    - Assess potential safety hazards.
    - Assess electricity.
    - Anticipate any pitfalls.

- Establish a plan.

- Gather equipment.

- Coerce/hire help.

- Set call time.

- Dress appropriately.

- Set up equipment professionally.

- Be unobtrusive.

- Make friends with everyone. (Bring donuts or bagels.)

- Focus on aesthetics.

- Be confident.

- Enjoy the experience.

Okay, right. So the difference between the studio and the location is? Location engineers do not have safety nets. You are committing to create a studio-quality recording in a space that is designed for everything other than recording. Planning is the only thing that can save a location engineer. The less time you have to set up on site at the gig, the more time you need to put into the planning and preproduction. You get one shot; there are no do-overs. Well, maybe there are do-overs. Okay, actually there are many do-overs, or overdubs—just listen to the Eagles' live album from the 1980s. The *Rolling Stone Record Guide* of 1983 claims it to be the heaviest overdub live album in history to that point. Bill Szymczyk claims that the perfect three-part harmonies were not live, but courtesy of FedEx, shipped in at a later date from other sessions in recording studios. Most people aren't the Eagles, and they were saved only by the foresight of their engineer to set the recording so it could be overdubbed.

Figure 1.9 Carnegie Hall, New York City, NY.

There is a point at which recording a rock band in a small club with a low ceiling becomes different than recording a 90-piece orchestra at Carnegie Hall (see Figure 1.9).

These jobs might seem vastly different from the start, but they have similar pitfalls. A small club will typically be full of blatant and obvious hazards and hardships. The hardships in a classic concert hall are still there, but they may be more subtle, hidden deep in the sub-basement to which you have no access. Both spaces can have funky power, no isolation, radio towers, and broken lifts. Planning, lugging, and preparing remain the same. The difference is in the art of the recording. What you set up, where you set it up, and how you set it up will be dramatically different, determined by the style of music, the nature of the space, and the budget within which you need to stay. The aesthetic of the final product is the difference. The end products may not resemble each other, but the fundamentals of getting the sound remain the same.

It might be more important for us to dwell on the commonalities for now—the networking that got us the gig in the first place, the professionalism, the confidence, the preplanning we will do to reduce surprises and disasters, even the schmoozing and glad-handing we will do to ensure that everyone we encounter during the process (from clients to stagehands, and from performers to stage managers) will be working toward a common goal (see Figure 1.10).

Figure 1.10 Happy people work together for a common goal.

That common goal will always be capturing the performance in a manner that results in obtaining the best recording while keeping the musicians as comfortable as possible so they provide the best performance (which makes us all look good).

Is It Live or Is It...?

Many audio professionals arrive at live recoding through audio schools or as commercial studio or home recordists. If you know how to record tracks and make a CD, you should be able to record live, right? Well, maybe. Certainly with some training, the basic knowledge of a recording engineer regarding signal flow and the behavior of sound waves can be applied to live situations. Once the gaps are filled in regarding acoustics, gear, methodology, etiquette, and such, you can easily proceed, but keep in mind that there are some other differences as well—the differences in methodology we mentioned could throw a studio engineer off his game.

The controlled environment of the studio allows the engineer to plot and plan everything, then make last-minute changes or adjustments even after the performance has begun. If a studio engineer is unhappy with the angle of a microphone during the first take, it can be adjusted before the second take. If a live recordist is unhappy with the angle of a microphone during a performance...well, it's just too late. The location engineer needs to know everything about everything, have a game plan, and get everything right the first time (see Figure 1.11).

Photo by Michael J. Lutch.

Figure 1.11 Boston Symphony Hall.

If not, you may have to fix it tomorrow in the remix (if you can).

The controlled environment of the studio is conducive to separation; live performance is not. You can put up gobos or otherwise isolate your sound sources in the studio, but that would be grossly inappropriate on stage during a performance. In the studio, you can choose to use a click track for consistency. Click tracks are rare in live performance. The list of differences rolls on. You can address these differences with the information contained in subsequent chapters and a little bit of experience, and an audio professional can combine his existing knowledge and experience with the information herein to create a working model for live recording.

With knowledge of microphone techniques and microphone types, the experienced engineer can achieve results that will amaze and wow his clients (see Figure 1.12).

Photo courtesy of Stan Coutant.

Figure 1.12   A properly chosen and placed microphone can make all the difference in the world.

The proper microphone techniques in the proper place will get the job done and will allow you to skip that expensive EQ. The trick is to find the combination of technique and sweet spot quickly, and for that you need to know a little something about acoustics.

Experience will inform you as to how sound will behave in a space and how other factors will affect that space. This will, in turn, affect your attempt to record that sound. The size and shape of the space, the reflectivity of the various surfaces within the space, even the size of the audience (both as individuals and en masse) will have a dramatic effect on what you hear, how you hear it, what you record, and how you record it. So, as we begin to examine the differences and similarities between live recording experiences, let's consider how sound behaves in space.

2 Sound in Space

It should be obvious that the manner in which sound behaves in space will have serious ramifications on your attempts to record in a particular space. As you determine how and where you record, you must take all factors of a space into consideration. Remember that the behavior of sound waves and your behavior in reaction to those waves in a space will always impact the quality of the final recording.

Found Space

As live sound recordists, we are often called to a particular space to record for a particular reason. Much in the same way that so many studio hits were produced in the early '60s at Columbia Records' 30th Street studio, a converted church known for its incredible resonance, many spaces are used due to the sound and feel they add to a live recording. A recording made at the Village Vanguard in New York will have a very different feel than a recording made at Carnegie Hall.

Artists and producers will seek to record their live performances in Lincoln Center if they are in New York (see Figure 2.1), in Royal Albert Hall if they are in London (see Figure 2.2), and so on—both because of the flavor these venues add to the recording and due to the history of the space. Some artists will travel specifically to record in these spaces or will arrange to be recorded during a tour at specific stops when they are performing in the classic concert halls. The sound of the Boston Symphony Orchestra is the sound of Symphony Hall (see Figure 2.3), just as the sound of the Saint Louis Symphony Orchestra is the sound of Powell Symphony Hall. Although we cannot change the history of a space, it is our obligation to consider the effect the space will impose on our recording.

Identifying Acoustic Issues

Even the most renowned of recording spaces will present issues to the live recordist. Some might be obvious; others might be buried deep in the bowels of a hundred-year-old building. Before we get to issues of safety, electricity, ground, and more, we should start with the more obvious and predictable behavior of the wave in this space,

Figure 2.1   The New York State Theater at Lincoln Center in New York, home of the New York City Opera.

Figure 2.2   Royal Albert Hall in London.

Photo courtesy of Stu Rosner.

Figure 2.3 Symphony Hall in Boston.

dictated by the walls, floor, and ceiling. Every time a sound wave encounters a surface, one or more of three things will happen. The wave will:

- Reflect

- Refract

- Absorb

Reflections

We can break down reflections in many ways. Let's start by looking at reflections inherent to the space, and then we'll look at the ones created by putting a band or orchestra in that space.

When a sound wave encounters a hard surface, such as plaster, brick, or polished wood, a substantial amount of the energy contained in the wave will be reflected, or sent back out into the room. The process begins with the direct, or *early*, reflection, which is the one that bounces straight to the observer's ear (see Figure 2.4).

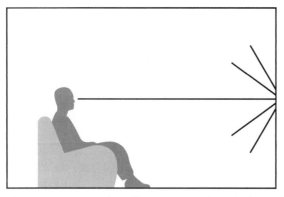

Figure 2.4 An early reflection goes directly from the surface to the observer's ear.

It continues as the wave spreads throughout the space, reflecting repeatedly every time it encounters another hard surface (see Figure 2.5).

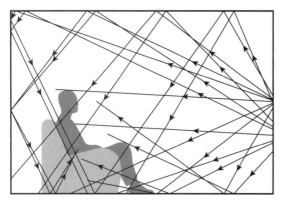

Figure 2.5 Reverberation is a series of random reflections, growing thicker and diminishing in level over time.

This process, known as *reverberation,* is a key element of a space's signature sound. These reverberations must be captured in order to record and reproduce the event accurately; at the same time, they must be controlled and used in a measured proportion to the original signal in order to replicate the original event and prevent the final product from becoming muddy.

In addition to the very predictable manner in which a sound wave will behave when it encounters a plaster ceiling or a polished wood wall, there will be other, sometimes less predictable, encounters. Suppose the band you are recording has monitor wedges on the stage to hear themselves and other band members as they perform. This is pretty common, especially for electrically amplified bands. Now suppose the rear of the stage is reflective. Frequently, great concert halls are designed in this manner to amplify the sound on stage out into the house. Here's the problem: Instead of reflecting the acoustic sounds of a string quartet out into the house in a balanced manner, the rear wall is reflecting whatever the monitor mixer happens to be throwing into that wedge. And the microphones out in the house? They are picking up those uncontrolled and often undesirable reflections.

A loud drum kit may also present a problem. Once again, the sound waves produced might bounce uncontrollably throughout the house, wreaking havoc on your recording. Keep in mind that drum sets, especially when played loudly and amplified, are rich with low-frequency information. Due to their larger wavelengths, these low-frequency waves will bend (high frequencies are far more directional) and retain more energy as they bounce. This means that low frequencies will be emphasized after repeated reflections, and due to their ability to bend and disperse, they will be even louder in the corners of the room. A little common sense will inform you that you do not want to place your microphones anywhere near the rear corners of a large, reflective concert hall as a result of these properties.

Absorption

After reading the previous section, you might think softer surfaces that absorb sound waves would be more desirable. Unfortunately, nothing is quite that simple. It is true that softer surfaces often found in concert halls and other venues, such as drapes, upholstery, and carpet, absorb sound waves beautifully. These surfaces help deaden unwanted reflections, such as the low-frequency bounce and the monitor reflections off the wall behind the performers (see Figure 2.6).

Figure 2.6 Placing absorptive material at the rear of the stage has both advantages and disadvantages.

Unfortunately, these surfaces also absorb some of the sweetest and most desirable of the high frequencies. Too many soft surfaces will suck much of the nice high end out of percussion and brass. They will absorb just the right frequencies to make a piano or cymbals sound dull, and they will remove clarity and definition from the high end of the mix. When you record in a very absorptive house, you might have difficulty getting enough high end and clarity into your final mix.

And if it weren't challenging enough to get good clarity through recording high-frequency information, there is another hitch. After you figure out everything you need to know about how a room will sound and the best places to put your microphones, someone goes and fills the house with big bags of water. These bags of water buy tickets. They claim to be there to enjoy the performance. They are really there to absorb high frequencies, because these bags of water, also known as the audience, are soft and absorptive. (Regardless of how much you work out, you are still soft in the grand scheme of things.) If you fail to take their presence into account, the final product will suffer.

Other Acoustic Issues

It is unrealistic to think that we can anticipate every manifestation of a sound wave in every space, but there are some recurring themes we encounter during our careers. We frequently encounter platforms in one form or another in live spaces. Drum risers are common on stage, often used to lift the drummer up so he is visible to the audience (see Figure 2.7).

Figure 2.7 A typical drum riser.

Stages themselves may be considered risers, and in small clubs stages are notorious for their deleterious effect on the sound.

When drum risers lack enough structural reinforcement or when a stage is poorly constructed (as sometimes happens in small clubs), the platform's softness can act as an acoustical damper, sucking up some of the high frequencies. A drum kit on a riser of this type will lack crispness in the cymbals. If the whole band is playing on a poorly constructed stage in a second-rate dive, the piano, vocals, and guitar can lose definition due to a lack of high-frequency information.

Sadly, even a well-constructed stage or riser can sometimes act as a bass trap. Low frequencies can get trapped in boxes of this type, and when they explode into the room, adding to the existing sound, they can accentuate the low-frequency information tremendously. As you record in these situations, you need to be ever vigilant of the projection of low frequencies.

Thinking in 3D

An engineer will sometimes be handed a stage plot scratched on the back of a napkin (see Figure 2.8).

Figure 2.8 A typical stage plot for a blues band.

If you are lucky, the band might even include all the stage monitors and amplifier locations. If you are unlucky, the napkin will have been used to wipe the beer off the lead guitarist's guitar case before he left the last gig. Beware of feet drawn as inches in *Spinal Tap* fashion.

The first problem, even with a nice, clean napkin, is that it is typically drawn in two dimensions. This is great if you are recording on flat land, but unfortunately, those gigs are few and far between. Nevertheless, the napkin is a start for your search for information. Every object that has been drawn in your stage plot will make lots of sound and will project lots of sound waves. You have a drawing of the sources but no idea of what or how those sources are going to project. From this plot, you can decipher the basic sound projections of the band. Typically, your primary issues and worst problems will not come from what is drawn on the napkin; your worst problems will come from that which is overlooked.

At this point, if you are not familiar with the space in which you are recording, you need to address that and become familiar with it. Head to the club and fill in the missing details on your plot. Most of the time, you need to add room shapes, or walls, windows, doors, staircases, bars, and even chicken wire. If the stage is already set up, take a look at placements of monitor speakers, the biggest sound source often left off the back of the napkin or covered up when the drummer blew his nose in it. Also include the location of the main house PA speakers. Now you can create a far more comprehensive drawing (see Figure 2.9).

Now you need to start imagining your sound sources, active, live, full, and tingly. Begin looking at your plot and try. The first things you should look for are the direct sound conflicts. Pay particular attention to where conflicts between monitor wedges and house PA speakers overlap the instrumentation. Often the club has taken steps to avoid outrageous issues between their PA system and instrumentation, as many of these direct conflicts can result in feedback.

Begin by imagining all sound coming directionally from your sound sources in two dimensions (see Figure 2.10).

We can see issues in two dimensions; the bass is close enough to the piano and drum kit that low-frequency bleed might be an issue. The bass player's monitor wedge is projecting directly to the back wall, resulting in a first reflection, which will flood the drum kit. The drummer's monitor looks harmless, and it is pointed off house right. The lead guitarist's and singer's monitor looks to be fine, although there might be an issue with reflection in the bass microphone, and on closer examination, a reflection back toward the piano is also a possibility. The PA system looks acceptable except for the placement

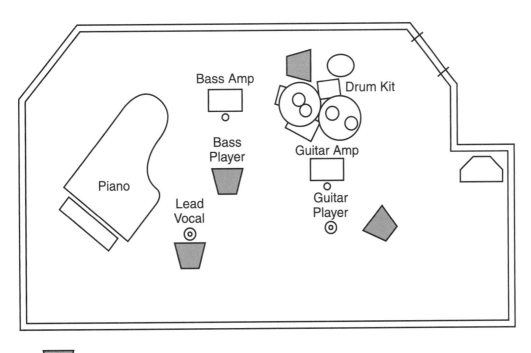

= Monitor

Figure 2.9 Actual stage plot of the band performing on stage at the Sheldon concert hall, with the added acoustic piano.

slightly behind the band, allowing for potential bleed in the piano, bass, drums, and guitarist/vocalist.

Now let's look at an elevation of the same setup (see Figures 2.11 and 2.12).

We get additional information here with a drawing that includes the height element. Now we can clearly see that the monitor of the vocalist isn't going to directly impact the bass as we had feared, because it will mostly end up in the null of the microphone. However, the initial reflections are still a concern due to the slanted hard-plaster ceiling pointing those reflections directly at the drum kit.

These second and third reflections might not seem to create much of an issue and might not be strong enough to create feedback in the PA system. Nonetheless, they could cause coloration of the sound in the recording due to the Haas effect.

The Haas effect is the integration of a sound source's reflections into the perception of the direct sound. These integrations happen with reflections that are shorter than

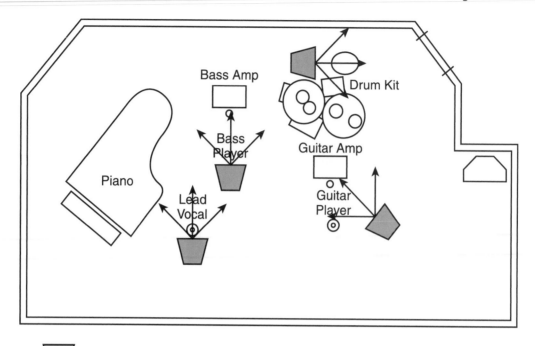

= Monitor

Figure 2.10 Directionality of sound sources, coming from the wedges on stage.

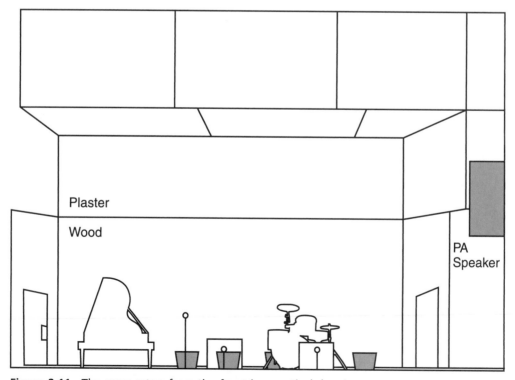

Figure 2.11 The same setup from the front in a vertical drawing.

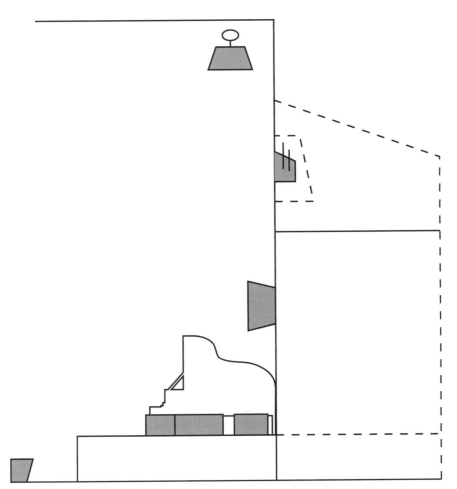

Figure 2.12 The same setup from the side in a vertical drawing.

35 milliseconds. Thirty-five milliseconds, while seemingly short, is actually quite a long time in terms of sound. In 35 milliseconds, sound in a club with a temperature of 70 degrees can travel about 39 1/2 feet! Consider the fact that the average height of the ceiling in a club or bar is 10 to 14 feet and the width of a large stage might be 10 to 20 feet. These reflections do not necessarily return to your microphones as happy, pleasant reverberation, but as possible negative coloration of the sound, particularly if a large amount of artificial reflection has been added by the PA system and monitor speakers. The Haas effect of an instrument in a particular space can be good, as long as it is a defining character of the space. It can add dimensionality and sense of space to the sound source, but only if it is natural.

Control Booth? We Don't Need No Stinkin' Control Booth

Well, okay, maybe we really *do* need a control booth. In the studio, the best way to find your microphone technique is to start with something you know and make adjustments based on trial and error, listening in your isolated control room. This is a luxury you don't have on a location recording. Good isolation and calibrated monitor speakers are even more difficult to find. The popularity of mobile recording trucks is a direct result of their ability to provide some of the benefits available in the recording studio's control booth. Unless you are extremely lucky and have a very large budget, a mobile truck isn't an option. You have to make do with found spaces.

Finding the space can be quite difficult. Most of the time, the proximity to the stage will be your driving factor. The acoustics of the temporary control position, while typically important, usually boil down to two factors. Is it close to the performance? How sonically isolated is it from the stage or performance? The key in finding the best space to set up is to find a location that has no direct sound, and we often sacrifice a direct line of sight in our quest for sonic isolation. Thanks to their infrared function, low-cost baby video monitors are often a good solution because they can help you see the performers if they are not in your line of sight, even if the house is dark. A low amount of first- and second-degree reflection would also be helpful, and obviously no direct sound is your primary goal. When you cannot find a separated space, you are better off setting up somewhere other than directly in front of the group. You don't want to hear the performance. You want to hear the recording of the performance that you are creating. Staying out of the direct sound will allow you to better hear and assess what is being recorded. To the side or behind the group can often yield better results than directly in front of the group.

Power of the Acoustic Space

You are on location because the found space has an element that is special. The event may be unique—or, more likely, there is an acoustical element, such as the reflections unique to a particular church or performance space. There may be a spiritual consideration, such as, "Dude, we never rock harder than when we play the Pageant!"

Man has known the power of acoustics for a long time. The opera houses in Europe have magnificent sonic clarity and tone for the music, allowing each member of the audience to hear the music in all its glory and color. The cathedral builders of the Middle Ages incorporated amazing acoustics into their designs to enhance the power and majesty of the new pipe organs to wow and assure the faithful. The ancient Greeks constructed outdoor amphitheaters, where you can hear a whisper uttered from your significant other on stage 200 feet away or the individual voices of all 50 of the bus tour members marching across the stage.

One of the more amazing phenomena from our forefathers of acoustic design came from the Mayan people (see Figure 2.13).

Figure 2.13 Tulum, on Mexico's Yucatan Peninsula, shares some amazing acoustic features with many Mayan and Aztec structures.

The Mayan city of Chichen Itza contains one of the more fantastic examples of acoustic construction. David Lubman and Mexican researchers under the leadership of Sergio Beristain are investigating the main temple structure, Kukulcan at Chichen Itza. They are looking into why the temple "chirps." If you have ever had the misfortune to record a concert in a concrete box at the bottom of a long set of stairs made out of concrete, you might begin to understand the issues Mr. Lubman has encountered.

The stairs act as a giant physical comb filter, creating massively and diversely phased reflections. The rise and run of these stairs are often a very short run with a very high rise. The rise can be so high that it has been determined to be unsafe for tourists to climb. It is quite steep, almost ladder-like. It's bad for climbing, but great for chirping. For recording, this is typically a bad thing. If you want to convince your followers that the feather serpent god Quetzalcoatl has heard your prayers, this might just be your thing. Mr. Ludman and his Mexican colleagues have come to the conclusion that the stairs built into the temple are intended to deliver a comb-filtered echo return of a clap that sounds amazingly similar to the call of the Quetzal bird, of which Quetzalcoatl is part. The other part is serpent, which some believe is the reason a rattling sound can be heard from the hall of warriors if you turn to the left and clap. Say your prayers, clap, and God answers. This makes for very impressive acoustics and a great place to have your gig if you happen to be the high priest of Quetzalcoatl.

If you are a recording engineer attempting to record a small chamber group at the bottom of the stairs, you are dealing with an extremely difficult situation (see Figure 2.14). Your stairs, like that of the ancient Mayan temple, will change the sound that is created in the space though a similar comb-filtering effect. A typical technique and approach to recording in this space will probably not work, because often the room's acoustic oddities will work against you. In some cases the stairs are not an insurmountable problem because it can be a fairly uniform change, and flutter can be dealt with to some extent by adjusting the microphone position. The larger issue with this room is a long, open hallway that turns it into giant resonating chamber. If a typical space microphone array is used, a noticeable buildup in energy will occur, throwing the image out of center. In a tricky acoustic space such as this, thorough preplanning (including carefully laid out

Figure 2.14   The Pulitzer Foundation for the Arts staircase gallery.

close-microphone technique) is required, with the addition of some dedicated room microphones to add back some of the oddity of the space if character is desired.

Finding the Sweet Spot

We all talk about the elusive sweet spot. Where is it? What is it? One can search a lifetime for it. Before you can search for it and find it, it would be good to know what you are seeking. Often the sweet spot is defined as the best space to hear something. In the terms of a hi-fi enthusiast, the sweet spot is usually centered in the middle of the grossly expensive stereo system, dead center between two enormous speakers that often have forced their owner's neighbors to improve their insulation. But is it really the sweet spot? That is somewhat subjective. The neighbors might think the sweet spot is somewhere about half a mile away, particularly if they don't share similar musical tastes and sensibilities.

When finding the sweet spot on location, it is wise to remember that all rooms are created unequally. Typically, it is best to find the point in a space where the direct sound balances the reverberation. First do this with the best microphones available—your ears. Next, check your thoughts by placing your next best microphones in that place and giving them an honest, objective listen. You can then make other adjustments, which we will explore as we examine methodology more deeply, but first let's see what happens before we even get the gig, as well as ways to make the transition from pre-planning to execution go as smoothly as possible.

3 The Key to Success: Planning

While we are all focused on reflections in our space, the gear that we have or want, and the new depths our bank account will reach as a result of this gig, the most important part of live recording is also one of the least romantic. Never underestimate the power of good planning. Proper planning, with all the forethought and legwork it entails, often makes the difference between a smooth, relatively stress-free recording process, resulting in a high-quality recording, and a train wreck. Let's do whatever planning is necessary to avoid the train wreck.

This does not mean that we will never deviate from our plan—quite the contrary. One of the hallmarks of a great audio professional is our ability to roll with the situation. An extra guitar player shows up? No problem, as long as we have planned properly for the elements we know will be present. The conductor decides after sound check that he wants to add timpani, a piccolo, and timbales? Rather unusual, but once again, no problem. More planning translates into the minimization of potentially big problems during the gig. If you are dealing with many problems due to your lack of planning, and on top of that you have a timpani, a piccolo, and timbales, you are headed for the train wreck. The addition of these three elements will be fairly easy to accommodate if everything else is calm and under control.

We all have too much to remember—the logistics of our lives, our other gigs, our families and relationships, and so much more. It is arrogant and unwise to think that we can also remember every aspect involved in planning the gig as we discuss the event with musicians, conductors, producers, assistants, house engineers, monitor mix engineers, Teamsters, and publicity teams. To ensure that we are covering all our bases, we need to take good notes throughout the planning process. If the conductor says the cello is the soloist, write it down. If the house electrician warns you about a particular circuit, write it down. If the house manager says he is allergic to mayonnaise, write it down. A pattern emerges: Write everything down. When you look back over your notes while estimating the job, while loading in your gear, while you are getting everyone sandwiches, or when you are about to start recording, you might find one little tidbit that you forgot—a tidbit that is suddenly very important.

These notes will become a blueprint for you. As you estimate what you will charge, you will refer to these notes. When you order gear for the gig, you will work off this ever-growing blueprint. As you set up your gear, you will refer to it again, as you will while recording and even during the mix. Take lots of good notes and refer to them often. For these notes to be as comprehensive as possible, you need to gather information in a thorough and efficient manner.

Gathering Information

There are different possible situations in which you might record live. A venue, artist, or someone representing the artist might call you to offer you the gig. There will be differences when you are booked by a venue, but it will be pretty much the same whether the artist or his or her agent contacts you. Either way, this is your client, and handling clients is a critical skill. You need to be nice and accommodating to the client without pandering. You must gather all the information that the client has to offer without overburdening him. You must draw out everything he knows that can help you with the gig while still retaining your status as the expert. This type of finesse will come naturally to some and will take others years to learn, but it is a necessary skill either way.

The first order of business is to always be positive. Perhaps the client is a band that plays a style of music that you find reprehensible. Your personal tastes are insignificant; they represent your musical choices during your personal time. This is work, and the client is paying you to record the band. You should never lie and say, "I love this band!" if you find it painful to listen to, but you should not insult them, either. They are the client, and they have hired you to do a job. Instead of saying, "I hate new country," try saying, "There are a lot of new country fans around here." Guess which one the client wants to hear? To be perfectly clear, the client probably doesn't care whether you like the music, but negative feelings about the craft are better left unstated (see Figure 3.1).

If an artist or representative has booked you, a good first question is where they want to be recorded. Ask about upcoming gigs. Ask if there is a particular venue where the artist is most comfortable, one where he feels his performances really shine. Often a venue like this will be best because when musicians are comfortable, they give their best performances. They may have called you because they have a gig coming up at a famous venue, one steeped in tradition and well known for its acoustics and the excellent recordings that have been created there in the past (see Figure 3.2).

Either way, your obligation at this first encounter is to try to establish the location in which the recording will take place.

Photo of Boston Symphony Hall courtesy of Michael J. Lutch.

Figure 3.1   Orchestral music might not be your personal favorite, but those ticket purchasers in the audience and the paid professionals on the stage have a job for you.

Figure 3.2   Some artists will seek out classic venues such as Royal Albert Hall for their recordings.

Once the client has established the location, ask who is in charge. Get the names, phone numbers, and email addresses of anyone in the venue. If it is a venue that the artist frequents, he will be able to give you far more information. Ask who the manager is. Find out whether this is the same person who booked the artist and who pays him. If not, find out who this other person is or who these other people are. Ask for names and contact information for everyone in the venue—the owner, the manager, the bartender, and the kid who helps people carry in their gear. Once again, there is no such thing as too much information.

Now that we have established the location in which the recording will take place, let's move on to something equally important. Ask the band what they want the recordings to sound like. This will produce some interesting responses. Some bands will answer that they want to sound just like their studio recordings. Some will answer that they want to sound like some other band's studio recordings. Many bands will cite a historical recording. Some will say they want to sound like Nirvana's *MTV Unplugged in New York* or the *The Allman Brothers at Fillmore East*. Some will say they want to sound like the early '70s Grateful Dead live albums. Some will say they want to sound like Jimi Hendrix at Monterey Pop, which may present a problem if they are a string quartet. Any reasonable request can be accommodated, as long as the artist or band has the budget to support it.

Which brings us to our next question: What type of budget do you have for this recording? If the answer to the previous question was that the band wants their live recording to sound like their studio recording, and the studio recording used $100,000 worth of signal processing gear, then they better have a big budget for this live recording.

During this process of gathering information, you also have the opportunity to do a reality check on your clients. If their budget cannot support the type of recording they seek, this is a good time to offer suggestions to "tailor" the setup to accommodate something close to their needs while beginning to trim the budget.

Finally, another necessary question is: How much time will I have to set up? Many factors will influence this, including other bands that may be playing, sound-check schedule, union rules, accessibility to the venue, and ease of loading in. Remember, no one will allow you to load equipment in while there is an audience in the house, so you must plan this in advance, in conjunction with personnel at the venue and in compliance with any other events taking place at the venue.

There will be other questions that come to mind, some of them unique to this particular gig. Do not be afraid to ask anything. Remember, the more information you have, the better prepared you will be when the time comes to create a plan of action.

Creating a Plan

Now that you have all these bits of useful information, let's roll them all up together and figure out how to approach this gig. As a lifelong optimist, I always start by planning for the ideal setup, and I suggest you do the same. Start by disregarding the equipment you already own. It might be convenient, but if the client can afford it and the budget can support it, there is probably something better out there. Start by assuming the ideal setup even if you are unsure of whether a perfect setup will tip the budget too far. There will be plenty of time later to pare things back if it becomes necessary.

Consider the microphones you would prefer to use. Consider the hardware and software you wish to use to record the event. Is there any signal processing that comes to mind that will help the recording? Visualize your ideal setup at this point—the best microphones, the best method of recording, and any other processing you will need. Don't forget to include cables, microphone stands and clips, and a snake in that vision. Remember, you can always cull some of this out later due to budgetary or space considerations.

Preliminary Paperwork

Now the time has come to create a track sheet for your recording (see Figure 3.3).

The paperwork at this stage is as critically important as the notes you took earlier while meeting with the clients. The track sheet is a fluid document—the one you make now, during the early planning stages, is a preliminary track sheet. Parts of it will hold up; parts of it will be abandoned. Nonetheless, it is what you start with as you contemplate how to isolate your tracks and spread them out in your recording device. As with gear, think big. Because you may be contemplating more (and better) microphones than the budget will eventually support, consider the ideal distribution of signal as you record it as well.

There are many important bits of information that you should enter on the track sheet. Along with information about microphone selections and the track a particular component will end up on, contemplate everything along the signal chain. Which snake input will you use? Will this input be split with the engineer doing the live mix in the house? Is there a special preamp you would like to use on this input? You should note all of this information on the track sheet at this time. As previously mentioned, you can modify it later, but a more solid plan at this point will result in a clearer picture in your head of the final setup.

The preliminary track sheet should be done in conjunction with a preliminary block diagram. In addition to everything already discussed, the block diagram should include all connections, such as power, ground, and all digital connections. This will help you

CLIENT: The Saint Louis Symphony Orchestra
PROJECT: Riech Festival
LOCATION: The Touhill Performign Arts Center
CONTACTS:
    Josh Riggs FOH eng.
    314, XXXX
    Jason Freely Tech. Director Touhil
    Robert McGrath
DATE: 04-13-2007

input	instrument	microphone	source	stand	SPLIT	PRE	A/D	Notes
1	bata hl	MK4	PG	short	x	RM 1	RME 1:1	
2	bata hr	MK4	PG	st bar	x	RM 2	RME 1:2	
3	squeak hl	M147	PG	boom	x	RM 3	RME 1:3	needs a/c
4	squeak hr	M147	PG	st bar	x	RM 4	RME 1:4	needs a/c
5	marimba oh	A7 RED	PG	boom	x	RM 5	RME 1:5	needs a/c
6	mar. kick	md 421	tpac	desk	x	RM 6	RME 1:6	
7	xylophone oh	km 184	tpac	boom	x	RM 7	RME 1:7	
8	xylo. Kick	md 421	tpac	desk	x	RM 8	RME 1:8	
9	vibes oh	A6 RED	PG	boom	x	RM 9	RME 2:1	needs a/c
10	vibe. Kick	md 421	tpac	desk	x	RM 10	RME 2:2	
11	congas oh	SM81	tpac	boom				
12	5 addconga	at4050	tpac	boom	x	RM 11	RME 2:3	
13	M kick	md 421	tpac	desk	x	RM 12	RME 2:4	
14	M congas	umt 70s	PG	boom	x	RM 13	RME 2:5	
15	M timbales	4011	PG	short	x	RM 14	RME 2:6	
16	H kick	md 421	tpac	desk	x	RM 15	RME 2:7	
17	H oh hl	sanken 44x	PG	boom	x	RM 16	428 5	needs a/c
18	H oh hr	sanken 44x	PG	boom	x	RM 17	428 6	needs a/c
19	A Dunnuns	umt 70s	PG	boom	x	RM 18	428 7	
20	A cowbells	4011	PG	boom	x	RM 19	428 8	
21	piano	MK4	PG	CLAW	x	RME 1:9	RME 1:9	

Figure 3.3 A typical track sheet.

further visualize everything involved in your recording and the manner in which it interconnects. Don't forget to include as much as you can of the front-of-house PA system. You may interconnect with FOH PA systems at times; either way, their signal will affect your recording, so they need to be addressed.

At this point, you can start filling out your microphone wish list and microphone stand ideas and flesh out the details of your track list. Plan out your basic gear structure. Determine whether you want to go with a full console—if not, then how many channels of microphone preamps will you want to bring? Basic assumptions such as these are good to consider during the site survey, as you begin to imagine whether it is feasible to load in and set up all this gear. It is unprofessional (and one of the worst feelings ever) to attempt to cram too much gear into a space that is too small, only to find another room that would be perfect when you are loading out. To avoid this, the site survey is critical.

Site Surveys Rule!

Now that you have an idea in your head of how and where your microphones will be and how they will interface with your recording device, you need to consider the space in a detailed manner. Nothing beats a site survey for this. You can visualize a space all you want, but you will formulate a far clearer idea of the ramifications of the space on your recording by walking around in the space, listening to your footsteps and the way the reflections of those footsteps return to your ear. You really want to do a site survey before you plan any further. Nothing changes your packing list faster than a site survey.

Here are a few things to bring to a site survey:

- A notebook and a few pens, or an electronic notebook

- A tape measure

- Business cards

- Swag

- Donuts

- Ears for listening to the house

- Ears for listening to people

- A good attitude

Just as important as bringing the right gear to the gig is bringing the right gear to the site survey. You need to bring some very important equipment with you to do the survey correctly. First of all, bring a notebook—either traditional or electric. Because you need to write everything down, this may be the single most critical piece of gear you bring along to the site survey (see Figure 3.4).

Also bring a tape measure. The laser type is the most useful because it helps you avoid climbing up into small areas to get an idea of the dimensions with which you are dealing. It also makes for a quick end to the discussion of hanging microphones from an extremely high ceiling by clarifying that the catwalk is 150' 2" from the stage floor.

Equally important are business cards; bring lots. These are not swag, but this is an important contact opportunity. Give business cards to everyone you meet—and I do mean *everyone*, from the CEO to the janitor. The higher-ups need them because they might need to contact you, either now or for a gig in the future. The other folks might contact you to save you pain by filling you in on details of which a CEO is unaware. This has the side benefit of validating these folks as important in the process, which of course they are.

Figure 3.4 A notebook and a handful of pens are critically important during a site survey.

Don't forget to bring swag, or free stuff, to give out. This could be as simple as offering gum, jelly babies, or gummy bears or as impressive as giving a flashlight or an LED key chain with your company logo printed on it. The trick is not to be tacky. It is best if the stuff is actually useful (see Figure 3.5). A quick clip, carabineer, or pen is useful. A brightly colored wristband with your name on it is annoying. If it is an early call, bring donuts, the all-purpose and always-welcomed gift. This treatment of people— letting them know you care about them and respect them—should always be at the front of your mind. It makes it easy to make a good first (and lasting) impression.

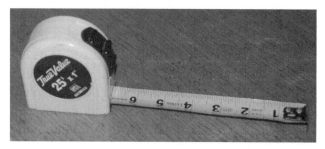

Figure 3.5 Even something as simple as a tape measure can be immeasurably important during a site survey.

The first step in a site survey is to contact the house manager or any other good contact whose information you have available. Try to pick a good time to call this person. Do not call him at a busy time; also try not to call during lunch. You really want this person to be your friend and ally, at least for the length of the gig. Introduce yourself and ask politely whether you can do a site survey. If the person starts hemming and hawing about it, be sure to use your best diplomacy skills. Tell him how wonderful his venue is and how many great shows you have seen and heard about in their fine hall, remembering to be as honest as you can during this process. Tell him how you have always wanted to record there, how excited you are to have this opportunity to do so, and how important it is to you to create the best possible recording—not only for your own benefit and the band's, but also so you can continue to uphold the reputation of their most excellent venue. As the house manager pulls out his shovel, ask him which is better, Tuesday afternoon or Wednesday morning, and hope that he is not hip to this oldest of sales tricks, the yes-yes question.

So what do you assess during a site survey? These items in particular:

- Power
- Ground
- Phase
- Voltage
- Setup location
- Isolation
- Easy access for loading gear
- Fire and safety codes
- Distance to stage
- Acoustics
- New friends

It is extremely important that you do a site survey. Look at it this way: If a picture is worth a thousand words, and there are 24 "pictures" per second in a movie, plus audio to go along with the pictures, this means you will need to ask questions quickly enough to get 30,000 words per second worth of information on the phone, versus going to the location. Seems like an easy call. Go on location.

More Power!

Now that you are in the venue doing your site survey, it is time to assess many of the features of the house. Acoustics, the shape of the room, and the materials that comprise the room are all important things to observe. Some of the most important assessments you will make during the site survey relate to power: How much is available, where is it, and is it clean?

Start by calculating how many amps your rig requires. In most cases, you will need a full, dedicated 20-amp circuit that is on the same phase as the event you are recording. If there is a PA system, you need to be on that system's phase. If that is not possible, you need to be on the same leg of power to ensure both safety and quality. Make sure the voltage is constant over a minimum of a five-minute period. The voltage should read a value between 110 and 120. Invest the two bucks in an outlet tester to check for proper wiring (see Figure 3.6).

Figure 3.6   A typical outlet tester.

Proper, clean ground and proper wiring are vital for a good and safe recording. Bad grounds can ruin recordings and fry gear. Almost as bad—bad grounds have killed people. If your goal is a high-quality recording and an injury-free experience, then you need to ensure that your power is good. If your recordings lack quality due to power issues, it will be hard to develop a following and get work. It is even harder to get live recording gigs when you are in prison for manslaughter, and it's harder still when you are six feet under. So check your power during the site survey and find a good circuit from which to work.

Where Do You Want This Stuff?

Another critically important part of your site survey is to ascertain where you will set up your gear. When you do the site survey, you will develop some ideas about this, and the representative of the house may have some different ideas. What are your criteria for this?

Obviously, you need good, clean power somewhere nearby, as previously mentioned. This is of paramount importance. You also need to be able to assess your recording during the performance. Because you are interested in the information you are record- ing, and because the sound in the house is unimportant to you, you need to select a location where you will be isolated from the house sound. Very few venues construct sonically isolated spaces for this purpose, so you have to be a bit flexible. If you cannot be completely isolated from all house sound, you have to ensure that, at the very least, you are not in the path of the direct house sound. That would color what you hear as you attempt to monitor your recording.

Another criterion for your ideal location should be access to easy load in and load out. It is not always possible to be right near the doors that lead to the loading dock, but if you have good power and good isolation and you are close to an outside door, you are doing pretty well. Of course, you cannot be *too* close to that door, because another criterion that determines your location relates to the local fire and safety codes. Blocking doors is generally frowned upon.

Another criterion is distance from the stage. A shorter run—in other words, setting up close to the stage—has several advantages. First of all, a shorter run usually means a higher-quality signal, because your signals encounter less resistance by running through a shorter wire. Also, it means you can get away with a shorter snake. Unfortunately, this can become a tradeoff between isolation and a short cable run, and many times isolation will win this argument (see Figure 3.7).

Now that you have established the location from which you will record this event, you need to measure some distances. Primarily, you will need two measurements—the dis- tance from the stage to your recording location and the distance from your recording location to power. It should be pretty obvious that these measurements are needed to ensure that you bring cables, snakes, and extension cords of the proper length.

Let's also revisit the acoustics of the hall at this point. What does the room sound like? How will that affect your recording? How much of the reflected sound will you want to include in the recording, and what will the relationship be between the direct sound you record and the reflected sound you record?

These Are Your New Friends
You've got some new friends now. They include:

- Managers

- House engineers

Figure 3.7   A typical setup for recording in a live venue.

- Other technical personnel
- Security
- Waiters and waitresses
- Bartenders
- Parking attendants
- The union
- Janitors
- Anyone else you run into

There is no better time to start making friends with the people who will help you create a successful recording than while you are there assessing the space. Start with the manager, who we will call the boss. This person needs to be on your side. Make friends with him or her. The boss can give you all the access you need, and he can also pull the plug. If the boss does not like you, great difficulties may be in your future, so try to get on his good side. If he *does* like you, he might recommend you to other potential clients.

Ask the manager how much time you have to set up, and try not to act surprised when this answer varies wildly from the one you obtained from the client. If you are not offered enough time to set up, ask whether you can come in earlier, set up, leave, and then come back. In this case, pre-rig anything you can. If you have this opportunity, then set up the things that cannot be seen and finish your setup later. We often find ourselves using this two-stage setup method in spaces that experience heavy use, such as cathedrals and other religious buildings.

Among your other new best friends are the security personnel. Seek them out and chat with them during your site survey. They will let you in when and where you need to be. They will also help protect your gear. Sometimes they are the only ones who can offer you access to an alley or a loading bay that will be the best place for your load in and load out. They are like anyone else you encounter in this process, so show them a little respect—ask about what it's like to work here, ask a few random questions about the neighborhood, ask about the weather or last night's game, and they will be inclined to like you (see Figure 3.8).

If the venue serves food and drink, befriend the wait staff and bartenders. There are several good reasons for this. You might need to kill some space in the venue for your setup—in other words, for you to do your job, they might lose a few tables and the income they would have earned. They will not be happy about this. Can you blame them? If they like you, they will be less unhappy about this, and no matter who they are, you want them on your side. Talk to the waiters and waitresses. Apologize in advance for the tables they may lose. If they like you, there will be no hard feelings about the lost tables, and they may even bring you a nonalcoholic beverage during the gig.

It is a good idea to plan to order some food from them the night of the gig, so that even though they may have lost a table to you, at least you can give them one paying cos-tumer. If they feed you and drinks are on the house, or even if they give you nothing at all, remember to leave a tip (even if you are not running for president).

Parking attendants should also be among your new friends. Sometimes when we load in our gear, we do so through a crowded parking lot. Sometimes there will be cars parked right up to the loading dock we want to use. If this is the case, the parking attendants

Figure 3.8 One of your new friends.

can be your best friends. Do not wait until the night of the gig. Like everyone else who may impact your ability to successfully record, befriend them ahead of time.

Last but far from least among your new friends are the union guys. If this is a union shop, then there will be union guys, and nothing will happen without their blessing. It is critically important that you establish a relationship of cooperation between yourself and the union.

Planning Gear

After you come back from your survey, you should have a better sense of what you will need to bring. You will also have an idea about how to get it there, the number of stairs, and whether the invention known as the wheel will actually help, particularly in the form of a cart or hand truck. As you consider gear, plan to take more than you need. Along with obvious gear, including your favorite microphones and recording system, bring extra microphones. Bring a laptop with another recording system loaded and ready to go for backup. Don't forget the microphone stands, microphone clips, cables, and a snake, along with a few extra clips and stands. How about a power strip and an extension cord? Better yet, bring a few extra power strips and few extra extension cords. Don't forget a ground lifter and a small tool kit, just in case. You also want to plan to do a mix on the fly—a live to two-track mix that is sometimes called a *safety mix*. This allows for instant playback and is a decent reference mix for judging takes and retakes. It also provides something when everything else fails. This can be on your main recording system, but a standalone allows for more security in the event that your main system crashes.

While planning, always consider bringing lots of everything—in fact, it is wise to bring more of everything than you think you could possibly use (see Figure 3.9).

Figure 3.9 More of everything than you think you will need.

That means lots of what you need, even more of what you need, and then backup for all those things you need. You can never have too many things in the trunk of your car, ready in case they are needed. When you actually hear the band play, you have the option to consider other possibilities. The style of music and the method of recording will influence the number of microphones you use and their placement. You might decide that less is more; sometimes you can create a far better recording with a pair of microphones at the front of the stage and another pair back in the house than you can with 20 microphones. But you still want those other 16 microphones handy, just in case. We'll discuss the aesthetics that influence these decisions later in this book. First, let's explore more closely the relationships we develop as we examine gig psychology.

4 Gig Psychology: Playing with Others

T he number-one thing that will get you more clients, gigs, recommendations, free booze, dinner, parking, movie passes, adulation, respect, gold fish, and any sort of coveted item or service is how you behave. Your number-one goal on location is to *appear* professional. *Being* professional runs a close second. Getting a fantastic recording is a large portion of what makes you a pro, but the other aspects of being professional include understanding the needs of others and how others view you, and getting them to work *with* you rather than *against* you. You also need to make everyone you meet comfortable and happy with every aspect of your presence. This takes many forms, from helping the client understand and figure out what they really want or need in a project, to helping the live sound engineer improve his reinforcement, to blending into the show so as not to distract.

Don't Be a Putz

Remember, above all else, you are a pain in everyone at the location's rumps—except maybe the client, because they asked you to be there. It doesn't matter how nice you are or how much cash is involved, you are not a known factor, and you are an additional potential problem to deal with while putting on a performance or event. Keeping in mind that perception rules, you should be in full schmooze mode the minute you begin to make contact in order to give the best impression. You need to foster the team ideal.

Your primary goal is to get the best recording possible. This is not necessarily the same goal shared by everyone else at the event. Taking this into account, everything—not just the recording—needs to go smoothly if you are to achieve the best possible recording. If things unrelated to the recording go wrong at the event, it will affect your product as much as a mistake or error on your side of the console. It is your job to keep all aspects of the recording running smoothly. You need to work with all others involved in the production—from the house manager, who is trying to seat people behind your very ugly and intrusive microphone stand, to the monitor engineer, who is afraid he won't be able to ring out the monitor speakers with that fancy recording microphone.

Figure 4.1 Putzes.

Obviously, the best time to deal with all the issues that may arise is well before the night of the gig. Remember to respect everyone there. Their jobs are just as important as (if not more important than) the one you are doing. Whether this is true is insignificant; it is a good rule of thumb to think that it is. The people you are working with perceive their jobs as the most important. Don't mess with that perception.

The Front-of-House Engineer

Imagine you come to a gig, and the front-of-house engineer has selected microphones you are unfamiliar with or you do not like. Your first instinct might be to replace all the microphones he has selected. This might lead you to create a better record in terms of a solid quality you'll be getting from the microphones; however, it might wreak havoc and cause you far greater problems.

If the front-of-house engineer is not used to working with a particular type of microphone that you have selected or if he is just not set up for these microphones, it is very likely that he will create feedback. This is particularly the case if you replace his microphones at the last minute, and he does not have the chance to re-EQ the sound system. Not only might this lead to a worse-sounding concert and a worse performance as a result, but it could also lead to wailing feedback. Feedback kills your recording. And then you not only make an enemy of the front-of-house engineer and the performers, you also don't get paid for the night. In fact, a stunt like that might mean you never get paid as a live sound recordist.

The Monitor Mixer

If the group you are recording has a monitor engineer, also known as a *monitor mixer* or *stage mixer*, you will need to make contact with him in addition to the front-of-house engineer. The monitor engineer is often more critical than the front-of-house engineer for the recording. The monitor speakers are far closer to the microphones and will therefore have more impact on the overall sound of the recording than the front-of-house sound system will. As we discussed earlier, the monitor speakers can introduce reflections into your microphones to give you undesired and undesirable sound. You really need to become friends with the monitor engineer, primarily because he knows more about the group than anyone else in the building. The monitor engineer deals with the group on a regular basis and knows their tricks, oddities, and habits. Typical placements of monitor speakers are not for the best quality of recording, but for the most accommodating position for the artist. Monitor speakers are there so the artists can hear themselves and their band-mates.

Typically, other than feedback and the convenience of the artist, not much thought is given to the monitors' location. With the invention of in-ear monitoring, many issues have begun to lessen. Nonetheless, monitors are far from gone, and you will encounter them almost everywhere you go. Badly EQed or bright-sounding monitors will be picked up clearly in the performers' microphones. Even worse is the possibility of rolling, roaring feedback. Unless you are recording Jimi Hendrix, this is typically a bad thing.

The key to solving these issues is prompt and timely discussion about what microphones will be used and where they will be placed, especially in relation to the stage monitors. Often you cannot reach an agreement on microphones. At this point, you need to consider other options for miking the sound source. Remember to be kind to your monitor mixer even if he does not see eye to eye with you regarding microphones. You need to get along with everyone in the human chain of production as much as you need to get along with all the devices in your signal chain.

Seeing Double

You might choose to ignore the PA system's microphones and mike everything with your own microphones. This can be a decent way to record a good high-quality sound. The issues created with this method of doubling up on all microphone stands, cables, and wiring may not be a problem for the front-of-house engineer, the monitor mixers, or even the band. Unfortunately, it might be a problem for the concert promoter, owner of the building, owner of the bar, or owner of the theater, as it becomes exceedingly ugly.

There are times when you will be called upon to record sound for a video shoot. Double miking becomes almost completely unacceptable because it creates a field or forest of microphones instead of a compelling view of the musicians and players, in opposition to the desires of the cinematographer or videographer. It would probably be acceptable to place one or two high-quality microphones in unobtrusive positions to get the particular sound you desire. You also might be able to use claw clips to attach a secondary microphone onto the same microphone stand in use for the PA reinforcement microphone (see Figure 4.2). The issue that presents itself here is that you might not get your microphone into the proper position to pick up the sound you desire because you are sharing the stand with the live front-of-house engineer.

Figure 4.2 A claw attached to a microphone stand for doubling a microphone setup.

The Audience Is Listening...and Watching

The most important group that we have yet to mention is the audience at the event. If they are not happy, comfortable, excited, and into the performance, the recording will suffer. Often an artist feeds off the positive energy of the audience. If this is lacking, the performance might not be as spectacular as it could be.

Keeping the audience safe and happy is one of your primary goals. If the best location for you to set up your control room allows for no way to safely cross a threshold, door, or walkway, with tables that create a tripping hazard, you must find a new place. It is important that you help the entire performance, including the audience's enjoyment, rather than hinder things.

It's also extremely important that you take into account safety measures provided for the building, such as the fire code, electrical code, and general public safety rules. Remember, as quaint as the saying "safety first" may be, it really *does* apply in a location recording. It is a smart idea to meet with the building manager before your concert to figure out where you can run cables in order to keep things generally out of the path of patrons. Typically, the house manager or building manager will understand the needs of the audience better than almost anyone else. They will also be the people who can help you deal with parking situations, coffee, bathrooms, power, as well as many other features unique to the building or house.

The main point when dealing with anyone you meet on location is to treat him or her nicely. Many people have been persecuted for this, but you really *do* need to be nice to everyone for a change. I cannot emphasize this point enough. Be nice. While we have given a few examples of how to stay out of the way and be helpful to your fellow production team members, the basics apply to anyone and everyone you meet at a recording location. If you are able to make yourself helpful and useful and make the gig run more smoothly than it does without you, you will be welcomed back. More importantly, you might become the preferred recordist for that venue, leading to glory, money, and general success.

Dress Codes

Putting people at ease is one of the most important things a recording engineer can do, particularly on location. We have discussed different ways your actions can put people at ease, but their first perception—the thing that starts everything off—is how you first appear. We have all been told and taught that appearance is nothing more than superficial. This may be true—it is very superficial. However, first impressions are very difficult to change. This being said, it is important to do basic human things such as showering; wearing clean, neat, appropriate clothes; combing your hair (if you have any); arriving promptly; and wearing pants without any holes in them (see Figures 4.3 and 4.4).

Figure 4.3 Clean-looking stage setup.

Figure 4.4 Inappropriate dress for stage setup.

Obviously, your level of dress, appearance, style, attitude, and how you present yourself can change, depending on your client. Dressing to go to the symphony probably wouldn't be appropriate to go to a Goth rock club, but it would be preferable to the reverse—going to the symphony dressed as if you were going to a Goth rock club. I'm not saying to take away all of your style, though. There are ways you can dress, act, and appear that are appropriate for any situation in which you may find yourself.

Also remember that while something might be appropriate for the club or venue, it may not always be proper attire for the load in and load out of the concert. Almost as important as bringing the correct microphones is bringing the correct suit to change into for the concert. This is especially critical if you are in a position that can be seen by the audience. In these situations you want to practice being invisible. Dark colors, conservative clothing, and appropriate clothing are the best ways to blend in. You can always rely on black clothing to help you disappear in a theatre or concert hall. If you have doubts about what level of dress is expected, it is always better to be overdressed than underdressed (see Table 4.1).

Table 4.1 Appropriate Attire in Some Situations

Type	Load In	Event	Load Out
Corporate	Khakis, comfortable shoes	Khakis, polo shirt, dress shoes	Khakis, comfortable shoes
High Culture	Khakis, comfortable shoes	Suit or tuxedo, dress shoes	Khakis, comfortable shoes
Everything else	Comfortable clothes	Dress in black	Comfortable clothes

Focus on the Band

It happens all too often that we record a band we like, and when we sit down to talk with them, we discover that the sound we love, the sound we know we can create, and the sound we are really looking forward to are not what the band wants. Maybe it's not even what they like. This is the type of information you need to get from the band at your first meeting.

During your first conversation, pay attention to what the band says, not what you want them to say. Be a good listener. Ask the right questions to get the answers you need to make them happy, rather than fulfilling you own idea of what they should sound like.

Here are some things you need to pay attention to. As you talk about your ideas regarding how you intend to record the band, ask them what they want to sound like. Do they want to sound like their last album? Do they want to sound like their first album? Do they want to sound like Judy Garland in *The Wizard of Oz*? As you ascertain their needs and the manner in which they want the recording to represent their performance, remain professional and engaged in the conversation, even if their requests seem odd to you.

Your job as a live recordist is very involved. There are many things you need to do in order to be successful. One thing you cannot be is judgmental about the band's direction and their desires. Even if you think their direction is silly and superfluous, your job is to discover within yourself a genuine interest in some aspect of the band's direction, beyond your interest in the paycheck at the end of the gig.

Creating the Language

The first step in figuring out how the band wants to sound is to actually go hear them play. While this seems obvious, I can't tell you how many times I've asked live sound recordists whether they have heard the band before, and they've said no. Go hear the band. Then go back and hear them again. Preferably, you want to hear the band at least two or three times. Each time they play, they do something slightly differently—either they are getting better or they are getting more comfortable with the music and morphing in a direction that is more interesting.

Another advantage is that you'll build a relationship with the band because they will see you at a number of gigs. Most importantly, you will be beginning to develop insight into the band's modus operandi. This continues to build trust with the musicians as they begin to feel you know them and understand their work, since you've seen them perform many times.

However, seeing the band perform many times is not always feasible. Another option is to ask the band whether they have a recording that they've done previously, either studio or live. From these recordings, you can gain a tremendous amount of useful information about how they like or dislike the way they've been recorded in the past. Find out whether they like anything particular, even in recordings they don't genuinely like. Find out whether they're looking to make a break from these recordings or whether they're just trying to improve on the quality of them. Or perhaps they have some new material and they would like to re-create the recordings they had before, just with new songs. In short, find out the reason for the record you will be creating.

At this point, you also need to figure out why they are hiring you for the recording. Are they doing it for an archival recording of the show, or is it for a CD release or an MP3 download, or perhaps a promotional piece? Each of these will bring a different set of challenges to the recording (see Figure 4.5).

Figure 4.5   iPod in dock.

In addition to their own music, find out what music inspires the band. Talk to each member of the band and find out who his favorite artists are and what his favorite recording is. What does he like to listen to? What's on his iPod? This will give you an idea of the sonic language the band members have in mind in terms of recording. It will be easier to talk about different elements of the recording if you understand the sound history the band brings with it.

For example, you might be working with a metal band that tends to like the hair-metal bands of the 1980s with the raw power of AC/DC and Led Zeppelin. By finding out which Led Zeppelin albums they like to listen to or which 1980s hair bands they really enjoy, you will be able to coax out the terminology that you will use to describe sound in a manner that they will understand. For example, you can describe a certain commonality of bass that is similar to that used by John Paul Jones and "The Lemon Song" from Led Zeppelin. You now have a point of reference from which you can start a conversation about the sound of the bass. The common thread of music and sonic experience that you develop with the band through effective communications will allow you to have a more accurate conversation about the sonic quality of the recording, thus enabling you to fulfill their needs.

This common language will come in handy when you're discussing what you'll be doing for the location recording. Let's take our metal band again. The drummer is a huge fan of trigger drums and wants to trigger his drums on the record. You may hate trigger drums and think that it is absolutely the wrong thing to do on a live record, mostly because they don't use trigger drums when they perform live. At this point, you need to persuade the drummer to your point of view. The question is, when do you stop attempting to persuade and decide that ultimately the client is correct? For me, this point comes after I've asked the client whether he would be willing to listen to another idea or thought. If the reaction is instantly negative, then I back off and develop a different approach, either to further convince him or to accommodate the client through acquiescence.

If I am still trying to convince the client, the other approach typically involves finding tragically bad recordings of someone who has used trigger drums in a location recording, and how it doesn't work. Other times this different approach requires me to go in with something like a small two-track recorder to do a quick demo of how the band actually sounds live. This is often an eye-opening experience for the band that has never heard itself. This technique is not as unusual as it was 10 years ago, with the proliferation of small, high-quality digital recorders. It can be a useful technique because you can start to highlight things you think might become a problem from where you sit with your two-track recorder. Occasionally, I find that my suggestions might actually not work, and then I change my ideas. This process dramatically increases the collaboration and leads to a more sonically pleasing product, increasing happiness and satisfaction for all involved parties.

These techniques might seem to be slightly exaggerated, particularly if you are a musician and you are accustomed to talking to other musicians to indicate your feelings about music. Many of us communicate about music effectively by simply employing standard musical terminology. When I was working with the late Hans Vonk, I discovered I was having a hard time understanding some of his requests. Hans was an amazing conductor who balanced the orchestra phenomenally well, creating a unique tonality. It probably helps that he started his life and musical career as a pianist, but in the end, the result he got out of an orchestra was a wonderfully balanced instrument. I thought I had been doing a good job until I started getting requests from the Maestro that certain things were out of balance. I'd sit down in my recording booth and play the recordings back, and I could not understand what he was talking about. His complaints were never that something was so out of balance as to be obscene, but that something was slightly low here or slightly loud there. After about three weeks of this, I finally asked the Maestro a question I should've asked at the beginning of the conversation: "What are you listening to the recordings on?" It turned out that Maestro Vonk's time, like that of all major conductors in the classical world, was extremely limited and that he had done most of his listening in his car, on the Autobahn between Berlin and Dresden.

These days, you will find that most people listen to their iPods on airplanes and such. Details such as this can give you great insight into the problems you will face when discussing either your recordings or someone else's. It is important to get a generally agreed-upon central reference point, including the playback systems being used, in order to understand what all parties are listening to.

We have been assuming that your client is a music group, but often you are meeting with a producer. Regardless, the same principles apply no matter what type of project it is and no matter whom you are working for. You might need to modify your choice of sonic examples, such as relying on classical examples before recording an orchestra or talking about a favorite television program instead of a favorite music program if you are doing a video shoot. If you are miking a speech, you might want to talk about really nice-sounding speeches, such as the miking technique used in most presidential press conferences of two SM57s side by side, or the traditional SM58 on a table stand for the reigning champion of any given sport. You need to analyze your client's sonic language and open a dialogue with him to understand what sort of sound he actually desires.

While doing all of this, you still need to take into account all the technical details of the space, the gear, the power, and the ground.

5 Understanding and Respecting Power and Ground

Some of the most important assessments you will make during your site survey are an examination of the power situation in the venue and a determination regarding the quality of the power and the all-important ground. Having clean, adequate, and safe power can, in the best of situations, make the difference between a quality recording and something that is not usable. In the worst-case scenario, bad power or ground could actually lead to fire, serious injury, or death.

We work with audio signals. By the time we receive audio, it has been transduced, or converted, at the microphone from acoustic energy to an electrical signal. We work in the world of electrical signals, and therefore any electrical issues that present themselves at any point in the signal chain are a component of our recording. The electromagnetic spectrum is far larger than many people realize, ranging from well below those annoying 60-Hz hums, to VHS and UHF radio and television waves, and far beyond into microwaves and ultrasonics. Magnetic resonance generated from moving electrical energy (inductance) and rogue voltages can travel down paths that we intend in order to avoid affecting our recording; they can also travel down paths where we do not want these errant signals due to poor maintenance, mishaps, or bad design.

The Basics of Audio as Electricity

As mentioned, our audio signals are electrical signals; specifically, they are current running through wires in a path we have determined—signals that are analogous to the original acoustic wave. We already know that we need to convert the acoustic wave to an electrical signal using a transducer. Let's examine this idea a little more closely.

A transducer is a device that converts one form of energy to another, such as a light bulb that converts electricity to light and heat or a tape-machine playback head that converts a magnetic signal into electricity (see Figure 5.1).

At the moment, the transducers with which we are concerned are microphones. All microphones are transducers; they convert the acoustic energy presented to them into an electrical signal that we can route through our system.

Figure 5.1 A light bulb is a typical transducer, converting electrical energy to heat and light.

Converting acoustic energy to electrical energy in a microphone requires a diaphragm, which is a surface made of a thin, flexible substance under tension, similar to a drum skin or the paper in a kazoo, which vibrates in response to the changes in atmospheric pressure caused by the compression and rarefaction of molecules of a sound wave. The physical motion of this diaphragm, analogous to the original sound wave, is converted into an electrical signal, which is also analogous to the original sound wave. There are several methods of accomplishing this. A general microphone type represents each one. Each of these types of microphones has assets and liabilities, and each will affect both the technical and aesthetic aspects of a particular audio situation.

Dynamic Microphones

Different types of microphones will convert acoustic energy to electrical energy in different ways and will present you with different advantages and disadvantages. We commonly use dynamic microphones, also known as *moving-coil microphones,* in live work. We obtain several advantages from dynamic microphones. Primarily, they are cheap and they are tough. Unlike in the recording studio, where a microphone can be stored in a stable, locked cabinet until it is needed, we throw our microphones into flight cases and anvil cases, toss these cases in the backs of our trucks and cars, and bump our way to the gig. Okay, we are not really that careless with our microphones (or any of our gear), but the reality of moving from one location to another *does* invite more wear and tear, and dynamic microphones are capable of taking a great deal of abuse before they cease to function.

Dynamic microphones work on the principle of inductance, in which electric current is created, or induced, by a wire or any conductor as it moves within a magnetic field (see Figure 5.2).

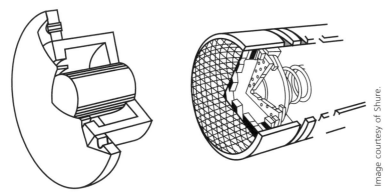

Image courtesy of Shure.

Figure 5.2   In this diagram, showing inductance in a dynamic microphone, the magnet, which is attached to the diaphragm, moves through a wire coil, which creates an electrical signal analogous to the original sound wave.

There are two types of dynamic microphones, moving-coil and ribbon, although when someone refers to a dynamic microphone, he is usually discussing the more common moving-coil variety, which we will explore first.

In a moving-coil microphone, a wire in a magnetic field is attached to the diaphragm, which causes it to move in concert with the diaphragm. The wire is surrounded by a magnetic field, and the free electrons within the wire will begin to flow as a result of this movement, producing electricity. To understand the relationship between electricity and magnetism, consider an experiment frequently done in high schools that involves spiraling a wire around a nail with electricity from a battery flowing through it, causing the nail to become an electromagnet. In the case of the high school experiment, the nail is converting electrical energy into magnetic energy, whereas a moving-coil microphone converts acoustic energy into electrical energy, but the principles are similar.

Because the movement of the attached wire causes the flow of electricity in a moving-coil microphone, and the diaphragm moves in response to the sound waves in the air, the electrical signal will be an analog of the original sound waves. A moving-coil microphone, which most audio professionals describe as a *dynamic microphone,* has one end of a spring-like wire coil attached to the diaphragm, while the other end of the wire coil feeds the microphone output. Either the wire coil is surrounded by a permanent magnet or the coil itself surrounds the magnet. Historically, moving-coil microphones do not have the best frequency response; however, they are inexpensive and durable, making them an ideal microphone in many instances.

Durability is not only a factor when a microphone is dropped or thrown into a flight case to be transported, it also is related to high sound pressure level (SPL) situations. Moving-coil microphones are not only difficult to break, they are difficult to overload with amplitude—in other words, they can be used in situations in which the sound source is very loud. This makes them useful for instruments with tremendous transients, such as drums, percussion, and guitar amps, as well as for instruments with high SPL. Their toughness makes them ideal for live sound as well as film shoots and other work outdoors or in distant facilities, because these situations involve travel, and dynamic microphones are less likely to be damaged in transit. Moving-coil microphones such as the Shure SM57 (see Figure 5.3) and SM58 (see Figure 5.4) and the Sennheiser 421 (see Figure 5.5) and 441 perform well on guitar amps and drums, particularly snare drums and tom-toms, due to their high resistance to overloading.

Photo courtesy of Shure.

Figure 5.3   The Shure SM57, a studio and live use workhorse of a dynamic microphone.

Photo courtesy of Shure.

Figure 5.4   Like its counterpart, the Shure SM58 is a studio-standard dynamic microphone.

Figure 5.5 The Sennheiser 421 is a dynamic microphone offering a different texture than the Shure dynamic microphones.

Bass drums require even more resistance to overloading due to the extremely high SPLs. The old-school recommendations for bass drum microphones include the Electro-Voice RE20 (see Figure 5.6) and the AKG D 12 E (see Figure 5.7) or D 112.

A 421 can also be used successfully in a bass drum. The Shure SM58 is also an ideal vocal microphone in live situations—whether music, broadcast, film, or video—where durability is a primary factor.

Figure 5.6 An EV RE20 is a classic choice for a bass drum and is also a favorite of many radio announcers.

Photo courtesy of Stan Coutant.

Figure 5.7 The AKG D 12 E attained status as the studio-standard bass drum microphone.

While the microphone choices outlined a moment ago are considered by some to be standards, meaning many audio professionals will use these without thinking about it too much, there are always new microphones worth considering and fresh ears (yours!) that should be making the final determination and microphone selection.

All of the dynamic microphones we have discussed thus far offer relatively small diaphragms. There is a new generation of large-diaphragm dynamic microphones that is gaining tremendous and well-deserved respect. This new wave of microphones is led by Heil Sound, with their PR-20 (see Figure 5.8), PR-30 (see Figure 5.9), and PR-40

Photo courtesy of Heil Sound.

Figure 5.8 The large-diaphragm dynamic Heil Sound PR-20 is excellent on vocals, snare drums, and drum overheads.

Figure 5.9   The Heil Sound PR-30, also a large-diaphragm dynamic microphone, excels on guitars and toms.

Figure 5.10   The PR-40, also a large-diaphragm dynamic microphone from Heil Sound, is considered by some engineers to be positioned to replace the D 12 E as the studio-standard kick-drum microphone.

(see Figure 5.10) gaining great success throughout the industry. The strong rear rejection of all of Heil Sound's products makes them as good for broadcast and interview applications as they are for live recording.

Ribbon Microphones

Ribbon microphones also work on the principle of inductance and are therefore another type of dynamic microphone; however, engineers never refer to ribbon microphones as dynamic microphones—they are always referred to as ribbon microphones. In the ribbon microphone, the diaphragm is a thin, metallic ribbon, which is extremely fragile. This metallic ribbon is thin enough to be responsive to the vibrations in the air. As with the moving-coil microphone, the ribbon microphone's moving conductor—in this case, the diaphragm—is suspended in a magnetic field, created by permanent magnets built into the microphone. Despite their excellent frequency response, ribbon microphones are much more delicate than moving-coil microphones and perform poorly in outdoor conditions when gusts of wind are present. They also do not respond well to transients.

A new generation of ribbon microphones has emerged that boasts a more rugged design, but many in the engineering community remain unimpressed by the quality of the sound captured compared to the "classic" ribbon microphones. To many audio professionals, there is still nothing as good as the sound of an RCA 77 (see Figure 5.11) on a cello; however, transporting so delicate and expensive a microphone might not be practical during live recording.

Photo courtesy of Stan Coutant.

Figure 5.11 The RCA 77 is a classic ribbon microphone, delicate and sweet, but it might not be the best choice due to transportation issues.

The most widely used ribbon microphones are older models, such as the RCA 77 and RCA 44 (see Figure 5.12).

Ribbon microphones are popular with voiceover announcers, and as with many types of classic or vintage equipment, they have become sought after and expensive. They are also used on string sections and brass sections; however, close miking is not recommended in this case because ribbon microphones are overly sensitive to the wind produced from the bells of the instruments and the high SPLs of some brass instruments. Ribbon microphones are commonly used for plucked gut- or nylon-stringed instruments as well.

Photo courtesy of Stan Coutant.

Figure 5.12 The RCA 44 BX is another classic ribbon microphone, popular with announcers and singers and delicious on string sections.

Condenser Microphones

Condenser microphones work on a completely different principle than dynamic microphones—the principle of capacitance. A capacitor is a device that, like a battery, is capable of storing and discharging an electrical charge. The turn signals and intermittent windshield wipers in cars have capacitors in their circuits, which store a charge for a user-selected or predetermined period of time and then discharge. Condenser microphones work on the same principle, where the stored charge is released in a fashion that is analogous to the original acoustic wave (see Figure 5.13).

Think of two buckets of water, each with a hole in the bottom. If these holes are different sizes, the water will trickle out of each at a different rate, just as electricity will trickle out of a capacitor at a specific rate unique to each capacitor. The diaphragm of a condenser microphone is a capacitor. This capacitor has a minimum of two opposing plates—one fixed in the rear, called the *base plate,* and one moving plate that sits in front. The stored voltage is discharged according to the distance between these two plates. Sound pressure waves entering the microphone cause the front plate (diaphragm) to vibrate. As the front plate vibrates, its relative distance to the rear plate changes. This is the means by which the output voltage is modulated (see Figure 5.14). The name "condenser microphone" derives from old terminology in which capacitors were called *condensers.* Although some audio professionals refer to these microphones as *capacitor microphones,* the vast majority in the engineering community continue to refer to them as *condenser microphones.*

Photo courtesy of Neumann.

Figure 5.13 The inner workings of a Neumann U 87, a popular condenser microphone.

Photo courtesy of Neumann.

Figure 5.14 The Neumann U 67 is another popular condenser microphone and is less expensive than the U 87.

The electrical charge held by the capacitor within the condenser microphone's diaphragm is supplied by an external source. Older models of condenser microphones have a separate power supply unit, which is generally tube-powered and about the size of a lunch pail, and which plugs into an electrical outlet to provide power to the microphone's capsule (see Figure 5.15).

Photo courtesy of Neumann.

Figure 5.15   The Neumann M 179 is a tube condenser microphone.

Newer models receive their power directly from the audio console or from outboard preamps. Known as *phantom power* (+48 volts DC), it derives its name from the fact that the power supply is no longer visible (and taking up loads of valuable floor space). More expensive modern consoles have switchable phantom power on each input/output module. Moderately priced and inexpensive consoles have one switch to enable all modules for phantom power. Phantom power should always be turned off while microphones are being plugged in or unplugged, because the resulting pop can damage monitors and other equipment. Phantom power is supplied through the microphone cables in DC, as noted a moment ago, and is blocked by capacitors from entering the console's microphone preamps, resulting in no effect on the audio signal passing through.

Condenser microphones are very sensitive and can break or overload easily; however, they offer superior frequency response. Due to their extreme sensitivity, they are considered by many to be the best vocal microphones and are capable of picking up the slightest nuance of a performer's voice, especially under carefully controlled studio conditions. Condenser microphones are exceptional all-around microphones and are commonly used on vocals, brass, woodwinds, strings, pianos, drum overheads, and any acoustic instrument. General-purpose condenser microphones may be inappropriate for live recording, broadcast, or film work due to their extreme delicacy and sensitivity. The Neumann U 87 is the most widely accepted and commonly used condenser microphone, featuring fine frequency response. Other Neumanns include the U 89 (a little brighter than the U 87); the vintage FET47 and U 47 (a tube microphone), which are both heavily sought after for their richness of tone; and the KM series, including the KM 84, KM 100, KM 130, and KM 140, fine microphones for drum overheads and pianos. The KM 130 is particularly well suited for live recording, often for picking up the ambience of the concert hall, because it is omnidirectional. There are also many other manufacturers, such as Audio-Technica, that make popular models of condenser microphones (see Figure 5.16).

Photo courtesy of Audio-Technica.

Figure 5.16 Not all condenser microphones are made by Neumann (as you might think by looking at the previous photos). Audio-Technica makes this condenser microphone.

The AKG 414 is also a widely accepted condenser microphone, useful in all situations except close miking, as is the AKG 451, which is excellent in most situations—particularly for instruments that need a strong edge at higher frequencies, including drum overheads and toms, and low strings, such as cello and double bass (see Figure 5.17).

Wireless Microphone Systems

You will sometimes encounter wireless microphones as you work in live venues. Wireless microphone systems are used anytime a microphone cable would be confining or unsightly. They have become very popular in sound reinforcement, particularly when

Figure 5.17   The AKG 414 is another studio standard condenser microphone.

the performer wants the freedom to dance or move around the stage (see Figures 5.18 through 5.20).

Figure 5.18   A Telex FMR-1000 wireless microphone system.

Wireless microphones broadcast on specific radio frequencies and require a transmitter, antenna, and receiver to broadcast and pick up the signal for routing to an audio console (see Figure 5.21). Often these microphones must be in the line of sight of the antenna attached to their receivers, and the batteries must be changed regularly. When used with a lavaliere, a wire runs from the microphone to a body transmitter with antenna, which broadcasts to the receiver. In handheld wireless microphones and wireless headset microphones, the transmitter and antenna are usually incorporated

Figure 5.19   The Elector-Voice REV wireless microphone system.

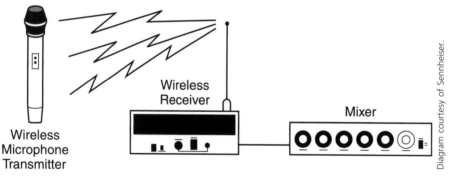

Figure 5.20   A wireless microphone system by Shure.

Figure 5.21   This is the basic theory of wireless microphones.

into the microphone itself. Because the signal broadcasts in the UHF and VHF bands, there is a risk of interference by ham radio operators or CB operators.

Polar Patterns

Before we follow the signal past the microphone, there is one more aspect of the microphone that we must examine—the polar pattern. A polar pattern is a map of a microphone's directional sensitivity, graphically depicting the way a microphone will respond according to the position of the sound source relative to the microphone's position. Also known as *pickup patterns*, there are three basic types of polar patterns: omnidirectional, or nondirectional, which is equally sensitive in all directions; bidirectional, which is sensitive only to the front and back; and unidirectional, or directional, which is sensitive only in the front. Cardioid is a commonly used name for a directional microphone with a heart-shaped pickup pattern, as are supercardioid, hypercardioid, and ultracardioid for shotgun microphones with tighter heart-shaped patterns.

A microphone's directionality is determined by the microphone type, because certain patterns are inherent to certain types of microphones, and affected by openings on the sides or rear of the microphone, which allow phase cancellation of sounds from certain directions. Openings close to the diaphragm cancel high frequencies, while openings further from the diaphragm cancel lower frequencies.

Moving-coil microphones are inherently omnidirectional (see Figure 5.22).

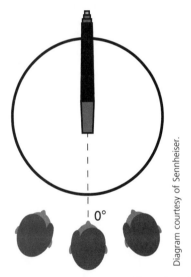

Diagram courtesy of Sennheiser.

Figure 5.22   The omnidirectional pattern shown means that the microphone is equally sensitive in all directions. This pattern is inherent to both dynamic and condenser microphones, but other patterns are easy to create.

Adding ports to the microphone casing and adding an acoustic phase-shifting network creates a cardioid pattern (see Figure 5.23).

This causes sound waves approaching the microphone from the rear to impact both sides of the diaphragm. These sound waves will have their phase reversed on either side of the diaphragm and are therefore greatly reduced in intensity. This increasingly reduces the microphone's sensitivity as the sound source moves off axis, with its minimum sensitivity located at 180 degrees off axis (the rear of the microphone).

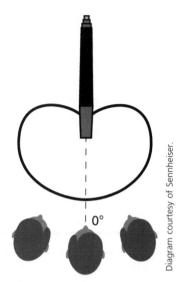

Figure 5.23   The cardioid pattern is most sensitive to the front and least sensitive to the rear. It is a common pattern for vocals and instruments when separation between sound sources is desirable.

Ribbon microphones are inherently bidirectional, making them most sensitive to sounds entering the microphone at 0 degrees and 180 degrees and least sensitive to sounds entering at 90 degrees and 270 degrees (see Figure 5.24).

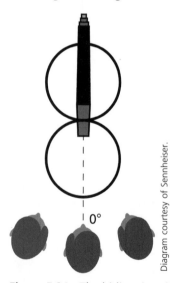

Figure 5.24   The bidirectional pattern is most sensitive to the front and rear of the microphone and least sensitive to the sides.

This pattern can be valuable when you are recording an interview or two singers singing a duet.

Condenser microphones are inherently omnidirectional; however, they can easily be made multidirectional, offering a variety of patterns, based on which plate is charged. Many condenser microphones have a third plate, and by variously reversing, reducing, or eliminating the charge to selected plates of the three plates, bidirectional, omnidirectional, and cardioid can all be made available.

Consoles

When the signal leaves the microphone and heads down the cable, the next stop is the mixing console, the center of everything. All signals pass through the console. The console's primary functions are routing and processing of input and output signals. A professional console has the ability to simultaneously route numerous input signals to a wide variety of devices and locations. Signals arrive at the console, where the audio professional sends them wherever they are needed. These amazing devices are simple to understand. This is due to redundancy, the seemingly endless repetition of modules, which makes them easy to understand and use. If you take the time to understand one module or strip in a console, you will understand them all, thanks to redundancy (see Figure 5.25).

Photo courtesy of SSL.

Figure 5.25 The redundancy of modules makes it easy to understand even the most complex consoles, such as this SSL XL 9000 K in Studio Davout, France.

Remember, versatility and flexibility of a console, more than the number of modules, are the hallmarks of a quality console. A state-of-the-art console will consistently give the audio professional many options for signal routing. Shifting the sequence of effects in the console and choosing different ways to bring signal in and then send it out allow the engineer to maximize quality and fulfill his aesthetic.

The first point at which the signal is manipulated by the console is determined by the type of signal present and selected. Consoles accept primarily two types of signals, line level and microphone level. Although DJ consoles will also accept signal at phono level, as will older home stereos, we will remain focused on the more common line and microphone levels. There is a need for two separate types of inputs because there is such a vast difference between the voltage levels of each of these signals. Microphones output tiny amounts of voltage, somewhere in the range of -60 to -70 dB—well below the console's optimal operating level—while a line level's signal is already roughly in the range of the console's standard operating level. As a result, these signals need to be dealt with differently when they arrive at our console in order to ensure maximum quality and proper preamplification of each signal.

Due to its extremely low voltage, between -60 and -70 dB, a microphone-level signal requires a tremendous boost so it will be sufficient to be processed by the console's components while retaining reasonable signal-to-noise characteristics. These signals will need as much as a 70-dB boost in order to reach your console's standard operating level. That is a lot of amplification, and if one were to treat it cheaply, a great deal of noise would be introduced to the signal, which would be unacceptable because it would go against the goal of quality audio. This signal therefore requires a large amount of clean amplification. The microphone input of a console contains a special amplification circuit, a preamp or mic pre, which performs this function. The microphone preamp is typically the single most expensive component and is considered by some to be the most important component on any console because it must have excellent signal-to-noise characteristics while amplifying the signal tremendously.

The microphone preamp is also one of the components that is chiefly responsible for the character of the sound, or the way a console will color a sound. The characteristics of a console—such as a Neve, which is known to have warm mic preamps, as opposed to a Solid State Logic console, which has a reputation for transparent mic preamps—will often determine an engineer's console preference. When customizing a console, a popular fix involves removing the mic preamps and adding replacements that suit the engineer's taste more closely. This type of modification can make an inexpensive console sound like a top-grade model; it could also give an engineer the versatility or cleanliness of one console combined with the mic pre characteristics of another. Several manufacturers sell rack-mountable or standalone boxes with high-quality preamps that may be used as outboard signal processing gear to improve the sound quality of the average console, and of course plug-ins are available that emulate all the most popular preamps. The aesthetic choice of a particular preamp can greatly affect the final product and can become part of an engineer's aesthetic as well as his or her signature sound.

While quality is always beneficial, it is less critical in a console's line input preamp. Because consoles operate at or near line level, line-level signals do not require much boost. An audio console's line inputs are typically used for the output of electronic musical instruments, such as electric guitars and basses, synthesizers, samplers, and drum machines. Another primary use for a console's line input is to receive the output signal from recorders and signal processors. The separate inputs on an audio console can be compared to the separate inputs on a home stereo amplifier. The home stereo has separate inputs for turntable, CD, DVD/TV, and auxiliary sources. Due to the varying output levels of these devices, it is necessary for devices that are being connected electrically to be well matched, as mentioned previously. If an improper signal is routed to an input with either too much or too little level, the result will be either damaged components due to excess of current or level, or poor signal-to-noise ratio, since the engineer will be unable to bring the sound up to an adequate level without also bringing up the noise, as mentioned above.

Impedance

The difference between microphone-level signals and line-level signals is not described as simply a difference in level, it is described as a difference in impedance, and that has other extremely important implications. A microphone-level signal at somewhere around −65 dB is known as a *low-impedance signal* and can travel long distances through cable without significant loss because such small amounts of electricity encounter little resistance. Conversely, a line-level signal is at or about optimal console level, somewhere between −30 dB and 0 dB, and is also known as *high impedance.*

Due to its higher level of current, a line-level signal sent through a long cable will experience resistance resulting in deterioration, or signal loss. Some consumer microphones are high impedance. These can sometimes be identified by their low price, their location on a shelf at a local discount big-box retailer, or the fact that they terminate in a 1/4-inch jack, also known as a *guitar plug.* There are several different types of 1/4-inch jacks. There is the type just described, which will only have one "ring" on the jack (these will typically carry a high-impedance, unbalanced signal); there is another with two rings, known as *tip-ring-sleeve,* which is balanced but still high impedance and typical of 1/4-inch patch cords; and there is a stereo 1/4-inch jack, frequently seen terminating a pair of headphones, which is also high impedance. Low-impedance signals typically terminate in a barrel-shaped three-pin connector known as an *XLR*, or *Cannon plug* (see Figure 5.26).

Photo courtesy of Neutrik.

Figure 5.26 Various connectors (left to right), male XLR, female XLR, RCA plug, 1/4-inch phone plug, 3.5mm mini plug.

On a regular basis, engineers will find themselves in situations in which it is necessary to turn a line-level signal into a microphone-level signal. This is common in both live recording studios and while recording an electric bass or a synthesizer. Basses and synthesizers output at line level, but it is a long way from the stage to the control booth. If you were to run a high-impedance signal all that distance, it would result in tremendous signal loss due to resistance. When the engineer wants to send a line-level signal a long distance, a direct box, or DI, is used. A DI is actually a step-down transformer that splits the signal, sends an unaffected high-impedance signal to a 1/4-inch jack (if the musician still wishes to send the signal to an amp), and lowers the level of the other signal to low impedance, microphone-level signal, routing it to an XLR output that allows it to be plugged into a microphone input or snake and make the long trip to the console without any significant signal loss. Although this method is effective on some instruments, other instruments, such as guitars, that benefit from the coloration of passing through an amplifier sound better if the musician plugs into his amp, upon which the engineer then places a microphone.

Once signals reach the console, you might need to adjust the first level of amplification. Microphone pres and line pres are controlled by mic trims and line trims. On some consoles there is only one trim pot (potentiometer) per module for both of these functions, while others offer separate trim pots for microphone and line. Sometimes there will be a switch to determine which signal the engineer seeks to amplify and use as an input; other times, the console will sense whether an input is plugged into a module's 1/4-inch input or XLR input and assume that it is a line or microphone signal based on the jack. In this case the trim will adjust whichever pre is associated with the signal that is plugged into that module, line, or microphone. If you have plugged in a microphone, look for a switch that says "microphone" if there is only one trim pot. If there isn't a switch and there is only one trim pot, and if you have a microphone and no line input plugged into that module, the module will probably know which signal you desire to amplify, and it will know which preamp will have the proper impedance to give you the proper range of amplification.

Trims are passive attenuators. They are simple resistors controlled by a rotary pot. A trim is used to vary the level of a signal before it reaches the amplification phase of a circuit. When set for maximum level, generally turned all the way to the right, the trim control is adding no resistance to a circuit. When turned to the left, the trim control is reducing the level of the signal by adding resistance. This allows a signal's level to be varied before it reaches the amplifier, which is a fixed gain stage and can therefore be easily overloaded if the input signal is too large. As such, it is a good idea when plugging in a microphone or other source to begin with the trim set to full attenuation, all the way to the left, and turn it up gradually until standard operating level is reached (see Figure 5.27).

Photo courtesy of SSL.

Figure 5.27 The mic and line trims on the SSL 6000, with the multitrack bussing and bus pan above it.

This is not necessary with line inputs because their levels tend to be more consistent. Although there will be some variation between the outputs of tape machines, computers, synthesizers, signal processing gear, CD players, and other line-level sources, these differences are smaller than the differences between the outputs of different microphones. Frequently, a line trim will provide a detent, or click-stop, at the twelve o'clock position as a normal setting for most line inputs.

Alternating Current

Now that you understand the flow of electric current from your microphones through your consoles, let's take a look at the other source of power upon which we depend, alternating current. Beginning at the point of generation, it will be useful to take a brief look at power generation and transmission. Power is generated at a plant somewhere out in the country and is sent down high-voltage transmission lines at about 110,000 volts—about 1,000 times more voltage than you wish to have arrive at your home or office's outlets. Transmission is sent using a three-phase system of alternating current that is offset by 120 degrees in phase relation to each other. The substation takes this high voltage and converts it to lower voltage, typically less than 10,000 volts for delivery across the grid. At the point of entry for a subdivision or large facility, you will often see a large green box. This is another step-down transformer for power delivery to the neighborhood or venue.

The voltage is reduced for delivery to homes and businesses at substations, allowing for transmission over small-gauge cables. Next, the power goes through a regulator bank that keeps the voltage near 120 volts. Now the power has been reduced and regulated and is ready for use, but it still is traveling in three phases. You need it broken down to a single phase for your equipment use. In a residential setting, this is "tapped" at the pole, using a single phase of the three-phase delivery. In most theatres, concert venues, and large event spaces, a direct connection to the three-phase input exists. Connecting to and using this power requires a three-phase distribution box, a device that splits the phases into three single phases and usually has a number of 20-amp, 120-volt grounded circuits, each with its own breaker. It is very similar to the power box that you have in your home, except that your home is one phase of the three that are delivered, also known as a *single-phase power box*. Now that you have gone through a three-phase distribution box (or a single phase box in your home), you have standard current that can be used for your gear. In the event that a three-phase hookup is required, the house staff, a union professional, or a qualified electrician should always perform this task, and a professionally designed and rated distribution box will be required (see Figure 5.28).

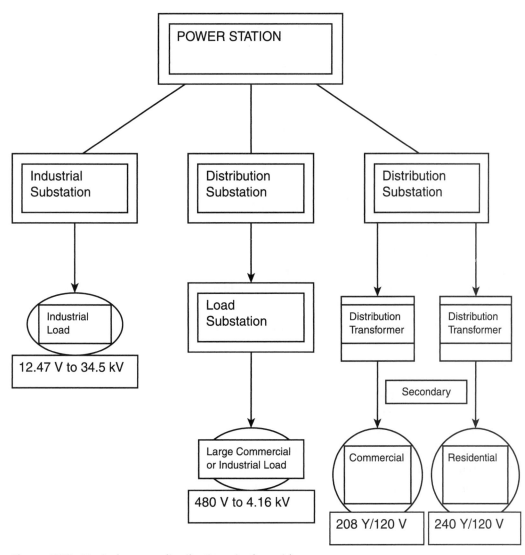

Figure 5.28 Typical power distribution via the grid.

Standard current here in the United States is alternating current, which arrives at homes, businesses, and venues at a voltage of 120 volts. Typically, this current is delivered to outlets through 15- and 20-amp circuits. Do not misinterpret this to mean that every outlet is associated with a dedicated circuit—quite the contrary. Typically, the outlet nearest your setup is one of several outlets sharing the same circuit. This permits the very real possibility of too many appliances placed on one circuit. Beware of overloading any one circuit by placing too many devices on it. If this were to happen, you could easily pull too many amps and trip the circuit breaker, which would cause you to lose power and lose your recording.

Watts = Volts x Amps   The ultimate equation and law governing electricity that should live in every audio professional's mind is often thought of as West Virginia—Watts = Volts × Amps. This simple formula allows you to calculate all elements of power draw when you are missing one element. Depending on your needs, it can be either W=VA, V=W/A, or A=W/V.

How many amps does a 100-watt light bulb draw? The only label has a description of the power usage in watts. If you are in the United States, you know that the power from the end outlet is supplied with a 120-volt current. Therefore, the light bulb burns at 100 watts with 120-volt current. To calculate the amperage used by this light bulb, simply calculate A=100/120, yielding A=0.833333 (repeating).

When checking power, always keep in mind that amps are additive on a single circuit—in other words, they are in series. The voltage is pushing the amps and typically will not change with the addition of additional equipment, unless you start to overload the circuit. You will usually trip a properly wired circuit before you see any significant change in voltage, due to overloading. *Do not overload a circuit!*

Keep a running total of the power consumption of all the equipment you are plugging into a single circuit to ensure that you do not exceed the number of amps to which the circuit is protected. In other words, if the breaker says 15 amps, be sure you don't attempt to load the circuit with 20 amps. Frequently, a power amp will be the culprit in a setup. Power amps are power hogs, but not all the time. They can draw spikes up to the top of their rating as printed in the manuals or on their bodies, but they don't consistently draw this power (see Figure 5.29).

Figure 5.29   The back of an Ashly Powerflex 6250 integrated amplifier.

Often they run with a much lower power consumption until they need to reproduce very high amplitude. At that point, they will suddenly draw full amps. This will not be an issue for you because you have plugged the amplifier or powered speakers into a circuit that you are confident can handle the peak amp draw, and you know you have not overloaded the circuit. If you have failed to make the proper calculations, things might seem fine until the power amp tries to pull full power for a transient and trips the breaker.

In addition to the consideration of the number of amps you will draw, you need to be mindful of the voltage draw as well. This is slightly less critical because recording on reel-to-reel machines has become rarer (they were far more voltage-dependant), but it is still a consideration. While the pull of amps is obvious—your breaker will trip if you exceed the number of amps that the breaker can bear—the pull of voltage is more subtle but equally important (see Figure 5.30).

Figure 5.30 A typical commercial breaker box.

To visualize the importance of voltage, imagine that your equipment is like a grindstone mill. The grindstone needs to turn at a specific speed to work properly—in other words, that speed, like your voltage, needs to be constant. If the speed varies, the grindstone will simply stop. You have engineered your grindstone to be powered by a waterwheel, which is dependant on a constant flow of water. If I go upstream and throw a few rocks into the stream or divert some of the water's flow to another use, the amount of water powering your waterwheel will be reduced, the speed of the wheel will be reduced, and the power to your grindstone will be reduced, thus reducing the speed of the grindstone and rendering it ineffective.

The same concept applies for electrical components that require a specific amount of voltage to operate properly. The components within the electronics are attuned to work on a specific sent voltage amount. Tape machines and other devices that have a motor or other moving parts make this equation more critical, because they will not run at the proper speed without the proper voltage applied. Other devices, such as computer microphone preamps or power supplies, contain circuits that have been designed with the intention of running at 120 V or 220 V (if you are in Europe). If the voltage requirements are not met, you might encounter serious problems. For example, if you lose too much voltage and your hard drive drops from a typical rating of 12 V in a ±5 V power supply to something that is high enough for it to continue to spin or too low for it to spin properly, you run the risk of dragging a head across the edge of the platter and destroying all the data you have recorded. Almost any device that has a power supply can encounter great difficulties if that power supply is expecting to see 120 V, but the voltage drops too low. In this case, the power supply will attempt to pull more voltage, overheat, and either burn itself out or blow the circuit. Either way, it ain't pretty when the voltage drops.

The best defense against low voltage and the many problems it can cause, both within your gear and in the circuit, is a UPS, or uninterruptible power supply. The UPS has an added benefit in that it will guard you against brownouts. The UPS contains a battery, which augments the voltage sent to its outlets. Most people purchase these for their computers to provide some sort of battery backup, which allows them enough time to save their files and shut down their computer in the event of a power failure or other problem with the supply of municipal power. As live recordists, we not only seek protection should we lose our power, we also look to the UPS to augment the voltage in the event that we should have a brownout, where the voltage drops below the 10-percent variance from normal voltage that our equipment typically requires. If your voltage drops from 122 V to below 105 V, you want to be protected. It is therefore critical when selecting a battery backup or UPS that you choose one that includes voltage regulation. There are also power conditioners that will try to continuously make up the voltage curve on your power stream. This type of device is the best option because it will constantly clean the power's voltage.

Understanding Ground

Many people are thrown by the concept of ground, but in fact understanding ground is not as daunting as it might seem. First of all, remember this one simple point: Like you after a long gig, electrical current just wants to go home. The ground is home to electrical current; from the moment it is generated, it wants to go home, into the ground.

Typically, the easiest way home for electricity is a completed circuit, in which you have the electricity coming in on the hot and returning on the neutral. In situations where this is broken or the system is otherwise compromised, the electricity seeks another way to get home, back to earth ground. So, electrical systems are grounded, typically through a grounding wire. If the grounding wire is lifted, disconnected, or broken off, the alternate route is broken, so the electricity will try to find another route down to the ground. If your guitar player's lips touched the microphone while he was holding an electric guitar whose amplifier had the ground lifted because of a hum, you might find that the electricity would decide to use that guitar player as the path to the earth ground. This would, of course, result in a shocking conclusion. In the interest of both sound quality and safety, ensure that your ground is locked on and solid at all times.

Power on Location

When considering power and ground on location, there are a few things you need to take into account. If the event you're recording does not involve a PA system or another audio or video setup, you do not need to be as concerned about the source of your power. If, on the other hand, you are recording an event that will be sent through an amplification system, PA system, or building speaker system—in other words, an event that will be amplified—it is critical that you use the same leg of power, if not the same source of power, as that other system. This will enable you to avoid potential ground loops and ground differentials that might exist between two different legs of power.

It is important to note that while you have a strong interest in using the same systems as the front-of-house PA system or any other amplification, you must be certain that the circuit is rated with adequate power to support all your gear along with the PA system. In the event that the one circuit does not have enough power for both, you will blow a circuit by sharing it, which would create a problem for everyone.

Testing the Power

One of your most important tasks during the site survey is testing the power. Some consider it the most important test you will perform. Regardless of whether you are connecting into the PA system, you still need to check the outlet or power source into which you will plug. Be sure to bring along a good-quality voltmeter that will allow you to read the voltage. There are three measurements you need to take to ensure good, clean power. The first measurement is a standard reading between the hot and the neutral (see Figure 5.31).

This measurement will show the amount of voltage available on this circuit. In the United States, it should read between 110 and 120 V. Voltage can sway as much as 10 V, from 110 to 120, and still be acceptable. Outlets that are below 110 volts or above 120 volts should be avoided.

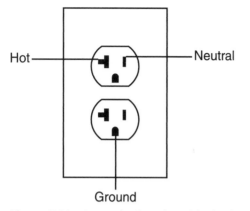

Hot ———

Neutral

Ground

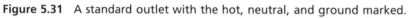

Figure 5.31   A standard outlet with the hot, neutral, and ground marked.

The next item to check is ground. If the ground is good, it should give you the same reading as between hot and neutral. If it does not, then the ground is not secure and could lead to serious problems (see Figure 5.32).

Figure 5.32   The difference between hot and ground should be the same as the difference between hot and neutral.

Next, you need to measure the amount of voltage between the ground and neutral. This should read zero (see Figure 5.33).

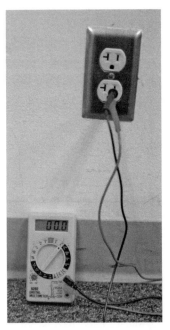

Figure 5.33   There should be no voltage read between the neutral and the ground.

Neither of these legs is intended to carry current, so the circuit should be left uncompleted, resulting in no voltage, or a reading of zero. Unfortunately, this often is not the case. In older buildings, mishaps with wiring can often lead to voltage between the neutral in the ground and connections of grounding. Badly grounded equipment could also be responsible for this reading. This may also cause hum in an audio system. Any reading more than 0 indicates a potential problem, but it is not unusual. Hum and buzz issues can be created by voltage between neutral and ground as low as 0.25 volts. This makes it apparent that somewhere on the circuit there is a problem where voltage is creeping into either the ground or the neutral. Either way, current between the neutral and the ground should be avoided. Just like in audio systems, it is the voltage getting into the audio path that causes trouble, and 0.25 volts is awfully low in an audio circuit.

Although these readings will not tell you whether you have adequate amperage on the circuit, they allow you to quickly judge the quality of the voltage and ground, which is valuable information. When considering amps, keep in mind that amps are used up on a circuit in series—in other words, amps are additive while volts are parallel. Voltage is not diminished within allowable parameters, but amps are. To ensure that there are enough amps to go around, you need to calculate the number of amps on the circuit by reading the power draw of all items plugged into that circuit, as already discussed.

Other Considerations

Another consideration for power is the gauge, or thickness, of the cables you use. Sixteen gauge, while acceptable at home for a lamp, is not acceptable for live recording, especially for a long run of power. As the gauge numbers get lower, the cable gets thicker. Any gauge thinner than 14 or 12 is generally unacceptable, and 10 gauge is preferable, especially for your amplifiers.

Like so many of your decisions before, during, and after the recording process, your power decisions will be based on what you are presented with in the venue. Ultimately, your goal at this stage will always be to find good, clean power and ground, preferably power that is on the same phase or leg as the PA, any other amplification, and any other elements with which you will need to interface. Lastly, make sure all your grounds are grounded. We cannot stress this point enough, for both safety and quality reasons.

In the event that there are issues with audio quality despite clean power and ground, hums and buzzes are usually caused by bad solder joints or broken shields. Due to the safety risks involved, radio interference, hums, and buzz should only be treated by lifting or breaking the ground as a last resort. Before you try anything as drastic and dangerous as breaking a ground, there are some simple checks you can perform.

First, check all microphone and line connections to ensure that they are at least one foot from any major power source. Power is an alternating current, and so is your audio. The power line may act as a changing magnetic field, similar in principle to the aforementioned dynamic microphone. This inductance infiltrating your very sensitive low-impedance microphone line could cause a hum. When crossing a power line with a microphone line, be sure to cross it perpendicularly to avoid inductance.

Here are some more simple troubleshooting tips. Identify the source of the hum. Is it in one channel or is it across the entire board? If it is in one channel, carefully check that microphone cable. If it is in the entire board, double-check that your console is grounded properly, then check that all outboard gear is also grounded correctly.

Ensure that the power to which you are connected is actually grounded. If you have done all this and you still hear a hum, disconnect all connections to the console and listen for the ground hum. Reconnect everything one piece at a time, listening for the hum to emerge. When it does, the last item connected is responsible for the noise.

Now that you have looked over the site and determined that your needs can be met as far as power, ground, and your location, let's examine the gear you will be using more closely.

Gear

6 Basic Gear

You will ultimately select the equipment you bring along when you record a live event based on the sound you are attempting to create on location. You will ascertain the ideas behind the approach, the basics of the sound, from the discussions you have had with the band and any other clients and from your site surveys regarding the properties of the location in which you will be recording.

Let's begin to consider what equipment you will need for a particular recording. Start by considering the track sheet, which you developed during conversations with the band and solidified during the site survey. Don't forget to consult the contract rider, which will also have valuable information and stipulations regarding the recording, the stage and PA setup, and whether the band prefers water in the green bottle or water in the blue bottle. At this time, you also need to take note of what other equipment you will need to interface with the PA system, location broadcast folks, video companies, or anyone you run into who is also working on site. But let's not get ahead of ourselves; we'll start with a look at the basics.

Recording live is pretty straightforward. A location recording is like any other recording gig—the main difference, obviously, is that you are on location rather than in a controlled environment, such as a studio. The fundamentals remain the same. You need to collect and store the sound in a professional manner.

A flowchart gives a great overview of the simple process of collecting audio information as you follow the signal from the microphone, which transduces the signal from acoustic energy to electricity—a form of energy that your equipment can comprehend (see Figure 6.1).

The microphone preamplifier boosts the signal to a higher level, loud enough to be either manipulated by a console, processed, stored to an analog recording device, or converted by an analog-to-digital converter into a digital signal. The digital signal is then either manipulated through the use of digital equipment or stored on digital media for later playback. By examining the simple flowchart, you can begin to sketch in what equipment you will need on location. Let's start with the beginning of the signal's path—the microphones.

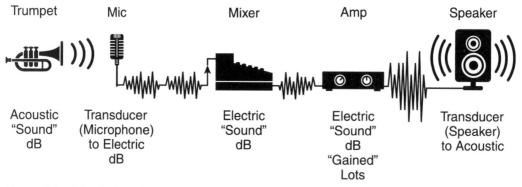

Trumpet	Mic	Mixer	Amp	Speaker

| Acoustic "Sound" dB | Transducer (Microphone) to Electric dB | Electric "Sound" dB | Electric "Sound" dB "Gained" Lots | Transducer (Speaker) to Acoustic |

Figure 6.1 A basic flowchart.

Microphones: Collectors of Audio Information

In the last chapter, we started talking about the properties of different styles of microphones, how they operate, and some of the advantages and disadvantages to the different types. Each of these microphones is a collector of sounds. Every one of them is a transducer, changing the acoustical energy of sound into an electrical voltage that we require in order to record. This process is the way sound is captured and stored. Different microphone designs will invariably introduce different styles of distortion and impose their own character upon the capture of audio, or the transition from acoustic energy to electrical energy. Although we may inherently think distortion is bad, try telling that to Jimi Hendrix, Nirvana, or the Sex Pistols. We need to take into consideration the ramifications of different collectors to determine the best microphones and microphone techniques for any specific project.

In a nutshell, dynamic microphones typically have the ability to handle high sound pressure levels. They also provide the sound engineer with a mellow approach to transients, or instantaneous peaks in level, while capturing sound (see Figure 6.2).

Photo courtesy of Shure.

Figure 6.2 The Shure SM58 is a standard dynamic microphone, common in both live and studio settings.

Ribbon microphones are typically more sensitive and accurate than dynamic microphones, but also far more delicate, making them more difficult to transport without damage and putting them at risk on a stage where they may get knocked over. Sonically speaking, ribbon microphones are also mellower than condenser microphones (see Figure 6.3).

Photo courtesy of Stan Coutant.

Figure 6.3 The RCA 77 is a classic ribbon microphone, delicate and sweet, but it might not be the best choice due to transportation issues.

Condenser microphones are the most sensitive and accurate microphones. They reproduce the most clear-sounding and realistic representation of the original audio; however, they are also the most vulnerable to transients (see Figure 6.4).

Incorporating a tube microphone with a high-voltage power supply can dramatically change the sound quality or characteristic of the captured sound. Tube microphones often introduce a warm, mellow sound to the audio they capture. This is particularly true at high SPL, near distortion levels, as the tube microphone is far more forgiving than a solid-state mic preamp when it comes to transducing a sound pressure level decibel to a voltage decibel.

Cables: The Interconnects

All cables are not created equal. In fact, all of the cables on my shelf are not created equal. Microphone cables have a number of different parts to them. There are the primary connectors, which are male and female XLR style, the type of wire running

Photo courtesy of Neumann.

Figure 6.4   The Neumann M179 is a tube condenser microphone.

between the XLR connectors, and the number of wires running between the XLR connectors. A standard XLR microphone cable typically contains a positive, a neutral, and
a shield (see Figure 6.5).

Figure 6.5   A typical multichannel snake.

There's another version of XLR microphone cable known as a *star quad cable*. Typical wiring for star quad cable is four wires and a shield, in which wires are paired and connected to the XLR connection, with the shield going to ground. A properly wired XLR star quad cable will avoid inductance and reject even the hottest radio signals. An improperly wired XLR star quad cable—for that matter, any standard XLR cable—will invite a host of problems, such as radio station hum or buzz. If the shield is broken or has a cold solder joint, the cable will often not pass 48V phantom power to the microphone. Another even worse possibility than not passing phantom power at all is passing it intermittently, providing the audience and your recording with pops and booms reminiscent of frying bacon on the Concorde.

A sometimes-asked question is whether you have to buy a $300-per-foot microphone cable? No, of course not. Good microphone cable manufacturers, such as Gotham, Canare, and Mogami, make highly dependable, oxygen-free star quad and regular XLR cables. Ultimately, each engineer will have to decide which cable best suits his needs and budget. The best approach is to believe your ears while assessing which cable provides the best signal quality and signal path. Generally speaking, spending less money on cables will ultimately deliver a lower-quality microphone cable, but the reverse is not necessarily true. There appears to be a certain value threshold that you can reach and easily exceed when purchasing microphone cable. The level of this threshold is a personal choice. Remember that interconnects not only refer to microphone cables, they also refer to connection points between devices.

Console Preamps or Outboard Preamps?

The next point in the signal path is the microphone preamplifier. Microphone preamplifiers are the point at which the signal enters most modern consoles. The preamplifier brings a signal up from microphone level to a usable level for mixing, processing, routing, storage, and so on. The quality inherent to this process is based on the design of the preamp, the quality of the components used in the microphone preamplifier, and the care given to the construction of the device (see Figure 6.6).

Photo courtesy of Solid State Logic.

Figure 6.6 The in-board microphone preamp from an SSL.

In most relatively small, inexpensive boards, the care given to the design and the construction is often lacking. As a result, many location recording engineers will opt to purchase an outboard, or external, microphone preamplifier. These microphone preamplifiers have a number of advantages. They can be located closer to a recording source if it's a remote-controlled mic-pre; also, they are simply better designed and built, and therefore they are better-sounding pieces of equipment.

The ability to locate your microphone preamplifier closer to your sound source and microphone gives you an incredible advantage in terms of the quality of sound that you will have to work with from the microphone. Locating your microphone preamplifier closer to the sound source and microphone will help, particularly in high-interference situations, such as a theater, or other live venues where the audio connections may run next to lighting cables for hundreds of feet. In these situations, it is useful to pre-amplify the microphone level signal as close to the microphone as possible. That way, you're sending a line-level signal (approximately 0 dBm) through the long cables, rather than a microphone-level signal (approximately –65 dBm), and any interference the cable picks up will be much lower relative to the desired signal. Many engineers also believe there are important sonic benefits in terms of frequency response gained from a shorter cable run; in other words, it sounds better.

Both Grace Design and Millennia Microphone preamplifiers have units that can be controlled by remote. Often these microphone preamps can even be controlled from within the digital audio workstation you are using to record the gig, in conjunction with stand-alone control options. Many of these remote-controlled microphone preamps also have analog-to-digital converters built into them. This means that if you use a digital audio snake, you can actually have a clean signal run regardless of the distance to the console after the short cable run to the microphone preamplifier, which doubles as a digital audio converter box. Eliminating such long runs greatly improves the sound quality of the location recording (see Figure 6.7).

Figure 6.7   Grace Design outboard preamps.

Remember, selecting your microphone preamplifier is as important as selecting your microphone. Either one will profoundly color or change the sound that you collect. A warmer tube microphone preamplifier will give you a radically different sound when compared to a solid-state microphone preamplifier. Think of this in the same terms as a large-diaphragm microphone giving you a different sound than a small-diaphragm microphone. Typically, the tube microphone preamplifier will give you a sound that is warmer, while a classic solid-state preamplifier will give you a more open, or clearer and brighter, sound. When planning your gear, you can add definition, color, and tonalities to the recording based on the individual equipment, as well as the equipment combinations you choose.

Give Us a Leg to Stand On

For a number of reasons, positioning and placing microphones on location is far more challenging than doing so in the studio. First and foremost, space is at a far higher premium onstage than it is in the studio. Second, you have far less control over the space. You need to share your space with a number of different people, including the artists, the house PA system, and of course the fire marshal. You also need to be sensitive to the staging and physical flow of the concert performance or event you are recording. It is completely unacceptable to block the audience's view of the lead singer by putting a large, heavy three-wheeled triangularly based atlas boom stand in front of him. Obviously, if this solution is not acceptable, then a smaller microphone stand and boom are required.

Elegant solutions can be found and sometimes result in being associated with a particular performer or style of music. For example, take Pavarotti and the tube-based Schoeps MK 4 microphone. The image of Pavarotti with a black windscreen on the long cylindrical tube is known to almost everyone. It is cleaner than the standard boom microphone, though not as maneuverable. It gets the job done.

As you get further back into the band and further from the audience's focus, it becomes more acceptable to place larger pieces of hardware to hold your equipment. For example, an onstage boom weighted stand is often an appropriate choice for a drum overhead (see Figure 6.8).

Aesthetics is your number-one consideration, but often aesthetics will lose out to necessity. For example, if you are hired to record a chamber music concert of a violin, cello, viola, and bass using a Decca tree microphone technique, a center stand that is sturdy enough to hold three microphones and their cables is required. Although aesthetics are important, safety needs to be the primary consideration in this case. If you have a microphone stand, such as a Decca tree, in a highly trafficked area, a large, stable stand that is difficult to knock over is preferable to a more attractive stand that may be too flimsy. This same concern for safety of both microphones and audiences is a good reason to bring sandbags and highly visible security tape to rope off your microphone

Figure 6.8 Onstage stand.

stands. At the very least, stake out a safety area on the floor. Protecting your equipment is important, but more important is protecting the audience and the musicians from having a heavy microphone stand come crashing down on them.

The easiest way to improve sightlines and protect the musicians, the audience, and your microphones is to hang them—the microphones, that is (see Figure 6.9).

Hanging the microphones is a great way to improve sightlines and protect the audience and your microphones. This is often easier said than done, because you need to have a facility that is able to accommodate the hanging of microphones, and more importantly, you need to have the time to position the microphones, as well as run all of the cables.

There are any number ways to hang a microphone. The common approach is to anchor the microphone and cable to some structurally sound portion of the building and to put

Figure 6.9 Hanging microphones.

in pull lines or guidelines of some type to pull the microphone into position. Remember when hanging a microphone that microphones are not that heavy. Some older models have more weight to them, but it's not the actual weight that is the problem while hanging microphones. The bigger problem is the tension applied to the microphone when it is pulled back into position. As the microphone is pulled back out of plumb while hanging down, the amount of kinetic energy placed on the microphones is increased, and the amount of tension and weight placed on the guidelines being used increase as well. To mitigate this issue, use a relatively high-strength fast fishing line to pull the microphone back at an angle.

If a large grid is being used, consider complementing it with galvanized 8-inch aircraft cable. As with all rigging, if you do not know exactly how much tensioner weight you are using or if there are any concepts in terms of using rigging that you do not understand, hire a professional who understands these things. This is a safety issue, and not a good place for you to be winging it. Schoeps and Neumann both make microphone-hanging equipment, often referred to as *auditorium hangers*. These hangers attach to the microphone cable, and a standard microphone clip screws onto the bottom of the hanger. If you attach the guide wire above the auditorium hanger, the auditorium hanger will hang in plumb. Then you can position the microphone's angle based on a 90-degree hanging point, rather than having to angle it by a guideline. The guideline should be used with the microphone in the correct spatial position on the front-to-back axis and removed from the evaluation of the angle.

Remember to bring additional line or specific microphone-hanging clamps to attach the top of the microphone line to the structure in the building. The microphone cable, not a guideline, supports the weight of the microphone. For a well-made microphone cable, this should not present a problem. Make sure the microphone cable is securely tied off to a structure in the building and not merely plugged into a snake or the console. It is not recommended to tape the microphone line to secure it to anything, because tape can loosen more easily than a solid knot.

Storage: Recording Devices

There is another major difference between recording in the studio and recording on location. Both have similar criteria in terms of trying to capture the ultimate performance, although while recording a live performance you generally have one chance (and only one chance) to capture the sound event. In the studio, if a hard drive crashes or another piece of equipment breaks, you can stop the session momentarily, execute a workaround, and repair or swap out the equipment. You might lose a few minutes or hours of studio time and a dollar or two, but the end result is not in jeopardy. While recording on location, the luxury of a momentary break and a quick repair is simply not an option.

Imagine you are recording a live concert. There is absolutely no way you can just stop a concert in front of 20,000 people and say, "Wait a minute, I need to get a new microphone." This is noteworthy, particularly when it comes down to data storage or the recording device you select to record the concert. The recording device you select must be rock-solid in operation. As the recordist, you must be intimately familiar with its operation; it must be easy to understand and easy to use.

Ultimately, your comfort level with the recording equipment should be a large factor when considering which recording device you will choose. The other dominating factor when choosing a recording device or storage medium is the format in which the end product will be released. If you are doing sound for a live broadcast event, you might be able to forego the recording device completely. If you are recording a live rock album and the plan is to record various stops along the tour, you will need to multitrack each concert. Each of these situations—and the many others in which you will find yourself—presents specific criteria that will steer you to a particular group of recording devices.

Thanks to major improvements in digital technology, multitracking is now inexpensive, easy to use, and straightforward on location. Using one of today's fast laptop's FireWire 800 cards, interfaces, and external hard drives, it is easy to do a 24-, 32-, or even 48-track recording in a piece of gear smaller than a telephone book. In addition to simplicity at the recording site, recording to your favorite digital audio workstation allows for quick and easy playback at the studio (see Figure 6.10).

Figure 6.10   A portable toaster-sized setup.

The concern with a laptop, a toaster-sized desktop, or even a full-blown desktop computer is that you are still dealing with a computer. Computers have made great strides in not giving the blue screen of death or the unhappy Mac sign, but crashes still occur in all machines, at random times and with dire consequences. Although this is particularly true if the machine is not constantly updated, cleaned, defragmented, talked to politely, and generally treated well, any machine can crash at any time. And they will. And usually it will be at the worst possible time.

A more secure and reliable solution is often a hard-disc recorder. This type of recorder is more stable and less likely to lose data. These are usually larger and more expensive than a laptop, but the ability to ensure recording without incident is priceless.

Right from their introduction, ADATs were tremendously popular on the digital multi-tracking front and were among the earliest inexpensive digital recording formats (see Figures 6.11 through 6.14).

The original ADATs were eight-track digital recorders that recorded on videocassettes and could easily be linked or synced up. The advantage to this, besides digital quality at a reasonable price, is that if a recordist owned three ADATs, he would have 24-track digital capability. If a client only needs eight tracks, the recordist can use one of the

Photo courtesy of Michael Conn.

Figure 6.11   A popular ADAT recorder/player, the Tascam DA-38.

Photo courtesy of Alesis.

Figure 6.12   Another popular ADAT recorder/player is the Alesis ADAT.

Photo courtesy of Sony.

Figure 6.13   Another ADAT recorder/player is the Sony PCM-800.

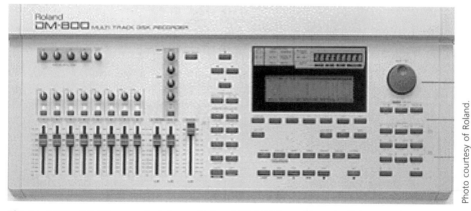

Photo courtesy of Roland.

Figure 6.14   ADAT recorder/player Roland DM-800 multitrack disk recorder.

ADATs. Of course, most ADAT enthusiasts have given up this now-outdated technology in favor of hard-drive recording, including the more modern ADAT disc recorders, but many of these tape devices are still available at bargain-basement prices through online auction sites.

Although ADAT disc recorders provide a stable recording format, many recordists prefer a hard-disc recorder, such as the iZ RADAR V or RADAR 24. These devices are more expensive, but they are extremely stable. Many recordists also claim that the sound quality available on the RADAR systems is superior to that available on other hard-disc recorders and software.

Two-Track Safety or Reference Mix

It is critically important to run a stereo mix in real time as a safety backup and as a reference mix of the event. At its most basic level, this allows for the client's instant gratification and a reference point when you begin the final production process. When you record multiple concerts by the same artist, intending to pick and choose the best performances from each, the two-track mixes will become a reference mix, which will help the musicians choose their best performances from each event. You can also use this mix to decide which tracks still need work and which ones are good enough to be considered "in the can."

Typically, a standalone real-time CD burner is used, such as the HHB Burn It PLUS or the Tascam 1000 DVD/CD standalone disc recorders. A DAT machine can also be used. Digital audio tape (DAT) was a functional mix format in the industry briefly, but it has now found its place for archiving and backups (see Figure 6.15).

Photo courtesy of Mark Trew and Trew Audio.

Figure 6.15 The HHB Communications PORTADAT.

Using the same mechanics as a VCR, with tape moving slowly across a rapidly rotating drum, DATs are an inexpensive digital two-track storage format, although DATs have mostly given way to CDs for archiving and backups due to the CD's attractive price and convenience.

Other ways to accomplish this safety backup include recording to a two-track flash recorder or directly to a laptop. An advantage to the laptop is that an efficient recordist could have the concert up and waiting for the client on his iPod at the end of the show. Little things like this tend to impress clients as much as your overall professionalism and the quality of your final product.

Power

In the previous chapter, we discussed power and the pervasive problems that are rampant as you draw power in various venues. There are a few devices you can bring along to help work with what you find and help you win the battle over power. It is wise to find and bring along a voltage-regulating, UPS (*uninterruptible power supply*) battery-based backup. This unit is primarily a souped-up surge protector with a battery to supply continuous power and a voltage regulator to keep your power steady—all built right in. These units are typically used by the computer industry to protect servers and other large, expensive computers and by some of the more obsessive among us on our home computers. Because computers do most of our recording, it makes perfect sense to incorporate this device to protect our systems, our computers, and our recordings.

While shopping for a UPS, ensure that the battery backup you purchase has an active voltage regulator. This keeps the sine wave complete in the voltage and at a usable level no matter what happens on the main power line. With a built-in battery backup, you have the added bonus that nothing will be lost in the unlikely event that some poor slob knocks out the power cord to your computer and recording setup. As long as it is plugged back in within three to five minutes, your data will be safe.

Many digital audio workstations require that the stop button be pressed for them to write the end of the WAV file markers or store all necessary data. In other words, a WAV file is not technically recorded until you press stop. This means if you have not yet hit stop, you are working without a battery backup, and someone pulls the plug out of the wall, your computer will lose all the audio to the point that it was last stopped. This could be called working without a net. Working without a net could be bad in that career-ending kind of way. Furman, APC, and many other companies make reliable battery regulators (see Figure 6.16).

Figure 6.16   An APC UPS, a typical uninterruptible power supply.

The most important thing to look for in a UPS is that it has batteries involved in assessing and maintaining voltage regulation.

Often while recording on location, you will need to run power from an outlet that is nowhere near the ideal location setup. Along with the UPS, it is very important to bring a properly gauged extension cord—one that is capable of sustaining this long run. Remember, the smaller the number of the gauge, the bigger the wire carrying the electrical current is. The bigger the gauge (the smaller the number), the more power the cable can handle. Using power cables that are at *least* 12 gauge is strongly recommended and always better. Although 14- to 16-gauge cable may carry enough power, you might experience a voltage drop as a result of the smaller gauge and possibly a percentage loss of power as well. Power is your lifeline and should never be taken lightly. Always ensure that you are securely attached to the wall; also make sure the plug is securely pushed down to where it cannot be pulled out accidentally.

Other Things You Need

Tape, tape, and more tape. Don't forget the tape. What kind of tape? Let's start with gaffer's tape. If you do not fly your cable runs and microphones, gaffer's tape is a necessity and will be your best friend. Do not confuse gaffer's tape—a high-quality, non-permanent, cloth-backed tape—with foil-backed duct tape or, even worse, plastic-backed Duck tape. Although duct tape and Duck tape are cheap, strong, extremely sticky, and highly recommended to fix anything that WD-40 doesn't, they are also extremely messy and hard to work with. Unlike gaffer's tape, duct tape and Duck tape leave a sticky mess wherever you put them—on the floor, on your microphone stands, or on your cable. The glue on those cheaper tapes is so invasive that such tape is often banned from venues. Unlike the distant past, when gaffer's tape was very expensive and only available from specialty stores, gaffer's tape is readily available and easily obtained via the Internet. It is absolutely worth the extra money. Gaffer's tape also comes in many colors, and it is a nice to have a selection of brown, white, black, and blue so you can match more closely the color of the venue (see Figure 6.17).

Figure 6.17   A roll of black gaffer's tape—my favorite flavor because everything goes with black—sitting atop a roll of boring old gray gaffer's tape.

While we are talking about tape, don't forget that it is also important to bring label tape. This is not a roll of masking tape—the best label tape is artist tape or photographer's tape. Like gaffer's tape, this is not permanently sticky, and it doesn't leave a mess after it is used. It is easy to write on because it is designed for that purpose, and it is clearer and easier to read than masking tape. It is more expensive than masking tape, just like gaffer's tape is more expensive than duct tape, but the additional peace of mind and efficiency from these tapes certainly outweighs the additional expense.

All live sound recordists should bring a standard briefcase to every gig that includes notepads, all pertinent information, and a hard copy of everything that has been discussed before the gig, including a copy of the contract with any riders, a release (if there is one), and a copy of the insurance papers if you carry insurance on your equipment or business. If you are working in a union house, it is wise to bring the union agreement that you have with the local. In short, bring all paperwork related to the project. Don't forget Post-it notes, pens, and most importantly, business cards. You might also want to bring a non-recording laptop that has your office information on it. You also need either a laptop or a notebook to keep notes about the session and track record.

One of the most important things a location recording engineer can do is to put together something called a *gadget box*. The gadget box is a tackle box or a toolbox filled with all the useful bits and pieces of audio gear that you might need in a pinch on location. My gadget box contains the following:

- Earplugs
- In-ear Shure ER 6–style earbuds as backups
- A multi-tool (Leatherman, Gerber, and so on)
- Jeweler's screwdrivers
- A hex-key set
- An LED flashlight
- An LED headband light
- A soldering iron
- Solder
- An A/C-to-D/C volt meter (small)
- Spare XLRs—male (unconnected)
- Spare XLRs—female (unwired)
- Markers
- Pens
- Pencils
- A small notebook or sticky-note pad
- Board tape (artist's tape, painter's tape, photographer's tape—*not* masking tape)
- Four ground-lift adapters

- Rubber bands

- Balloons (to capture impulse response for reverb in a pinch—also great for parties)

- Batteries (four each: AA, AAA, 9V)

- Eight XLR male to XLR female barrels

- Eight XLR female to XLR male barrels

- Four male XLR to TRS 1/4-inch female

- Four TRS 1/4-inch male to XLR female

- Two XLR isolation transformers (inline style)

- Two XLR 25-dB switchable pads

- Two stereo bars

- Two XLR barrels with ground lifts

- Two XLR or TRS impedance-matching adapters

- One-foot FireWire cable

- One-foot USB cable

- Two-foot TRS to TRS

- Two-foot MIDI round cable

- Various adapters for FireWire and MIDI connections

- Two-foot coaxial 75-ohm clock cable

- One RCA-to-RCA cable

- One insert cable, 1/8-inch TRS to 1/4-inch TS and RS (useful for connecting laptop soundcards)

- 1/8-inch TRS to 1/4-inch TRS adaptor

- Coaxial BNC-to-RCA adaptor

- Chewing gum

- Bit of wire

- Aspirin

- Cold or allergy medicine

- Tums

- ACE bandage

- Two dollars in change case

Sometimes elements can be replaced and repaired from the gadget box if you carry a full-blown toolbox in addition to the gadget box. Obviously, a soldering iron is something you should never leave at home when you go on a location recording. The location recording engineer should also always carry a flashlight and a multi-tool, such as a Leatherman, Bucktool, or Gerber. In a pinch, almost anything that doesn't need to be soldered can be fixed using the tools on a Leatherman. An LED headlamp is always a wonderful addition because it allows you to keep your hands free while pulling cables, crawling under stages, or soldering a fried connection back onto a wireless microphone.

With your equipment and all your accoutrements firmly in place, you are ready to record. This would be a good time to take a closer look at your options for data storage, data retrieval, and file management.

7 Where We Keep Stuff: Data Storage

We have discussed some difficult decisions we face as live recordists, including setup locations, where we draw our power from, and more. One of the hardest decisions you will make during a location recording deals with storage. The storage media you choose has as much to do with the quality of the sound and the aesthetics of the final product as the selection of microphones, pre-amps, signal processing, and consoles or control surfaces. Just as location factors into the rest of your selections of equipment and gear, location will contribute to your decision regarding the storage format. It would be difficult and impractical to haul a two-inch 24-track analog tape machine to a location recording. This scenario would get you major points for being cool up front, but would cost too much in the end as you failed to give the client what they wanted in a reasonable fashion at a reasonable cost (see Figure 7.1).

Figure 7.1 A 24-track headstack. While lugging a 300-pound machine along to a gig might make you look cool, it is hardly practical in this day and age.

In this situation, a well-designed computer the size of a toaster with a quality bus-based audio converter or a FireWire-based audio converter would be adequate to accomplish the job at hand. Every device and every medium available today has pros and cons. Ultimately, selection of the storage device will come down to the engineer's personal preferences, tempered by the limitations of budget and space.

Digital versus Analog

In the days of bearskins and stone knives, prior to the advent of the ADAT blackface recorder and the Tascam 8mm recorder, multitrack location recording was a difficult and onerous process. The digital revolution that brought multitrack recording to the masses also allowed location recording to become more readily available, easily portable, and affordable. In the old days, even stereo recording was a difficult and arduous feat, because quality two-track tape machines were heavy, delicate, expensive, and large (see Figure 7.2).

Figure 7.2 A Studer A807 two-track analog machine—pretty to look at, sounds great, but too heavy and delicate to lug to the gig.

Anyone who hauled gear for live recording during these prehistoric times remembers the nightmares of backaches and the necessity of van ownership. Fortunately, brighter days were ahead of us—first, briefly with multitrack digital recorders using dot and dash formats, then eventually with the joy and simplicity of the hard disk.

Ultimately, the tape-based digital recorders lost favor due to the same issues as multitrack tape recorders—excessive size, weight, and expense. The industry gladly moved to hard disk systems. Radar, Mackie, Tascam, and Alesis all make versions of a 24-track, 24-bit hard disk recorder. These devices, easier and more affordable in every way than their predecessors, do not require an external computer and write universal digital audio files. As computers and audio interfaces have become cheaper, smaller, and faster, computers have emerged as the audio storage destinations of choice.

File Formats

Analog recording has lost popularity in recording studios. This loss in popularity is even more pronounced while recording on location. Nonetheless, the question lingers: Which format should I use? As we discuss format, we are not (yet) talking about software, software platforms, or hardware platforms; so far, we are only discussing the type of file format in which the audio data will be saved. Sometimes the end user will dictate this, and other times the decision will be made based on the project itself and the goal of the recording. Ultimately, a smart engineer will save all files in a format that can be opened on virtually any platform. This allows the maximum flexibility when files and tracks need to be used on a number of systems, which frequently occurs.

While offering some benefits when used in the company's hardware structure, systems that use a native, proprietary format do not allow for portability and therefore reduce your flexibility. Saving in a proprietary structure might also cause problems at some point in the future. In the event that the recording is revisited in the future for a remix or other purposes and the proprietary machine or playback unit is no longer in existence, the files are as worthless as 50-year-old tape that has turned to dust in its box. This issue has already reared its ugly head. Some recording was done on early digital formats, such as the F1 beta recorders (see Figure 7.3).

Figure 7.3   The Sony PCM-F1 system, which recorded digitally on a Betamax video cassette tape.

Finding an F1 beta recorder in working operation, let alone one that has a functioning modern digital output, is quite difficult. The DAT machines of the '80s and '90s, once considered an excellent format for storage, are clearly headed in that same direction.

Even worse are the Exabyte and tape backup systems that were in use in the early and mid-1990s (see Figure 7.4).

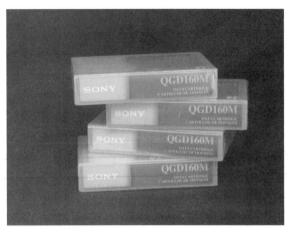

Figure 7.4 A stack of now-rare Extabyte tapes. Just try to convert these to a modern, useable format. I dare you.

Less common formats and systems such as these create a real problem today, and as a recordist you do not want to be contributing to tomorrow's problems. Rare or outdated formats used for storage or backup effectively become a hardship for someone down the line, because it will be harder to replay or retrieve data from your recording. A widely recognized advantage of analog tape is its universality in terms of how it is played back. A mono 1/4-inch tape can be played back on a stereo 1/4-inch tape machine despite the difference in head configuration because the basic format of magnetic storage (the way the audio is placed on the tape) remains the same. A 1-inch 4-track recording can be played back on a one-inch 8-track machine; as long as the spindles on the analog machine can handle the tape width, some version of the audio can be heard. With a digital tape and varying file formats, this universality is not possible.

It is always a good idea to conform to standards and procedures as laid out by the Audio Engineering Society (AES). Following the procedures for the AES 31 and digital protocol is highly recommended when creating a recording session. Basically, this consists of recording your files to a broadcast wave file, otherwise known as a *BWAV*. A BWAV is very similar to a WAV file, except it can contain more data in the basic track, such as artist name, dates, recording details, and space, similar to the CD text. Most importantly, it contains timestamps for all data. This timestamp will allow the recording engineer to reassemble a multitrack in any digital audio workstation that can accept a BWAV file. It allows for simple, accurate alignment of the multitrack so the different internal elements will play back in correct time, or in sync. This methodology allows for the ultimate compatibility.

AES 31 is also a file format exchange structure that allows edit decision lists to be transferred between different workstations. Although AES 31 may not always transfer all information contained in your recording, it will move the big chunks, the most important audio and text data, from one workstation to another. It certainly beats moving things around by hand and then trying to line them all up.

Standalone Gear versus the Computer

It is often a tough call to decide whether you would prefer to record on the computer or the standalone. This is one of those debates (like digital versus analog or Neve versus SSL) that has been raging for a while in the audio industry, and there is no one answer (see Figure 7.5).

Figure 7.5 RADAR by iZ Technology—a standalone digital multitrack recorder that records in BWAV.

This debate is so ubiquitous that Tascam has come out with something like a hybrid with their X-48. As previously mentioned, this is ultimately a call based on preference and budget. Standalone recorders are typically rock solid in operation, and they rarely hang up or freeze; in other words, they do what they are designed to do—record audio. These recorders are basically stripped-down computers, complete with disc operating systems, CPUs, and video cards (at least those that support a video monitor). The analog-to-digital converters that are built into these devices are critical components and vary substantially, as one would expect, largely based on price. Most have a fixed track count that shrinks when the sample rate is increased, since doubling the sample rate means twice as much data needs to be transferred. The simplest way to deal with the increase in data flow is to reduce the number of tracks available. The functionality and design of these units are similar to those of a tape deck. Simply connect all analog audio sources to the inputs on the deck, create a session, enable the tracks, and record. Easy.

The computer-based system is very similar to the standalone recorder, and with good reason. The standalone is little more than a stripped-down computer that is designed and built just to record audio. The same elements are required on both; an analog-to-digital converter, an interface, a program that allows for encoding the data into an audio file format, a storage medium, a video card, and so on. The computer offers more flexibility because it is more easily upgradeable, less proprietary, and less expensive to replace. You can add more memory or additional hardware as needed to increase track count or sampling rate.

For example, to increase an RME Fireface 800–based system from 28 tracks of 24-bit 44.1-kHz sample rate recording, you only need to add another RME Fireface 800 interface to double the track count. Now here's an asterisk, which should be a permanent figure in all audio professionals' minds when it comes to configuring and looking at digital audio workstations. The asterisk in this example is the assumption that you connect the Fireface using a FireWire 800 cable and you have a bus and other computer hardware that are fast enough to handle the data throughput and run the software, graphics, and so on *and* has been set up properly.

Let's also assume that both of the interface boxes have the same firmware updates installed. The firmware is the basic program that allows the interface box to operate as an interface box. This is a lot of assumptions. If this sounds seriously complex and unreliable, then you are paying attention—it is. It can be quite reliable if you pay attention to the details and keep everything clean and neat. The reward is the ease and flexibility you gain by having your favorite DAW on location. Often it can replace a mixer and other elements.

One word of caution regarding your DAW: This is *not* your all-purpose home computer. You are performing and executing important, professional work on this machine. You might be tempted to add an email program, a web browser, or even some word processing and spread sheet programs to this unit. Don't. These programs will pollute your machine and make it less stable. Remember, this unit is dedicated to recording and needs to be as stable as possible. Because any other program compromises that stability, you should refrain from loading anything on here that is not necessary for the gig.

The Two-Track CD Safety Mix

Our two-track mix serves several functions: It is a reference mix for the musicians and something fun for them to take home after the gig. More importantly, our safety mix is extremely important because any computer can crash. It doesn't matter how stable you think your system is—it doesn't even matter how stable it really is—all systems can crash, and the day you fail to run a safety is the day it will crash. For the lowest risk in your safety, mix on a separate board, splitting the signals at the microphone. These clean signals should be sent to a very reliable recorder, preferably one that retains all audio information in the event that power is lost. I prefer sending my safety to a stand-alone two-track recorder. Some people like to make a safety on a real-time CD-R (see Figures 7.6 and 7.7).

Photo courtesy of Marantz.

Figure 7.6 The Denon C550R Professional CD + CD-R/RW Recorder Combo-Deck is ideal for recording a two-track safety.

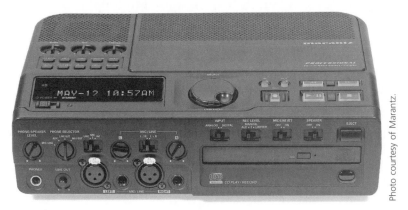

Photo courtesy of Marantz.

Figure 7.7 The Marantz CDR420 Portable CD Recorder is also ideal for real-time two-track recording.

This has the added benefit of instant gratification, and we all love instant gratification—especially the band members. There are some very high-quality and extremely stable CD recorders, including the HHB CDR882 CD burner, the Tascam 1000 (which is pretty cool with the DSD option), and the Masterlink by Alesis.

No Such Thing as Overkill

If recording is a good thing, is it possible to have too much of a good thing? Not in my world. In a perfect world, we would have all the tracks split, going to a hard disc recorder as well as a multitracked DAW, all backed up further with our two-track safety. Now everything is backed up, and backed up again. Our safety mix or real-time mix on the fly would come from the outputs of one of the devices in this case, but with this level of backup, we could proceed with the utmost confidence.

Mix Live, Mix Well, Live Well

This might seem obvious, but it is critically important to try to get some sort of functioning mix while doing the recording. Although this mix does not need to be broadcast quality, it will be helpful if it is a good quality mix. This mix allows you to focus on the tracks, assess them, and know what you have and what you lack in real time. Instead of watching the meters, trust your ears. This will gain importance when it comes to making changes.

Remember, a track cannot be heard as an isolated sound source; it needs to be judged as one component within a complex mix. Each element is like one voice within a choir; it is a color in a whole painting and has to be viewed or heard in context. This context needs to be established on site to know whether the tracking will work in post-production, to ensure that you are getting all the data you need to fulfill the project's requirements.

What if Nothing Explodes?

The importance of backups cannot be overstated. Without them, you risk too much. If you have two multitrack safeties and a real-time stereo mix when the show ends, you are in very good shape, but you can never back up enough. Typically, it is a good plan to make three copies of each format of the recording. This means three copies of each multitrack and three copies of the two-track mixdown. Then spread them out.

If getting to the post-production facility requires travel, or if you need to mail any of the elements, be sure to make backups. Leave one on site with the client, take one with you, and send one in the mail. If the two with you don't make it, the client still has a safety, and you can try again. One of the advantages of digital is the lack of generational loss, so the fifth copy will sound as good as the first, unlike analog, in which each time noise and distortion are added to the recording.

Leery of the Laptop

Basic laptops are not terribly robust. Frankly, they are pretty weak. They are designed to maximize stamina for enhancing battery life, and they typically will reduce performance in any way they see fit to achieve this. There are exceptions, of course, and as technology improves and capabilities increase, the ability of the laptop to become the primary recording device will increase as well.

One of the most debilitating issues regarding the laptop is the lack of a second independent hard disk, which some consider a basic requirement for digital recording. When recording to a computer, it is a good idea to record to a clean hard drive that is used exclusively as an audio storage drive. If you record to your master drive, or main drive (some PC folks call it the *C drive*), you might run into conflicts as the computer accesses the main drive for lower-level program functions, such as virtual memory and running of other software, both of which could interfere with and slow down the writing of the data you need. Because audio recording occurs in real time, it is important to remember that speed counts. You are asking the drive to do a lot of work; writing multiple files to a drive all at the same time is more taxing to a hard disk than writing one giant file. Remember, a multitrack recording is just that; you are recording multiple data streams. An alternative to the laptop is the toaster-sized box, which can take a high-speed processor, a full-size motherboard, and a power supply and is basically a compact but extremely powerful computer (see Figure 7.8).

Figure 7.8 A toaster box multitrack recording computer is a fully capable and powerful computer in a smaller package.

Keeping Track of All This Sound

Once you have decided upon the particulars, assuming you have not hired sherpas to lug an analog tape recorder to your gig, you need to think about file structure and labeling in order to easily access all your digital files anytime you wish. Most workstations will create a system of folders that will organize your audio. Make sure that there is a master folder in which these folders are stored. I give my master folders the same name as the initial session. Then the sessions folders—usually named something like Audio and Fades or Profiles—can be contained in the master folder. If you don't create a master folder, confusion may result when you arrive at the transfer and backup portion of your session (see Figure 7.9).

Figure 7.9 A Nuendo screenshot.

There are many different naming conventions and processes for your digitally stored information. All require the same basic information. The project name needs to have the client's name, the name of the location, and the date of the session. The date is often stamped with the time at the time of the file creation; however, it is not always readily displayed. For example, many project recorders will not show this information. An example of a good project name would be 071201SLSOPSH. The name breaks down this way: the date (2007 December 01), the client (the Saint Louis Symphony Orchestra), the location (Powell Symphony Hall).

If you are recording directly to a digital audio workstation, then you might want to add a version number to the end of the file name to keep track of the version number. So our name would be 071201SLSOPSHv1. Resist the temptation to use special characters such as periods (.), dashes (-), or even spaces. Although *your* system might support the use of these characters, other systems might not. If you feel you must separate your names, use the underscore (_). A descriptive name can save you when you are looking through the mass of files and folders later.

Track names need to follow a similar description. For example, a snare drum track should reflect the snare (SNR) and possibly even the microphone being used (such as SNR_SM57). The idea is to provide the mix engineer with as much information as possible, as easily as possible, and with the greatest chance of him understanding your notation. If your DAW supports comments or notes on each track of the edit list or mixer window, put as much information as you can squeeze onto the track. Include microphone pre-amplifier type, analog-to-digital converter type, whether it was split with front of house, and even positioning information if space allows. If you need to reconstruct the mix on a different DAW, these track names will be invaluable.

Choices such as file structure and a toast box can be pretty clear when you are in command of your equipment and you have a lot of gear and good racks, or if you are building a recording truck.

Because we are talking about building a recording truck, let's look at the advantages and disadvantages to mobile units, anvil cases, and board feeds as we proceed to the next chapter.

8 Decisions, Decisions—To Wheel In or Not to Wheel In: That Is the Question

So far we have talked mostly about gear that you put in your car, truck, or van. There are some other options at this juncture, such as putting your favorite console in an anvil case (or some other strong case) to protect it. If you do not want to bring your own microphones and console for any reason, maybe you want to split the feed and get your signal from someone else's console. Perhaps, instead of loading in your gear by pulling up to the loading dock and unloading and wheeling cases into the venue, you want to drive up in a fully capable mobile recording truck, essentially putting wheels on the studio instead of on the cases.

Taking a break from planning and looking at some options for general location recording, let's review the possibilities. The most unique aspect for location recording is the location itself. It is often the primary reason why the recording is taking place outside of a studio. The location has some allure to it, some history, perhaps a certain resonance that has brought you out from your natural habitat—the dark, cave-like studio. In this Part we have examined the different types of equipment and gear that you need on a location recording, and we all know there can be quite a lot.

So far we seem to be attempting to re-create our "home"—the studio—in the newfound location. We have to lug our prize microphones, microphone preamps, converters, and computers to this strange and unfamiliar place. As with any good sensitive gear, we need decent cases and packing to protect them. Two-hundred dollars might seem like a lot to spend on something that does not pass signal, but without quality protection, your gear will not pass signal when you arrive at the gig. Consider for a moment that cases will protect your $4,000 board, computer, and/or hard disc recorder. Add to that the confidence inspired by the knowledge that the gear will work when it arrives at the venue. It seems like a much better deal now, doesn't it? Think of a high-quality road case as an insurance policy that your recording equipment will arrive at the gig in a functional state.

Remember, the cardboard box or crate that the gear was in when you purchased it was designed to protect the gear only from the factory to you. It is not a road case. The only use the factory box has is to transport the gear to you, and its only subsequent use is to return the gear to the factory when it gets broken from not being carried in a road case.

Safe Cartage: Basic Protection

Lucky for us, the recording industry has set standards for protecting rackable equipment. Because most of the gear we use is rackable for installation, we can rely on the industry standards and load it up in a rack for road use. As with every other type of gear we use, there is a wide variety of rack-mounted cases available. They run the gamut from mass-produced metal and plastics boxes to expensive, custom-designed and built flight cases; the selection is virtually infinite. When choosing a case, you need to consider the following things:

- **Can I use the gear in the case without removing it?** This is important for a quick setup—for example, if you are using a computer interface with microphone preamplifiers, can they be connected in the rack when you assemble it, long before you get to the gig? If your plan necessitates a snake, can the tails be prewired in a rack before you get to the location? Timesavers like these free you up to spend more time on the really important things, such as schmoozing the house manager about killing the first row of seats or sweet-talking the wait staff into giving you free food. A pin system of snakes and connections can make your rack systems quick and easy to set up, saving you stress and making you look like a pro (see Figure 8.1).

- **Is the case too heavy to lift, or does it need to roll?** Often the desire to keep all the gear close and in the same rack outweighs (quite literally) our good judgment. Gear is getting lighter and smaller, but a thousand pebbles can weigh as much as one large boulder—or one hard-disc recorder. The trick in the weight department comes down to two elements: stacking and rolling. If you make the cases stackable, with quick interconnects, to divide the weight and make them manageable, you are halfway there. When you use the greatest invention ever, the wheel, you are making things as easy for yourself as you can. A very smart stagehand once told me, "Don't carry what you can push." Another even smarter stagehand once told me, "Don't push it if you can get someone else to," but that may be a point for another chapter.

Whether fitted to your road case, attached to a pallet, or installed on a cart, wheels will save your strength and your back. Because most location sessions are

Figure 8.1 A pin-out system, with tails of a snake pre-patch.

marathon affairs with load ins and load outs, not to mention the actual recording, you will need all the strength and stamina you can muster. Don't squander it all on the load in. There are also stairs, of course. If it is a modern facility, make sure you are not missing a wheelchair-assist device on the staircase. If one does not exist, your pre-production planning should have forewarned you of this, and you should have planned well in advance, having packed in cases that you can lift.

- **Can the case withstand the trip?** Obviously, this depends on the trip. Are you recording within this universe, somewhere beyond the galaxy, or right here in our own solar system? The Mars Microphone sent on the Mars Polar Lander failed, smashing into the surface of Mars at hundreds—perhaps thousands—of miles per hour. The recording engineer couldn't run back to the shop and get another 58, so that location recording would have to be deemed a failure. Monday-morning quarterbacking may be easy, but if only NASA had spent more time and energy on the road case…. The later Cassini-Huygens mission did successfully return audio from Saturn's moon, Titan, successfully recording the atmosphere of an extraterrestrial body for the first time.

When you take a trip to Mars or Saturn, you might expect to spend hundreds of millions of dollars for a road case, but for a trip to the high school to record the local concert band, you won't need quite the same level of protection. Instead of an airbag or parachute landing system, one would hope that a simple plastic case and metal rack would be adequate to protect all your gear from both the elements and the odd accident. Let's think of the gig at the local high school as a mere trip to the moon. If you need to go to Mars instead—in other words, if you need to go on the road for a long tour—loading in and out of a semi each night, a stronger case becomes necessary. A popular option in these situations is a PVC-skinned plywood case with foam padding and heavy-duty wheels. Throw on some strong door hinges, and your gear is protected from the dangers of constant loading and unloading on the truck (see Figure 8.2).

Figure 8.2 Flight mechanics from Jet Propulsion Laboratory lower the Cassini spacecraft onto its launch vehicle adapter in KSC's Payload Hazardous Servicing Facility. The adapter is later mated to a Titan IV/Centaur expendable launch vehicle that lifts Cassini into space.

Now that the gear is safely protected and all racked up and ready for travel, you need to move it to the location. Often this is done using personal vehicles—vans and trucks. Be aware that if you do indeed rent a truck, and you are recording in a facility that has a union crew, you will need to make sure that you are not required to have union truck loaders load and unload the truck. Try to imagine a worse situation than getting to the gig right on time, with everything as planned, and being unable to unload your own gear. Even worse, imagine yourself explaining it to a client.

The Wheels on the Studio Go Round and Round

Tired of carrying things around, loading them out of your garage or warehouse and into your van, then into the venue when you get there, only to load them back out after the gig and still have to move all that gear out of the van and back into the warehouse or garage after everything else is done? Just writing that sentence made me tired. Imagine how you will feel after handling hundreds, perhaps thousands, of pounds four times. Consider another option. Perhaps the easiest way to get the studio to the location is to just put wheels on the control room and drive it to the location.

Prior to the advent of digital technology and the portability it brought to professional recording, this was pretty much the only way high-quality live sound could be recorded. For many years this has been the primary way to do location recording. Many of your favorite live albums were probably recorded using a mobile truck; they have been in use for a long time. Famous trucks include Metro Mobile Recording, with credits including James Cotton and His Big Band, Koko Taylor, Mannheim Steamroller, Styx, Branford Marsalis, Indigo Girls, Barenaked Ladies, Buddy Guy, and Albert Collins. Another such truck is On The Spot Recording, with credits including Beth Orton, Spin Doctors, Ludacris, Chaka Khan, Bell Biv DeVoe, Teena Marie, the Gap Band, and Dishwalla. Le Mobile has credits including Gwen Stefani, Puddle of Mudd, Tom Petty, the Eagles, Fleetwood Mac, the Pretenders, Paul McCartney, John Mellencamp, U2, Melissa Etheridge, REM, Martina McBride, Stone Temple Pilots, Diana Ross, Don Henley, Sting, Madonna, Eric Clapton, CSNY, the Family Values 2001 Tour, Cher, and Garth Brooks. Among remote trucks with a longer history, Record Plant Remote stands out, with credits including Peter Frampton, the Rolling Stones, Mary Chapin Carpenter, Faith Hill, James Taylor, Guns N' Roses, Prince, Nancy Wilson, Bruce Springsteen, Hootie & the Blowfish, the Who, Billy Joel, Al Kooper, Delbert McClinton, Col. Bruce Hampton & the Aquarium Rescue Unit, Cornell Dupree, Def Jam, Emmylou Harris and the Nash Ramblers, Frankie Valli and the Four Seasons, Nanci Griffith, Radney Foster, REM, INXS, Wynton Marsalis, Elton John, Al Jarreau, Ricky Skaggs, Spin Doctors, Whitney Houston, Jimmy Buffett, Paul Winter, Trisha Yearwood, Aaron Neville, Meat Loaf, Rollins Band, Bill Cosby, and Garth Brooks.

Although digital technology has reduced the size and price of gear, effectively reducing the workload available for these mobile homes on steroids, there is still work for them. Larger-budget projects, in particular, still like the additional comfort level afforded to producers and musicians by these rolling recording studios. They feel

Figure 8.3 The control room in the Record Plant Remote truck.

Figure 8.4 Like most top-of-the-line remote trucks, the Record Plant Remote truck contains state-of-the-art recording gear.

more confident looking at a truck in the lot than they do looking at a lunchbox. Although you might question the sensibility of this, it is unwise to question your client's perception.

Typically, remote trucks have all the amenities of a full-blown recording studio—a major console, quality signal processing, and state-of-the-art recording devices. They also feature an acoustically controlled environment that is completely isolated from the performance, allowing the engineer to be confident in the monitor mix. As if that weren't enough, these converted Winnebagos and Airstreams often keep their kitchens and sleeping quarters despite the renovations; they have all the comforts of the studio and all the comforts of home (see Figures 8.3 and 8.4).

Sharing Is Good (Maybe)

Was your kindergarten teacher right when she said you needed to learn to share? Maybe. There are times in any of the aforementioned situations when you will be asked to split the signal coming out from the microphone and share it with the house engineer. Reasons for this request may include:

- Audio aesthetics

- Visual aesthetics

- Budget

- Client's unexplained request

You should consider splitting the signal when the house engineer has better microphones than you do—especially if you trust his skills at microphone placement. This is an audio aesthetics criterion. If the final product will sound better because you shared the house engineer's exceptional microphones, you should consider it.

If the client or house manager has made it clear that he does not want too many microphones onstage, a good recordist will respect and conform to those wishes by splitting the signal, getting double duty out of the existing microphones and retaining the visual aesthetics without compromising the sound.

In the event that the client has given you a limited budget with which to work, splitting the signal out of the existing microphones rather than renting additional microphones could be an effective cost-cutting measure. Finally, on occasion, a client will simply state that they want you to share the microphones with the house engineer or broadcast engineer. They might not give you a good reason. They are still the client, and even though they have not articulated their reasoning to you, your job is to serve them. You can try to talk them out of it if you think the overall quality of project will suffer as a result of the split, but ultimately you need to respect their decision.

When splitting microphones, use a splitter with outputs isolated by a transformer (see Figure 8.5).

Figure 8.5   A splitter with outputs isolated by a transformer.

This will protect the integrity and quality of your signal. Using a simple Y adapter might not give you the quality you hope for.

Okay, let's run down the checklist. Location? Check. Power? Check. Signal? Check. Storage medium? Check. Spares, tape, markers, business cards, and lollipops for the kids? Check. Time to get recording, so let's go to the gig.

The Gig

9 Recording Big (Because We Always Record Big): Clubs, Rock, Jazz, and Blues

Here we are, equipment set up in our location of choice, all safety considerations adhered to. We have made friends with everyone from the wait staff through the union, up to the venue's owner. We are ready to record. But where are we recording and how did we get here? Are there special considerations based on the space itself, the size of the gig, and even the type of gig? Of course there are.

Maybe your favorite bar band has discovered that you are a recording engineer, and they want you to record them live on location at the pub. Maybe you've been doing a demo in the studio with an unsigned band, and they want to add some live tracks to their CD. Maybe it's not Carnegie Hall or the Blue Note. Do you take the gig? Of course you accept the job. You plan, you assess the space, you pack, and you head out to the gig.

A rock-club recording can have many unique challenges, some of which we have already addressed and some of which we will explore here. In this chapter we will take a closer look at microphone techniques, including placement and patterns, along with the traps and pitfalls that are exclusive to location recording but rarely affect us in the recording studio. With proper planning, some common sense, and a little luck, you can produce a recording that is better than a studio recording and that captures the feel, spirit, and ethos of the live event.

Microphones for the Mix

It might seem odd that the very first thing we talk about is the mix when we have not yet set up, but the mix—the final product or the sound of the final product—will dictate all of the steps that come before. You might think of this in either direction, moving forward or moving backward. The microphones you choose and where you place them will give you the elements from which your mix develops, so all of your choices regarding microphones become part of the final mix. Looking backward, your final mix is the culmination of the elements you have available, and those are determined by your microphone choices.

Let's take this discussion to the next logical step. Everything you do affects everything else you do. That seems simple and obvious enough, yet it is often overlooked. Every professional mixer knows that as you EQ a certain frequency out of a particular source to reduce masking, other forms of masking between unrelated sources will either increase or decrease—in other words, everything you do affects everything else. In terms of placing your microphones with an ear toward the mix, moving a microphone by an inch or two or changing its angle can have a dramatic effect on the final product.

In the category of obvious, suppose you move a microphone a little bit and inadvertently pick up some of the signal from the monitors. The resulting feedback will certainly sour your recording (and get a whole room full of people pissed off at you). While slightly more subtle, that slight microphone change most certainly would have altered the phase relationship between your microphones, affecting the relative timbre and introducing the possibility of phase cancellation. These seemingly minor changes as you adjust the angle of the microphone by four or five degrees will have a profound effect on the final mix. To gain a better understanding of these relationships, let's review our microphone polar patterns.

Polar Patterns

As mentioned earlier (but worth repeating due to its importance), a *polar pattern* is a map of a microphone's directional sensitivity, graphically depicting the way a microphone will respond depending upon the position of the sound source relative to the microphone's position. Also known as *pickup patterns,* there are three basic types: omnidirectional, or nondirectional, which is equally sensitive in all directions; bidirectional, which is sensitive only to the front and back; and unidirectional, or directional, which is sensitive only in the front. Cardioid is a commonly used name for a directional microphone with a heart-shaped pickup pattern, as are supercardioid, hypercardioid, and ultracardioid for shotgun microphones with tighter heart-shaped patterns.

Understanding these various patterns will enable you to place your microphones effectively, minimizing bleed or conversely using some bleed to get a looser feel if indicated by the genre and reducing the possibility of feedback. As an example, choosing the proper pattern and angling the microphone correctly will give you more of the vocal on the track to use in the final mix, while lessening the odds of feedback in the vocal microphone due to bleed from the monitors.

A microphone's directionality is determined by the microphone type, since certain patterns are inherent to certain types of microphones and affected by openings on the sides or rear of the microphone, which allow phase cancellation of sounds from certain directions. Openings close to the diaphragm cancel high frequencies, while openings further from the diaphragm cancel lower frequencies.

Moving-coil microphones are inherently omnidirectional (see Figure 9.1).

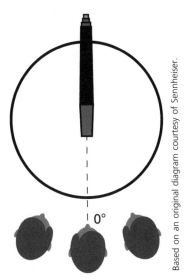

Based on an original diagram courtesy of Sennheiser.

0°

Figure 9.1 The omnidirectional pattern shown means that the microphone is equally sensitive in all directions. This pattern is inherent to both dynamic and condenser microphones, but other patterns are easy to create.

Adding ports to the microphone casing and adding an acoustic phase-shifting network creates a cardioid pattern (see Figure 9.2).

This causes sound waves approaching the microphone from the rear to impact both sides of the diaphragm. These sound waves will have their phase reversed on either side of the diaphragm and therefore will be greatly reduced in intensity. This increasingly reduces the microphone's sensitivity as the sound source moves off axis, with its minimum sensitivity located at 180 degrees off axis (the rear of the microphone).

Ribbon microphones are inherently bidirectional, making them most sensitive to sounds entering the microphone at 0 degrees and 180 degrees and least sensitive to sounds entering at 90 degrees and 270 degrees (see Figure 9.3).

This pattern can be valuable when you are recording an interview or two singers singing a duet.

Condenser microphones are inherently omnidirectional; however, they can easily be made multidirectional, offering a variety of patterns, based on which plate is charged.

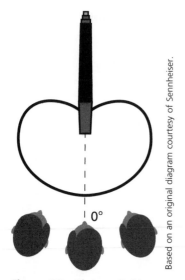

Figure 9.2 The cardioid pattern is most sensitive to the front and least sensitive to the rear. It is a common pattern for vocals and instruments when separation between sound sources is desirable.

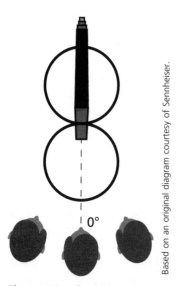

Figure 9.3 The bidirectional pattern is most sensitive to the front and rear of the microphone and least sensitive to the sides.

Many condenser microphones have a third plate, and by variously reversing, reducing, or eliminating the charge to selected plates of the three plates, bidirectional, omnidirectional, and cardioid can all be made available.

Critical Listening

An important concept in the entire field of audio, which becomes particularly significant when discussing microphones, is how to listen, understand what you are hearing, and trust your ears. Learning critical listening takes time, but it begins by simply listening to the sounds around you. Next time you walk up a concrete stairway, listen to the reflections of your footsteps bouncing off the walls. Listen to the combination of the reflections and the footsteps themselves. Close your eyes and listen. Next time you walk through the woods or down a city street, listen to the layers of sounds. If you are in the woods, what do you hear close to you—your footsteps as they crush leaves and twigs, and perhaps the sound of a nearby stream? What do you hear that is a little more distant—the chirping of a bird, the croaking of a frog? How about in the distance—perhaps an animal moving through the woods or the wind quietly rustling the leaves atop the trees? If you are in a city, stand on the street and listen. What sounds close—traffic noise and perhaps people's voices? A little further away, do you hear the sound of a bus or a car without a muffler? Perhaps a siren in the distance? And what about that underlying ambient rumble that most cities seem to have? If you listen at a moment when there are no voices and no traffic, does the city have a certain basic sound—perhaps a combination of distant sounds that combine to become indistinguishable? Identifying and analyzing these layers is the beginning of ear training, or learning how to use your ears most effectively.

Much in the same way that you can tear apart the layers of sound described a moment ago, you can dissect what you hear in an audio situation. Instead of simply accepting the complex, aggregate sound, an audio professional is constantly listening to the layers that comprise that sound. In addition to tearing apart the layers of sound on the basis of loudness, as described a moment ago, we analyze the frequencies and locations of the various sounds that arrive at our ears. What is the highest sound in pitch of everything we are hearing? Perhaps it's the chirping of birds, the wail of a siren, or the squeal of faulty brakes. We also ask where sounds are coming from. Is the full-frequency, white noise–rich sound of the wind moving from left to right? Is it coming from behind us? If we were able to change the timbre of the wind, would it be easier to carry on a conversation on our cell phones?

These are the same questions we will ask throughout the audio process. When we compare two microphones on a single instrument, the criteria that determine which microphone we will ultimately use are the same. What frequencies are we hearing? Are we hearing enough of the high and low ends of this particular instrument? Are we hearing too much of any particular range of frequencies? Does it sound as good through the microphone as it does when we stand on the stage in front of the instrument? How do we know that? These questions are not always simple to answer; often it is a matter of comparing sounds between different microphones until we determine which one (or which combination of them) sounds best to our ears. And the answer to the final question—how we know that—is simple. We answer all these questions by keeping our ears wide open and using them in every situation, discerning and dissecting all the information we are given.

This is not simple to learn, but the way to start is by using your ears critically every day. Use your ears to listen to and analyze everyday sounds. Every sound event can be analyzed; do not pass up any opportunity to pick apart a sound, especially complex sounds that offer interesting entertainment. This will enable you to listen more critically in the studio, on the set, or in a live situation. There is little right and wrong in critical listening; it is subjective. The ultimate goal is simply to understand what you are hearing; increase your understanding of what you hear and increase your trust in your ears. Trusting your ears is the ultimate aesthetic goal.

Microphone Placement

Based on our ideas of critical listening, we know how crucial microphone placement can be. Where a microphone is placed on an instrument is as critical a decision as which microphone the audio professional chooses. Musical instruments do not always produce sound in the way one would expect, so it is important to understand the advantages and disadvantages of various locations on various instruments and to understand unconventional pickup patterns, such as middle-side (MS) (see Figure 9.4). The most important criterion in choosing and placing a microphone is listening. If one microphone does not produce the desired sound, try another. If you are unsure of the best location to place a

Photo courtesy of Stan Coutant.

Figure 9.4   The Shure Model VP88 stereo middle-side microphone.

microphone, have the musician play while you circle the instrument, listening closely to select the best location. Odds are that the microphone will sound best in the same location where it sounds best to you. That being said, here are some ideas for various instruments.

There are numerous ways to place a microphone on a drum set. The simplest form, placing two microphones at a slight distance, will give a nice airy sound, but the bass drum and snare will lose much of their power. With jazz, bluegrass, or folk this might be adequate, but with rock or dance the snare and bass drum, or kick, are critical because they drive the tune. As such, most modern recording professionals favor a minimum of four microphones on a drum kit, one each in the kick and snare and two at a distance. Typically in the studio, if you have enough microphones and a console that is capable of enough inputs, the ultimate setup would include one microphone each on the kick and snare, one for the hi-hat, one on each tom-tom, and two overheads. When you are recording live, however, the four-microphone setup on drums will usually suffice.

When placing microphones on skinned drums (everything except the overheads), always use a dynamic microphone so close to the drumhead that it is almost touching. Aim the microphone at an angle to prevent standing waves from occurring between the head of the microphone or the diaphragm and the head of the drum. For overheads, you'll achieve better results by thinking of each microphone as picking up half of the drum kit, rather than simply miking the cymbals. For the left overhead (from the engineer's and audience's perspective, not the drummer's), think of the microphone as the center of a triangle described by the toms and the cymbal. Similarly, think of the right overhead as the center of a triangle described by the snare, hi-hat, and cymbal. Also be aware of the potential for phasing between microphones. Left and right overheads can cause phasing unless they are tilted away from each other, and the right overhead can have a poor phase relationship with a hi-hat microphone if it is placed too high. Generally, overhead microphones placed at a height of about six feet are pretty safe.

For a kick drum, an AKG D 12, a Heil PR 40, a Sennheiser 421, or an Electro-Voice RE20 is an ideal choice. Any of these microphones will avoid the problems of overloading. Place the mic deep into the drum and remember to angle it against the skin. For a snare, try a Shure SM58, a Heil PR 20, or a Sennheiser 421. On the hi-hat a Shure SM57 is a good choice; it is identical to the SM58, except it is more directional, and the narrower pattern gives better separation between the snare and the hi-hat. Any of the Neumann KM series would also be a good choice for the hi-hat. If you choose to mike the toms, try a Sennheiser 421 or, for a brighter, crisper sound, use an AKG 451 or a Heil PR 30. On the overheads, a Neumann KM 84 or an AKG 451 is always a good choice, as is a Neumann U 87 or an AKG 414.

An electric bass is often best miked without a microphone in the studio. Using a direct box on a bass, bypassing an amp entirely, not only gives a superior sound with a rich, full bottom and a lot of pop on top, it also avoids the potential problem of the bass amp bleeding into all the other microphones in the room. In live recording, the bass player will still want to be in his amplifier, so many engineers prefer to split the bass signal in a DI, or direct box, sending the clean signal to a microphone input and sending the high-impedance output to a bass amp so it can be miked. Sometimes in a mix the direct signal and the miked amp can be blended successfully.

With an electric guitar, use of an amplifier is necessary because taking a guitar direct results in a thin sound. When miking a guitar amp, use a Shure SM58, a Heil PR 30, or a Sennheiser 421 less than an inch from the speaker and on an angle. This will maximize the depth of the sound of the amp, while the angle will prevent a standing wave from forming between the diaphragm of the microphone and the speaker cone in the amplifier.

With an acoustic guitar, the sound will vary, depending on the guitar itself. The base of the neck, just above the sound hole, is often a sweet spot, as is the bottom of the guitar. Avoid the sound hole itself because this is often too reverberant and muddy to record well. As with most instruments, a good audio professional will walk around the instrument, listening closely to decide where it sounds best. Try a Neumann U 87, a Heil PR 30, or an AKG 451. In a pinch, a Sennheiser 421 will work well.

Pianos offer several interesting problems and different sets of problems between live recording and studio recording. In a studio, if there are no other musicians playing in the room, an audio professional will typically open the piano to full stick and record it both close and from a distance. If there are other musicians in the studio, we will close the piano to half stick, microphone it close, and throw a few blankets over it to avoid leakage into the piano track from other instruments. When recording live, the status of the piano lid will often be determined by the visual aesthetic, and as the engineer you will have to accommodate that choice. The piano player or the band's manager may prefer the piano open because a grand piano on full stick looks cool; conversely, they might want the piano lid closed to avoid blocking the audience's view of the stage.

Either way, when recording a piano, please remember where the sound comes from. The vibrations of the strings may create the sound, but the richness of the soundboard gives a piano its fullness. Ultimately, the sound you are looking for will determine your microphone technique. When you need to place microphones inside a piano on half stick, you might be better served by placing them close to the soundboard, rather than pointing them at the strings. Engineers use a variety of microphones on pianos, although virtually any decent condenser microphones will do the job nicely. Try a pair of Neumann U 87s or AKG 414s, one over the high end (where the short strings meet the soundboard) and one over the low end (where the long strings meet the sound-board). A pair of Schoeps MK 4 microphones in an ORTF or XY pattern, about 8 to 12 inches back from the hammers and 6 inches from the strings, can provide a realistic, lush sound. Ultimately, the best plan may be to compare the sounds of miking the soundboard or miking the strings themselves: Each has its advantages, and what sounds best will often be determined by the type of piano and the style of music.

Brass instruments provide us with a bit of a paradox. On one hand, they can easily overblow condenser and ribbon microphones; on the other hand, condenser and ribbon microphones accentuate their sound. A condenser microphone, such as a Neumann U 87 or FET47 (see Figure 9.5), or a ribbon, such as an RCA 77, placed two to three feet from the horn of the instrument solves this problem.

Photo courtesy of Stan Coutant.

Figure 9.5 A Neumann FET 47, as pretty to look at as it is to listen to.

As long as the microphone isn't too close, the problem is solved. Brass instruments produce sound from the horn, making microphone placement obvious and easy.

Woodwinds also sound best with ribbon or condenser microphones, such as a Neumann U 87. However, the sound does not emanate from the horn; it comes from the finger holes. As such, miking the bell of a clarinet will give an inferior sound to miking the finger holes toward the top of the neck. This is also true for saxes, oboes, bassoons, flutes, and piccolos. Commonly, when recording an orchestra configuration, the placement of wind spot microphones can be easily achieved through the use of established and conventional stereo microphone technique over the entire section.

With high strings, such as violins and violas, the best sound is captured from about two to three feet above the instrument, using ribbon or condenser microphones. Neumann

U 87s or U 89s, RCA 77s, and AKG 414s are all good choices. Cellos tend to sound best with a Neumann FET 47, M147, or other good condenser microphones with a strong, round low end set about one foot or less in front of the instrument. For a double bass, try a Neumann KM 84 or an AKG 451, either of which will accentuate the high end of the instrument and reinforce the strong bottom. Like a cello, a double bass should be miked from in front of the instrument, from a distance of one foot or less. In some high-SPL situations, such as a gospel concert, even the best cardioid condenser microphones can be overwhelmed and even harmed. In these situations, a small lavaliere microphone such as the Sennheiser MK2 or the DPA 4061 may be incorporated. This technique gives a clean, isolated sound but does not permit the natural blending of a sectional sound to be captured.

Due to the wide scope of percussion instruments, it would be impossible to include them all with specific instructions. They can, however, be divided into three groups: mallets, including marimbas, vibes, and xylophones; skins, including tympanis and congas; and toys, including tambourines and shakers. For all percussion instruments, condenser or ribbon microphones can be used as long as care is taken to avoid placing them too close to the skins. A pair of Neumann U 87s placed four or five feet above the percussionist's setup will work nicely as he moves back and forth through a piece, playing timpani sometimes, marimba other times, and triangle still other times.

As we get further into orchestral setups, we also need to consider moving away from isolated close-miking techniques and moving toward miking the entire orchestra. Once again, there are many acceptable ways to do this. A simple stereo microphone technique of a full range X/Y pair set about 12 feet behind and above the conductor's head can yield spectacular results. The ultimate position of the pair in space needs to be determined by listening. The overall balance of the entire ensemble, as well as the balance between direct and reverberant sound, can be adjusted by a simple move of the microphone. If a group of instruments is too loud or bright in comparison to instruments that are toward the rear of the group, sometimes something as simple as moving the microphone higher up will fix the problem. Sometimes a good-quality stereo pair of microphones placed in the center of the house about three or four rows back, complemented by a few omnidirectional microphones placed up along the stage to catch both the direct sound of the performance and the ambience of the house, could be all you need to capture a larger orchestra (see Figure 9.6).

You can apply this same idea and concept to any recording situation in which you are attempting to balance multiple sound sources into a stereo microphone technique.

Once you have your center microphone configuration set, consider adding a few accent microphones back in for soloists or quieter instruments to supplement this setup.

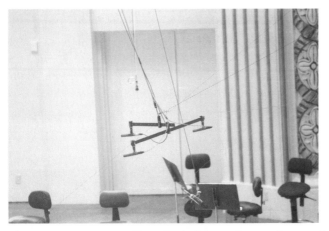

Figure 9.6 You can adjust the balance of an orchestra simply by moving a microphone position in space.

Consider using your omnidirectional ambient microphones even if you are close-miking a rock band. Sometimes the magic of the venue is captured in these ambient microphones. They also will act as a reference when you bring the recording back to the studio. The pair will give you the "you are there" sound to determine information about the recording. From here, you can get a great sense of where you will need to pan your close-miked instruments so that the bleed or off-axis sound recorded by your close microphones can be more in phase.

The ultimate rule, as stated earlier, is to use your ears. Each situation, whether miking to record or miking an orchestra pit for a live performance, is unique. Never allow yourself to be so confident with your setup that you stop listening and start relying on what you think you know. That sometimes happens to old engineers shortly before they are taken out to pasture. Never stop listening. Always take the time to listen critically.

10 Recording Bigger: Large-Ensemble Recording on Location

Let's continue the discussion we ended the previous chapter with—talking about recording a symphonic orchestra—only this time let's dive into larger ensembles and the differences and similarities we will encounter. The basic ideas and fundamental concepts for placing microphones on larger groups are very similar to doing so on a smaller orchestra.

Obviously, there are many ways to record larger and more intricate groups, but ultimately these methods break down into two separate styles of recording. The first is based on recording the sound of the large ensemble in the space in which it's playing—in other words, utilizing the ambience and presence of the space as an element of the performance. The second is an opposite view, based on recording each individual as closely as possible in an attempt to completely eliminate the space in which it is being played—in other words, removing the performance from the venue. Both styles of recording can be effective, depending on your criteria, and both have their advantages and disadvantages. Predictably, both have elements in common.

Common Elements

Note: Beware the stage plot with 27 8″×10″ colored glossy photographs with circles and arrows and a paragraph on the back of each one explaining what it is about.

Regardless of approach—whether you choose to place your microphones close or use the room—documentation during the recording sessions and performances is vital. Beyond the standard track sheets, equipment, microphone notes, and track logs, the most important piece of documentation you can generate is the layout and position of all the microphones in relation to the instruments and monitors during the recording. This is a *location plot*. This plot or chart should show as accurately as possible the location of all sound sources—that is, instruments, singers, and PA speakers, in addition to your microphones. This plot or chart is more than just a convenience during setup; it will become vital during the mixdown process.

Recording and storing the location of all the elements in the recording is now much easier, thanks to the invention of the cheap digital camera. A digital camera should be part of your standard gig box or pack. Basic shots you should always take with your camera include a wide view of the stage or performance area that shows all elements, including microphones, from a distance. Even if you can't see everything in great detail, it should not concern you. The image is primarily a tool to remind you what things look like at the time. Next, you will want to take smaller zonal pictures. For example, you might want to take a picture from the center of the stage to stage left and from the center of the stage to stage right. Also, photos from the left and right edges of the stage toward the center might be helpful later. Anything that is odd or unusual should also be documented with your camera, such as cable runs through a mouse hole that is hidden or typically inaccessible. These photographs, in conjunction with your hand-drawn stage plot, will be invaluable later because they contain the details about where everything was in space, and therefore in time as well (see Figure 10.1).

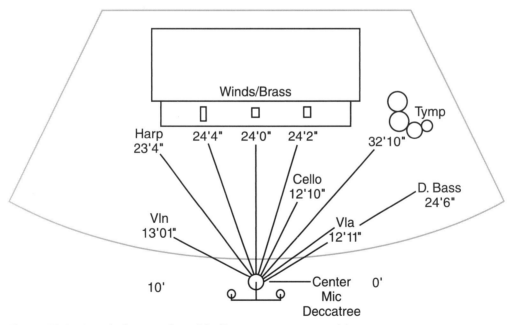

Figure 10.1 A typical stage plot with distance-to-center markings.

Time and Space

The digital revolution has brought us numerous advantages in day-to-day life as well as in recording. While recording live, one of the elements the digital-recording revolution has brought us is the placement of microphones in time and space. Because we know the speed of sound is 1,130 feet per second (fps) at sea level at 70 degrees Fahrenheit, we can calculate how long it will take for sound to leave its source and arrive at our microphones. For example, we can predict that when the sound leaves the soundboard of a violin and travels 20 feet to the center pair that we have so delicately placed above the head of the conductor, it will take approximately 17.7 ms to arrive. The sound from the concertmaster might only take 4.4 ms, because he is sitting within 4 feet of the conductor. This difference in time and the way that we perceive it helps give us our perspective on where in time and space in the recording we perceive the instruments.

If we were to add a spot microphone on a player toward the back of the orchestra, placing it six feet away from the sound of the instrument, and then proceed to mix that electrically in with our center pair, we would introduce a signal that is not natural, because the spot microphone will hear the sound milliseconds before it is picked up by the main pair. If the delay is below the Haas effect 40 ms (our threshold of perception), the image generally will be perceived as a thickening of the sound. It is also possible that phase elements may create some unpleasant comb filtering. Although this is not always a big problem for the instrument for which the spot microphone is intended, it can often wreak havoc with the other sonic elements in the mix.

The off-axis sounds that are not intended to be picked up while in a live event make it almost impossible to get a close, direct spot sound. In fact, on some things it may not be desirable to do so, as getting this phase information from the off-axis elements of the microphone becomes critical in maintaining a solid three-dimensional sonic image. Thanks to the invention of the digital console and the ability to have a delay on every channel, we can now correct this, and because we know the speed of sound and can measure the distance between our microphones and a center point or main pair, we can calculate the time of arrival of the sound from the spot microphone at the main pair.

Depending on what room-miking technique you are using for your main microphone collections, such as a Decca tree or an XY pair with outriggers, you might need to consider at which point to time-align your microphone. Typically, the center point of the XY pair or Decca tree is an ideal point to check much of this, depending on how you mix your front microphones. Typically, the center microphones run hotter than the outriggers and thus require the point to be delayed. This may not be true when the sound source is closer to the outrigger than the XY pair and therefore appears stronger in the outrigger rather than the XY pair (see Figure 10.2).

Client: The Saint Louis Symphony Orchestra
Date: 12-07-2007

MICROPHONE DELAYS

Temp F	in C	(at time of concert)
73	22.7778	

Mic/Position	Ft	In	D-ms
solo left	5	0	4.4
vln spot left	13	0	11.5
cello spot right	12	5	11.0
percussion Left	24	6	21.7
bass	24	10	22.0
horn Left	27	10	24.7
harp spot	23	4	20.7
ww	24	4	21.6
tymp	32	10	29.1
chr 4	40	9	36.1
chr 2,3	35	3	31.2
chr 4	40	6	35.9

NOTES:

Bass Microphone may need alignment more to outside right. Check on playback.

Figure 10.2 Chart with feet, calculation of time of arrival.

Microphone Placement and Selection

As previously discussed, your choice and placement of microphones should be governed by one primary principle: How does it sound? Of course, in the real world there are many other considerations. You are forced to take into account what microphones are available to you and how much time is available to place the microphones. Aesthetics are also a factor—in other words, what spaces and positions are actually available for you to place microphones or hang microphones without impinging on the visual effect of the stage? When you take all these considerations into account, ultimately all of your choices will be governed by the simple fact that it needs to sound good, and you need to end up with a nice-sounding recording when all is said and done.

When you place your microphones on a large group in an uncontrolled environment, the off-axis sound we discussed earlier plays a large role in the sound you are recording. Typically, the direct sound is your only concern within the studio space, where you are in a situation in which you have control over the sound. Things are different when you are doing a room recording, because you need to consider not only the sound you are intending to pick up, but in fact an entire snapshot of the sound you are gathering or collecting. Because you are collecting so many sounds from so many different sources, angled wide-frequency response is desirable—particularly a frequency response accurate from the low- to high-frequency bands. It works well to have a smooth microphone in terms of frequency response, so that all instruments sound equally pleasing. Typically, small-diaphragm condenser microphones are well suited for this sort of response.

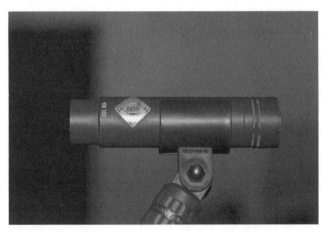

Figure 10.3 Small-diaphragm condenser microphone in hall.

In some situations, large-diaphragm microphones offer a warmer, more desirable response, because a larger diaphragm tends to cut down the transient response time, thus creating a more mellow sound. However, most large-diaphragm microphones today have an emphasis bump on the mid to high frequencies from about 3 kHz and higher, because they are typically used for speech recording. Ultimately, whether you are selecting a large-diaphragm microphone, a small-diaphragm microphone, or a phantom-powered condenser, your selection should be based on how the microphone sounds and responds to the situation in which you are using it.

Top-quality microphones set up in a stereo technique, such as an XY or an ORTF, in the right spot in the auditorium can provide the best recordings of a very large group. If you can find the sweet spot where all instruments are heard, you can eliminate your spot microphones, thus eliminating all the phasing issues and other baggage that comes with them. Often, even with the best microphone placement, a single stereo setup will not give you the ultimate recording because you sometimes need to make adjustments for poor players, softer instruments, and other performance-based issues. Nevertheless, finding the sweet spot will get you to 90 percent of where you want your recording to be.

Every hall will have a different sweet spot, so finding the sweet spot in each location ultimately will be the result of trial and error plus experience. In general terms, a good place to start looking for the sweet spot is somewhere above the conductor's head, away from the instruments. The distance and positioning of the microphones will vary depending on the size of the room you are miking, the size of the group you are miking, the amount of reverberation you want in your initial recording, and other factors, such as balance and tonality of the instruments in the mix.

Sometimes groups are large enough that a single stereo microphone technique might not be sufficient to capture the width or the breadth of the group that is performing and the space they are in. The spaced microphone pair might not seem to give you the size or image of the group that you would expect or feel when you actually watch it live. In this case, it might be time to consider a different spaced microphone technique, such as ABC, or three microphones across the front.

Another option would be to add outriggers to your XY or stereo pair. Outriggers are microphones typically set between 6 and 12 feet to the outside of the stereo pair left and right. It is important to observe the 3:1 rule when placing your outriggers. Effectively, when you are using outriggers, they offer the ability to increase the width of the image that you are creating in the stereo field. In addition to effectively adding space to the direct sound, your outriggers give you good phase information to expand the image.

Using the 3:1 rule is pretty simple—in situations like these, where two mics must be side by side, there should be three times the distance between them that there is between the microphones and the sound source. In other words, for every unit of distance away from the sound source, your microphones should be at least three units apart. If your microphones are one foot away from the source, then they should be three feet apart. This greatly reduces problems associated with phasing resulting from close miking.

Keep in mind that it is important when you add outriggers or additional microphones to stay true to the front pairs so the image you are creating stays intact. If you do not stay consistent, an image that has holes in it or seems absurdly wide may develop. When recording a large group like this, be sure to maintain a realistic perspective in your stereo spread.

This will be more difficult in situations when you must mike a pit orchestra as well as keep the action onstage accurate. Singers and actors frequently receive instructions from directors that require facing in many different directions. Depending on the blocking, they could be facing almost any direction at any point. Often, small radio microphones are employed to attempt to keep some semblance of on-axis pickup, but a blocking chart should be kept if a mix is to be done later to make sure that the proper position and perspective of the singers and chorus can be maintained throughout the final mix.

The pit orchestra also presents certain problems. Most pits are just that—pits. It is important to listen to your pit. Depending on the location and size of the pit, a typical orchestra recording setup can work, particularly a well-designed pit. Often, pits are located at least partially underneath the stage. This means that often, percussion, brass, winds, and the occasional stringed instrument will be in a less than desirable location. Spot miking to gain proper balance might be required. Most of the balance should be created from main pickups to create a sense of the space.

Similar to opera are large Broadway-style musicals. Both have moving-target singers, choruses, and pit orchestras. The major difference between the two styles is just the style of music. The Broadway show has a music sound that is more pop-oriented, and closing miking is more appropriate and conventional. Each instrument should be close miked and treated as a studio session. Most of the mixing in this situation will be done in post-production, with the similar goal of simulating the tightness of the studio sound.

The cast, and indeed a lot of the chorus, are often closed miked for the live sound, and these inputs can be split. If prerecorded click tracks and vocal tracks are used in the production, it is important not only to get original source copies of the recordings, but also to track at least one channel of the prerecorded material to sync up the master recording later. Often these shows are quite preprogrammed, using MIDI and other protocols for triggering sounds and such. You should record in real time all MIDI data and the resulting audio in real time. By capturing both the raw MIDI data and the triggered audio, you can then re-create the same event or change the triggered audio back at the studio.

Now that we have looked at events that are big and bigger, right up through large concert halls, let's take a look at the biggest of events we will ever have to record—sporting events and stadium shows, some with only one stage and some with multiple stages.

11 Recording Biggest: Stadiums, Sporting Events, Music Festivals, and Made-for-TV Events

As technology marches relentlessly forward, it is safe to assume that eventually, maybe not too far in the future, every sporting event and music festival that you could possibly want to see or hear will be made available to you in a variety of forms on a variety of media. This is already beginning to occur thanks to the Internet, between podcasts and streaming broadcasts. We already see people sitting in parks, enjoying on their iPhones a game that is taking place halfway around the world, and we can only expect technology of this sort to become more common and accessible as we move forward. And someone has to be there to record it for these assorted media; it might as well be us. To accomplish this, we need to take into account a variety of criteria—some similar to that which we already discussed, and some new, different, and bigger.

Differences in Venues

Recording in stadiums or large enclosed arenas is vastly different from recording in a concert hall, club, or theater. Big, boxy convention centers and large ballrooms also typically fall into this category. There is a variety of criteria that shift at this level, as the size and shape of the space are so radically different from venues that were created to make events sound good (see Figure 11.1).

The first thing to remember, and the one you must keep in mind throughout the process during these larger events, is that these spaces are not designed for standard performances in the traditional Western sense. These spaces are typically designed to showcase an event. Those who construct convention centers are more interested in creating a space that will produce a maximum of income through creative flexibility than they are about creating an acoustically aesthetic space (see Figure 11.2).

While many more modern stadiums are now being designed with the concept of broadcast included, they are more focused on eliminating reflections that will produce confusing audio for both broadcast and the live audience—the warm reflections that might enhance the experience of the podcast and streaming audience are simply not their

Figure 11.1 A really big indoor venue presents certain challenges.

Figure 11.2 A really big outdoor venue presents different challenges than indoor spaces, and without the benefit of acoustic design.

concern, and neither are our criteria for a space that is good for recording. Let's break down some of the different types of venues and some approaches that might help in specific recording situations.

Multiple-Venue Recordings: Festivals, Events, and Games

One of the most challenging and intimidating recording situations involves multiple venues, such as music festivals with a main stage, a second stage, and possibly even a third stage, or a sporting event such as the Olympics or the X Games, where there are multiple events in locations near each other (see Figure 11.3).

Figure 11.3 Each event of many occurring simultaneously, such as this snowboard halfpipe competition, will present its own issues.

At first glance, clusters of this type seems difficult to record, but if you tear apart the layers, you can easily understand each component as an individual.

Perhaps the best way to approach recording multiple events occurring in one general location is to examine each individual location as if it's a single recording in a single venue, keeping the thought in mind that this location's sound will eventually need to mesh with the overall sound of the project. This will, of course, affect the approach you select for the venue. If other engineers at other sub-venues of the same large event are close-miking groups, you must consider close-miking within your sub-venue rather than going for a big, ambient sound by using room miking. Ultimately, the sound of the sub-venue or location in which you are working will need to mesh seamlessly with the overall event sound (see Figure 11.4).

Figure 11.4 Approaching each component event individually makes multiple events easier to handle, even if this BMX bike event is occurring right next to a dirt bike race.

Even the smallest of gigs are easier, less stressful, and more successful as a result of pre-production meetings. At this level, those meetings become even more critical, transcending the need for major power distribution, the construction of towers on the field, and all the wireless frequencies you will need. The new topic that needs to be introduced at the multiple-venue level is the commonality of our final product. Engineers and recordists from each venue need to coordinate and agree on an approach to recording that is reasonable and achievable for all. Frequently, this will be supervised by a head engineer or sound supervisor for the entire venue, who will oversee the A-1 from each sub-venue—a sound supervisor for all venue engineers, who will make decisions regarding microphone techniques, signal routing, and recording platforms for all sub-venues.

If the event promoters and producers were wise enough to spend the money on an overall sound supervisor, a commonality between the audio products of all venues will be more likely.

There are occasions when it makes sense for the sound to be somewhat different between sub-venues. If you are in the skating rink recording the extreme curling exhibition, while another engineer is at a different location within the same event doing audio for the extreme snowman-building contest outside in the field, it would make sense that your location would sound more like a skating rink, and the other recordist's location would sound as if it were out in the open. If you are working at the X Games, recording a snowmobile uphill climb competition, no one would expect your product to sound the same as that of the Boardercross (see Figure 11.5).

Figure 11.5 Each individual event, such as this snowmobile competition, offers an opportunity to the recordist to achieve a sound that is unique while still compatible with the whole of the event.

Typical Sporting Events

When you are called upon to record a sporting event, the best and most realistic way to approach this is to consider that the client probably wants you to provide both a live broadcast from the event and a recording for podcast or other methods by which the event can be retrieved and replayed at a later date. This approach—treating it as a live broadcast as well as an archive—can be very similar to the approach of designing sound for a live-action play or a concert.

The first step is to analyze the elements of the event you have been hired to capture and prioritize the importance of the various elements that comprise the whole: What is the order of importance of all those elements when you transmit this information to your audience? Consider the audio information that your audience deems most important within the whole of the audio experience. Let's take the example of tennis. There are layers of sound within the audience experience that are easy to identify. The most important sonic element could be the crowd's reaction. Another very important element is the sound of the ball bouncing off the surface of the court, which differentiates between grass, clay, and concrete in the minds of the audience. The sound of the ball smashing against the racket is integral, not only enhancing and identifying the experience, but also giving the audience an understanding, inherent to the sound of the racket, of the different tensions on strings due to the material from which they are made.

Another significant element that you always have to remember is that your commentators must be heard over the din of the crowd and any other ambient sound. This becomes even more important if you are doing an audio-only broadcast, such as a radio broadcast or an Internet streaming podcast, without video, and it can be difficult when recording or broadcasting an event such as motocross or auto racing, or if there are 60,000 screaming fans in the grandstands.

So how do you approach all these factors and resolve all these issues? First, prioritize the various layers of sound that are available and necessary: What is the most important identifier of the event to the listener? How do the other layers interplay with this top layer and all others? As you create a complex mixture of the assorted bits of audio information, how do you keep it realistic, subtle, and believable? One popular method similar to mixing music starts with the most important element(s) on top, supported by the lesser and lesser elements as you move through the possible contributors to your eventual combination. Don't forget to include panning along with level relationship as you descend from most important to least important among your sound sources.

Consider, for instance, how you might assemble the elements for a tennis game. The commentators should probably be at the top of the audio mélange, because their comments and play-by-play are primary to audience involvement in the event. If you think of this as an audio pyramid, as many mixers do, the next item below the announcers' voices might be the sound of the players on the court moving back and forth, sneakers squeaking and bouncing against the court, the smack of the balls, and the cries of the judges and referees (see Figure 11.6).

Supporting the whole thing is the element of the auditorium or arena in which the tennis match is being played—the ambient sound of the live audience reflected in the venue,

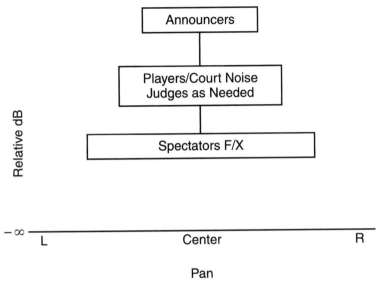

Figure 11.6 The audio mix as a pyramid.

along with the sound of the reaction of the crowd. These sounds enhance the audience's experience; in fact, without them, the audience will not find the event believable.

Another good example of incorporating ambient sound in a pyramid fashion to make the event believable is a baseball game. Along with your announcer microphones, you might hang an ORTF pair of microphones out in front of the location where your commentators are working. This ORTF pair will give you a relatively wide sound, including the crowd and the athletes, depending on the size and shape of the facility. This setup could be ideal for smaller venues with minor league or college games.

In a larger, more crowded venue, you might consider microphones near the home and visitor benches to catch some of the athletes' chatter. You may also want to consider placing the microphones behind home plate; in addition to catching both the visitors on one side and the home on the other side, you will also catch the sounds of the ball hitting the glove after a pitch, the crack of the bat when contact is made, and the umpires' calls for balls and strikes. This method is particularly attractive if you have limited microphone inputs, because you will get more audio information from fewer channels by centering your microphones in this manner.

Always ensure that your microphones are well protected, because all it takes is one 100-miles-per-hour fastball to do a lot of damage to a $2,000 DPA 4006-TL. Also remember that one of the most important things when doing a sports audio-only broadcast is to get the feeling of the crowd in the sense of the space. Although this might be the lowest element in your mix, the bottom of the pyramid, it is as critical as any other layer in your final mix.

When considering a sports broadcast for television, hiding microphones becomes more important. Another consideration for television broadcast is the importance of the new HDTV specifications, including surround sound. If the venue in which you are working is large enough, then hiding microphones will not be an issue; however, you will need to figure out how to get distant sounds from the edges of the venue into your mix. Space hyperbolic microphones are an outstanding option for this job, but they require many assistants to keep moving and aiming their microphones at the specific locations you need to capture. If you watch a football game, you have certainly seen this method employed, as audio assistants run up and down the sidelines with something that resembles an umbrella, pointing the long shaft toward the huddle to capture audio (see Figure 11.7).

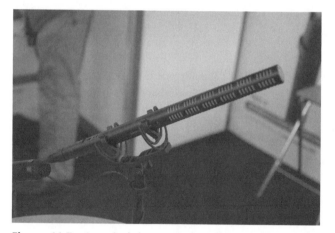

Figure 11.7 A typical shotgun microphone is at the heart of the hyperbolic microphones.

Your standard microphones will still work to capture the general sound and feeling, the ambience of the venue. You may supplement those with a lavaliere or lapel microphone on each of the head coaches. In the early days of location recording, during broadcasts from large sporting events, the announcers would use table-based microphones that could be turned off and on. In a more modern setup, announcers are typically given headsets with microphones that have coffer kill switches. It is important to remember when your announcers are using headsets with coffer kill switches that background audio information, either from the crowd or from the rest of the venue, continues throughout in order to prevent the dreaded silence. Even with constant audio information in the background, the kill switch can present a problem, particularly if the announcer is a soft-spoken person, because the audience noise will seem to go up and down when the button is pushed, since the announcer microphone is still picking up some of the crowd noise. Another factor that will affect this variance in level is whether the announcer is in an open or closed booth, because more crowd noise will infiltrate the microphone in an open booth.

Location of your announcers is, of course, critical. Beyond the way an open versus closed booth affects audio information, as already mentioned, their proximity to the action is also critical. Announcers need to see the game in order to understand what is going on and get a feel of the crowd's reactions. As audio professionals, we would like to see the announcers shut off in a booth somewhere away from the field, completely and totally isolated from the ambient noise and activity. In other words, this is another situation in which our needs as recordists are directly contradicted by the requirements of the event—we want the exact opposite of what they want and where they need to be. Obviously, the needs of the event supercede our desire for an isolated feed, so we do our best by using directional microphones and headsets to obtain the best audio we can while the announcers can still be where they need to be to do the best they can at their job.

Doing It in HD

With the advent of HD technology and the broadcast of HD sporting events, this new standard creates new challenges—that of the 5.1 sporting event. The HD specifications allow for broadcast in surround sound. It is therefore critical that you adhere to basics for mixing in 5.1. Always remember to keep the action in front of the viewer, because that is where the action is happening on their television (see Figure 11.8).

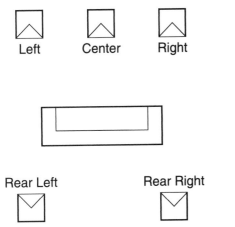

Figure 11.8 Typical 5.1 surround sound configuration.

Consider utilizing the same rules that are typically applied to 5.1 surround sound in film; these rules will translate well in the sports world. The game action should always be in front with a nice stereo spread and the subwoofer handling 80 Hz and lower information. The center channel and rear speakers will define your surround mix and differentiate it from regular old stereo television. Use this new technology so your audience ambience can be heard clearly. It will be the main element in your rear channel, just like being at the game. This differs from the stereo mix, where you would place the ambient crowd noise on the third level of the pyramid.

Frequently, the stadium PA system can be heard clearly, as can the calls and hoots from the stadium. Beware of the fans near the microphones, as expletives and such will be beyond your control. The announcers are typically placed either exclusively or primarily in the center channel, removing or attenuating them from their typical home in the left and right channels. This keeps them in perfect phase for the downmix to a stereo signal and opens up the left and right speakers for more accurate sound for the game noises. It also minimizes masking between the announcers (center), the game sounds (left and right front), and the ambience (left and right rear).

One of the most compelling features of sporting events mixed in 5.1 surround is the ability for the sports fan to finally experience and hear the event as if he were in the stands. If the listener at home wishes to enjoy the experience as closely as possible to being in the stadium, he can get rid of the announcers by unplugging the center channel. If the producer or director is concerned about the end user doing just that, you can pan the announcers between the left and right channels and the center channel, which will still work in the stereo downmix while reducing the ability of the viewer at home to eliminate the announcers and the important messages from their sponsors. Be careful, though—too much information in all three speakers (the left, right, and center) may result in a downmix with too much boost on the announcers, as it sums the center channel to both the left and right speakers of the stereo playback, a boost that has the potential to throw the mix out of balance. Always double-check your downmix to ensure sonic integrity regardless of the viewer's available technology.

Music Events

Recording a music festival offers a different set of criteria and therefore different problems and solutions. For the event that you only have to record on one stage, things are fairly straightforward—pretty much like recording any other venue, even if it is an outdoor festival. A location recording truck might make the most sense in this situation, given its many advantages, as previously discussed in Chapter 8. The controlled environment, free of unpredictable weather, is an ideal place to work; also, it will be easier to deal with the potentially high number of different artists coming in and out through your setup (see Figure 11.9).

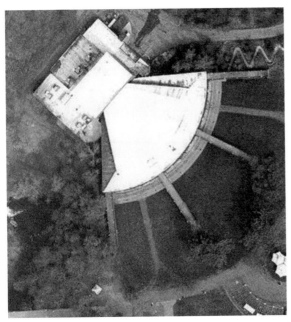

Figure 11.9 A large music venue, the Saratoga Performing Arts Center, as seen from outer space.

If the event is multi-venue—in other words, there is a second or even a third stage—then things get a bit more complicated. A costly but complete solution to this problem is multiple trucks—one for each smaller venue or stage within the overall venue. Often this is not feasible, sometimes due to the extra expense and other times because they have chosen you as the engineer and they want you to oversee all the recordings (as difficult as that is to do simultaneously). This setup does require fewer complete setups, because you can snake your signals from each sub-venue into your master truck, dedicating each subset on your console to its own recording device. This sort of central control has its advantages in uniformity of sound and streamlining of gear, but it takes tremendous advance planning and exceptional organizational skills on your part to ensure a good, clean, isolated product from each of your sub-venues.

In an attempt to simplify this approach, suppose you have two sub-venues at a music festival—the main stage and the second stage. If you bring in a snake from the main stage and dedicate your first 24 inputs to that snake, then send those modules to one hard disk recorder through your Mix Bus A only for that side of the console, you have a good start. Here is your other snake, the one from the second stage. If you dedicate those signals to inputs 25 through 48 on your console and bus those modules to Mix Bus B, which sends to your other hard disk recorder, you are discretely recording two events through one console.

In larger multi-venue events, such as the Olympics or the X Games, where there may be four or five events occurring simultaneously, all needing both sound reinforcement and recording, this same concept is used. Perhaps inputs 1 through 16 will be dedicated to Venue A, 17 through 32 to Venue B, 33 through 48 to Venue C, and so on. Each of these groups of modules can be sent through an aux send back to the venue for the crowd's benefit, as well as to separate recording devices. This requires tremendous organizational skills, but ultimately the central control room gives the entire event some uniformity.

Information Still Rules

Just like with simple events in small clubs or concert halls, the more information you have, the better off you are. For multi-venue sporting events, what are the unique criteria for each sub-venue? Obviously, you will approach the roar of the engines in a motocross or snowmobile climb differently than you would the scraping sound of the snow in a boardercross event. Meetings with sports organizers and athletes to understand what they do and how they do it will be valuable as you attempt to capture the essence of these different events through sound.

Similarly, when you are recording a music festival, gathering as much information as you can about every band that is performing, as well as the flow of the event, is critical. Get this information as far in advance as possible. Turnaround times between groups are critical and sometimes limited. Obtain information from the bands, the promoters, and the producers about how fast they envision the turnaround times should be. Often their ideas are unrealistic; this is a good time to introduce them to reality.

Sometimes in festivals you get lucky, and the instrumentation between groups is similar. If you are recording a blues festival, a typical blues band will have an electric bass and drum kit, an electric guitar, and a singer. The singer might play harmonica, but he can use the same microphone for that. Some of the players will also sing backup. Instead of doing a separate and unique setup for each group, you can do one basic setup that will accommodate all the bands with only minor modifications during turnaround.

Assume that every position will have a vocal microphone. If that musician doesn't sing in one particular group, you can simply shut off his microphone during that group's performance. If the groups agree to use the same amplifiers and basic drum kit, it will save a lot of change over time and speed things up dramatically. During turnaround, the drummer walks on with only his sticks, the guitar and bass players walk on with their ax and plug in, you make minor adjustments to a few microphones and turn a few modules on or off to accommodate their setup, and you are ready to go. Some engineers believe that this is the only way to do a festival. One word of caution, though: To retain your sanity and a sense of order, set up your microphones from left to right as they will appear on your console. Also, number each of your microphones on stage with the same number as the input on your console. This way, as the eighth band hits the stage and things have been moved around a bit, you can still easily identify which microphone goes to which input.

Organizationally, as you set up the event, the recording engineer should set up basic tracks based on the basic microphones setups and make tweaks and adjustments as the band changes. Ideally, you should set up three extra lines per side of the stage to accommodate any additional instruments and specialty items—or the possibility that members of one band will spontaneously decide to jump onstage with members of the band currently playing. During a festival, spare microphone lines will save your butt some days—less is more is not the case in these multi-band situations. As these tracks are sent back to the control room, less is definitely not more: The more tracks you have when you mix, the greater your flexibility. Try to keep things simple and fast on the front end so the audience and musicians will flow freely, unencumbered by your needs during the festival, but ultimately it is up to you to ensure that the tracks you have recorded are of the highest quality and offer the maximum in versatility as you mix. This can be a difficult balancing act at times.

Other Considerations

There are some other important criteria as you record a festival or a major sporting event. It is likely that you are splitting microphones with the front-of-house or television crews. Communication needs to be in place between all parties to ensure that everyone is ready before the signal is given to begin the show. In a music situation, this communication will typically take place between the house engineer, the recordist, and the stage manager. At a sporting event, there are also race starters (also known as *red hats*), sports organizers, television directors, and cameramen, all of whom need to agree that they are ready. Frequently, you will rely on radios at these events, so everyone on the same radio frequency can state that they are ready before an event begins.

If you are recording in a remote truck or some small hole somewhere hidden deep in a venue, you might be left out of the information loop. In that event, it becomes your job to do your best to ensure that everyone knows when you are ready. Direct communications with the stage manager and the front-of-house engineer will certainly help. This is where professionalism, schmoozing, and a well-placed cash tip can come in very handy. Good communications cannot be emphasized enough, both during the gig and during advance planning. The information you gathered beforehand should be compiled for all of the groups. Ask each artist you will be recording on each particular stage or venue about what they do and what they are looking for, and then analyze similar elements in each group to plan out your moves and the equipment list based on all that information. Remember to keep things as simple as possible. That might mean leaving designer microphones, such as your favorite AKG C24, at home.

It is important to consider microphone choices in the context of not only the band and the venue, but also the type of event. You certainly would not bring out our favorite condenser microphones for a motorcycle race featuring high SPL. I would be similarly reluctant to bring a condenser microphone to an outdoor venue of any type during rainy season, because they are particularly sensitive to moisture. Frequently in these cases, dynamic microphones are a better choice.

Also, don't forget the basics. Just like communication, people skills and microphone choices are common to all gigs, big and small. So is power, so don't forget to test it. Some of these simple ideas that were laid out early in the process still hold water—in fact, they become more important as you approach larger venues and more complex recording situations. Never overlook the basics.

As we discuss basics, remember some of the other things from earlier discussions. Good communications may need to extend beyond you, the FOH engineer, and the stage manager. Is there a satellite uplink or is the show streaming on the web? You need to communicate with the engineer handling that end as well. And don't forget the union; in many large venues, you will be heavily involved with union workers, so bring donuts and make new friends.

Are you scared yet? You shouldn't be, because good technique and paying attention to the basics all around will lead to success in all situations. Having looked at the biggest things we can record, let's move on to look at some that can be the smallest. What happens when we go out to do field recording?

12 Location Recording for Visual Media

Just as there are 10 types of people in the world (or 2 in binary code)—those who understand digital and those who do not—it can sometimes appear that there are 10 (2 in Base 10) types of directors in the world—those who understand audio and those that do not. The greatest directors of all time—Welles, Hitchcock, Allen, Landis, Spielberg, Cohn, Sayles—were or are very focused on their soundtracks. Every good director starts shooting a film or video with a picture in mind of the final product—he visualizes the film in its final form, and shooting and editing simply fill in the space in his vision. The great directors also hear a soundtrack under their final product, before one note or line of dialogue is recorded.

Making Your Case

Unfortunately for us, to many directors, the audio of their video and film projects becomes important at about 12:31 a.m. the night before their final cut is due for distribution. At this point they will typically come searching for an audio engineer who can sweeten up their mix and save their film. By "sweetening," they often mean making dialogue intelligible or even just audible. This is most common on small-budget video projects but will also occur on occasion on medium-size film and video projects. Often larger-budget projects have sound designers or sound supervisors assigned to cover these issues; their focus remains on audio as part of the whole throughout the project. Let's look at some of the basics that can make a low-budget video shoot a successful recording, since we often find ourselves in exactly this position.

Working with the Director

You might not have noticed the word "teacher" in the job description when you signed on to be the recordist for a low-budget film or video, but it is often important to educate the director regarding what will be needed to successfully record during a shoot. For many directors audio is the hum that comes out of the speakers, so you will need to teach the director what makes good audio.

You also need to be alert regarding the placement of equipment and the ambient noise inherent to the location, as well as the possibility that this ambience will interfere with your efforts to capture dialogue (see Figure 12.1).

Figure 12.1 Non-audio equipment and the noise it produces can be detrimental to your efforts to get good, clean audio on the set.

A romantic rendezvous in front of Niagara Falls would certainly be a wonderful visual image—one that could be incredibly annoying and distracting to the viewer if all that can be heard is the roar of the waterfall. If the final viewer needs to struggle to hear the dialogue, someone somewhere has failed in his job. As with all problems, there are reasonable and sometimes simple solutions, but it takes understanding and teamwork between the video and audio sides of the production for everyone involved to accomplish their common goal—a film or video that the viewer will enjoy.

The Basics

The basics of good audio always apply, and recording soundtracks for film or visual media is no exception. Distortion, phase, noise, hum, and digital overload are as bad in this world as they are anywhere else in audio. The same basic technical quality tests and aesthetic considerations that you apply to an audio-only recording will be applied to an audio-for-video recording. All of the planning, pre-production, and packing that you would typically do on a standard location recording apply directly to a field recording for video. Communication, teamwork, and preparation are still 90 percent of the battle.

Although the goal of recording quality audio remains the same, the equipment that you use for a video shoot will frequently be slightly different than what you would use for an audio-only recording. First of all, out of respect for and to enhance the visual aesthetic, your gear has to be out of shot, or not seen in the picture. You have to capture natural, high-quality sound of only what the director is intending to capture for the frame shot, and your gear needs to stay invisible during this process. One great example of this is the magnificent recording done on the movie *Kansas City* by Robert Altman. All of the scenes of tremendous jazz being played in the juke joint in Kansas City were shot live and multitracked with modern microphones hidden within the scene (see Figure 12.2).

Figure 12.2 Small, high-quality microphones such as the Neumann KM140 can be hidden in the set, maintaining the visual aesthetic while capturing audio flawlessly.

Although this is an extreme example of what may be asked of the recordist on a video shoot, it provides a great allegory and possibly even a roadmap of what needs to be done. The jazz bands in the movie sounded as if you were there, listening to them live, yet the scenes also had to meet the standards of our modern ears.

Extraneous Noise

Additionally, the recording for *Kansas City* also had to deal with the noise of the camera crew and everything else that goes on during a film shoot. The music needed to be captured live for the set, since the director felt it necessary to capture the emotion of improvisation between the musicians live on film. Ultimately, this is what you need to do as the recordist. You need to capture the emotion of the action, regardless of whether that emotion is music, romance, or action. The event is simply being recorded as accurately as possible while eliminating all extraneous noise created by the process of capturing the event, including all the video and film equipment, the makeup artists, the airplanes flying overhead, the power generator in the background, and the whirring and clicking of the camera.

Typically, when you are called upon to work on a film shoot, the most important thing to capture is not the ambience of the area around the setting of the scene, but the dialogue that is spoken or delivered by the actors (or the subject, in the case of a documentary). Because we need to keep our microphones out of shot as much as possible, the recording engineer will often employ a shotgun microphone in a hypercardioid, ultra-cardioid, or supercardioid pattern at the end of the fish boom or boom arm. A Sennheiser ME 66 and an Audio-Technica AT835b are typical mid-price-range microphones that can achieve the necessary quality at a reasonable price (see Figure 12.3).

Figure 12.3   This shotgun microphone, made by Audio-Technica, will work well on a film shoot.

One of the most important criteria while using this boom shotgun or any supercardioid microphone is to know the script and who needs to be recorded and at what time. It is also vital to identify the noise elements in the area and keep them off axis of the microphone. Often in the movies we are shown the soundman holding the microphone up over his own head and the heads of the actors as they make a dramatic play for the camera. Although overhead booming can be effective and can deliver a decent sound, after about an hour your arms become quite tired (see Figure 12.4).

Figure 12.4   Holding a boom above one's head looks stylish, but it can be quite tiring.

A less exhausting alternative positioning for the microphone is out of shot of the camera, with your hands below the picture. It is much easier to guide the microphone from the lower half because you do not have to support the weight of the boom, the microphone cable, and the microphone over your head, and you can concentrate on aiming the microphone at the appropriate actor (see Figure 12.5).

Figure 12.5 A boom held low can be maintained for a far longer period of time.

Even better than a fish pole, depending on the situation and the budget, another solution might be a sound crane. Like a camera crane, this allows you to mechanically move the microphone into the proper position so your arms can stay resting quietly and comfortably at your sides. Sound cranes are often expensive to rent, and they take up a lot of space, so typically they are exclusive to projects with large budgets.

Prepare for the Unexpected

Regardless of the equipment you choose, things will not always go according to plan. Suppose you have your microphone on the end of your fish pole. It is a bright, sunny day, the birds are singing, and everyone is positive and happy. You know where your sound sources are and where the ambience is. You absorbed the script, and your microphone is aimed straight at the correct actor. The director yells "action," the actor gets into the scene and begins emoting like never before, and you are catching it all. Everything is going well. Then the actor screams out his last line loud enough to distort your levels. You look down at your portable hard disk recorder and see the level spike to above zero. As we all know, spiking above zero is unacceptable in the digital world and typically translates into not just distortion, but complete and total noise combined with significant signal loss. The director yells "cut," says "bravo," claps the actor on the back, and says, "That was amazing. We've got it!" You now have to tell the director, "Oh, actually, sir, we don't have it—he distorted the last line." Now you get to reshoot a scene three or four times with the ire of the entire crew, who were ready to go to lunch, focused on you.

This could have been prevented if you double-tracked a single feed from your microphone. Basically, set one level where you believe it needs to be, then set a secondary level on a separate recorder, 6 to 9 dB below your first level. This will give you a safety net if your first level overloads or distorts and ensures that you will capture all the audio as it happens, without incident or angry stares from the rest of the crew. In the days of analog recording, this was not nearly as important because analog was far more forgiving, and even slightly distorted audio could frequently be used.

Often video shoots are done outside, where controlling the wind is not possible. In this situation, the windscreen can be your friend, but do not go for the simplest of windscreens. You often will find when you record outside that you need an audio blimp—a case for your microphone that covers it completely and totally (see Figure 12.6).

Figure 12.6 An audio blimp is a particularly effective windscreen.

Typically, an audio blimp is made out of fur or mesh with nylon cloth that reduces wind flow and air movement over the microphone. Although the basic foam windscreens can reduce the wind flow and protect the microphone from low-end rumble, foam also colors the sound more than fur or cloth blimps.

Beyond Mono

So far we have focused on mono techniques for recording dialogue. There might be occasions when you need to create or capture a stereo recording or image of the action or dialogue in the shot. Mid-side (MS) microphones or a stereo microphone can provide you with great detail in a highly mono-compatible signal. When coupled with an MS decoder, MS microphones allow you to adjust the width between mono and a fairly nice stereo image.

Mid-Side Microphones Mid-side is a coincident technique that employs a bidirectional microphone facing sideways and a cardioid microphone at an angle of 90 degrees facing the sound source. One microphone is turned upside down over the other so they are the same distance from the sound source. The left and right channels are created in the following manner: Left = Mid + Side, Right = Mid − Side, where you reverse the phase of the bidirectional microphone 180 degrees using your phase reverse switch at the console's input. The advantage to this approach is that you produce a mono-compatible signal, which you can then manipulate later, during the mix, to the desired width.

Most televisions, computers, and video players have a stereo playback system, and soon all will. Unfortunately, they are usually equipped with cheap speakers, mounted so close together that they are effectively a mono system. For an audio professional, this means that while mono compatibility may not be completely required, it is still a good idea to ensure that the end user has an enjoyable experience, particularly when dialogue is being recorded.

Another type of microphone that is now becoming more common during location recording is the surround-sound microphone. The ATSC standard for high-definition television broadcast includes a provision for 5.1 digital surround delivery. For us, this translates into more interest in recording on location in 5.1. Most production shoots for fictional shows may not need this to be done on location, since the sonic setting is frequently developed and designed in the studio later; however, nature documentaries and other productions that require accurate spatial recording during the shoot will demand delivery of 5.1 from the shoot (see Figure 12.7).

Of course, if you want to stay ahead of the pack, you can start developing those skills now: Tom Dowd started recording in stereo long before there was a consumer format to support it. As a result, when consumers could play back in stereo, Atlantic Records (Dowd's employer) already had a huge catalog ready to ship.

Figure 12.7   A Soundfield microphone can record in 5.1 and allows manipulation of the field later in the studio.

Other Considerations

Often on a budget recording, you will find that you only have access to a lavaliere microphone. If this is the case, be sure to check whether the lavaliere is a directional microphone or an omnidirectional microphone. An omnidirectional microphone can be placed closer to the mouth without distortion and with less interference from the subject moving his head back and forth, while a cardioid lavaliere microphone will be more susceptible to signal loss due to head swing. This can be difficult to overcome. In a situation in which the actor is speaking to another actor, try to place the microphone on the side closest to the other actor (see Figure 12.8).

Figure 12.8   A cardioid lavaliere microphone.

The idea here is that the speaker will be looking at his partner and therefore facing toward the microphone. Basically, think about where the speaker will be looking most of the time and put the microphone on that side of his body.

Many location multitrack recorders have microphone preamplifiers and microphone power supplies built directly into the unit. Be sure to save battery load while working on location; be aware of power consumption in film recorders. Often these units will provide power in the form of *T power*. Most engineers are familiar with phantom power, which is a 48V power source sent up the microphone cable to power condenser microphones. T power is very similar to phantom power, except instead of 48V, it sends 12V. Many microphones don't like to see this type of power. Get to know your microphones. Most microphones designed for location dialogue capture can operate on T power, such as those made by microphone manufacturers like Schoeps that allow you to select a microphone that will operate on either T or phantom power. Both get the job done, but it is important to know what you are working with.

As with all other recording, it is very important to take scrupulous notes about the location, tracking, and takes. One last thing you can take with you from location recordings in general is an impulse response for use in an impulse response reverb engine, such as Altiverb or IR by Waves. These are impulse response reverbs that model reverberation based on the impulse response inputted into them. They provide a quick and easy way to re-create the locations in which dialogue was recorded. This can be invaluable when you are trying to match after-dialogue recording (ADR) to the location dialogue track.

ADR is often done when the location recording is too noisy or unintelligible, obviously by no fault of the location engineer. There are some places that are just too noisy to use the original dialogue for the film. A good example of this is the dialogue for *Master and Commander*. The film was shot mostly on a set built out over the ocean with machines, hydraulic cranes, crashing ocean, and generally noisy things. As a result, 90 percent of the film is done with ADR. The location recorder can be invaluable when doing ADR because it allows the actor to get a sense of the rhythm, timing, and emotion of the original shoot.

Ultimately, when doing location recording for film and visual media, despite having a few unique tools, you follow the same basic principles that you use in any location recording: Be professional, plan ahead, take notes, and leave nothing to chance.

We briefly touched on surround sound in this chapter; now it's time to examine 5.1 surround a little more closely.

13 Surrounded!

Surround sound has long been a staple in the film industry, making its first real appearance in the 1980s. It first appeared with laserdiscs and then with the introduction of DVDs for home theater. Surround sound has made inroads beyond the movie theatre and into the moviephile's and audiophile's homes. The transition from analog to digital television has also been an engine for the popularity of surround sound, and as a result, the need to record in surround sound is increasing exponentially.

The new digital standard includes specifications for a 5.1 discrete surround sound transmitting capability. Most sporting events, concerts, and general programming are beginning to demand from the recordist and offer the consumer a surround sound mix of some sort. Most current surround sound is decoded through the end user's home theater system. These systems typically consist of five speakers and a subwoofer. The speakers are placed in a semicircle around the listener, with left, center, and right channels in the front and rear left and rear right speakers placed behind the listener (see Figure 13.1).

With these five speakers and a subwoofer, the listener can be placed inside an audio bubble or sphere created by the engineer.

Types of Surround Sound

There are two basic categories of delivery for surround sound: discrete and matrix. Discrete surround sound obviously refers to any signal that carries discrete channels—in other words, any format that contains an individual audio stream for each speaker is considered discrete. For a 5.1 surround format to be discrete, six individual channels of audio will be embedded. A matrix format will encode multiple channels of audio onto a lesser number of channels. The most common is Dolby Pro Logic (see Figure 13.2).

Dolby Pro Logic typically encodes a single mono surround channel in the out-of-phase information carried on the left and the right channels. This is a typical method for sending a surround signal on analog channels, where bandwidth is limited. Most network broadcasts are broadcast in this manner.

Photo courtesy of JBL.

Figure 13.1 Components of the JBL LSR6300 surround system, very popular for both home and studio use.

Figure 13.2 A Pioneer DEQ-P8000 Audio Processor with Dolby Digital, DTS, and Dolby Pro Logic II.

The most common matrix encoding systems work on similar principles of phase equalization in order to derive multiple channels from the two-track signal. The most common are Dolby Pro Logic, Pro Logic II, and SRS, with its family of surrounding coding matrixes. Matrix encoding was the first wave that made its way from the movie theater to the home in the 1980s.

Currently, the most common surround sound format is Dolby Digital, or AC3. This format is most prevalent on home DVDs. Dolby Digital is also the surround specification for the new digital high-definition television broadcasts. AC3 is typically an encoding signal for a 5.1 surround sound system. Another example of a discrete encoding system is made by DTS (see Figure 13.3).

The DTS system is similar to the Dolby Digital system because it is a discrete format. As a result, it carries more information on each channel and therefore provides a clearer, richer sound.

Figure 13.3 A DTS system.

Both Dolby Digital and DTS use data compression and audio manipulation to compact the sound for easier transmission. Dolby Digital uses audio-frequency band limiting as well as channel band limiting to achieve a smaller data footprint when compared to the DTS signal. DTS delivers true full-range audio signals to all five channels. In the age-old battle between power and quality, this gives you a sonic advantage; however, it dramatically increases the amount of space dedicated to transmitting the audio. Considering the implications of available space on the DVD versus the desired quality, this can become a problem if you want to include a plethora of special video features on your DVD.

Basic Surround Sound Concepts

As with the introduction of stereo, CDs, and any new technology that has come before it, surround sound mixing has taken some time to mature and grow into its own. As audio progressed from monitoring in stereo, early adapters of stereo were often fascinated by the idea of multiple speakers. Many live stereo records were produced for xylophones running from the left channel all the way over to the right channel, for the simple reason that now they could do it.

Early stereo mixes were fraught with oddities—Doors albums with the guitars and keyboard on one side while the drums and bass were on the other, Mamas and the Papas albums with lead vocals on one side and harmonies and answer vocals on the other, and other albums with the vocals on the left channel and the guitar on the right channel.

Debate still rages on among audiophiles and aficionados regarding which version of The Beatles' *Sgt. Pepper's Lonely Hearts Club Band* album sounds better—the mono or the stereo mix. As engineers began to play and use stereo more and more, the mixes became more solid, predictable, and familiar.

Surround sound has a head start, as we have already been through the evils and errors of quadraphonic, or quad (see Figure 13.4).

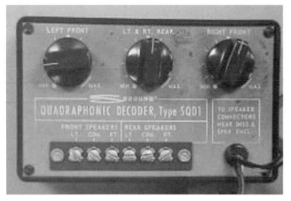

Figure 13.4   Quad.

Quad was a four-channel earlier version of surround sound that arrived and died in the 1970s. The major issue was the failure to find an acceptable delivery method. Engineers today have a huge advantage because we have learned from the mistakes of quad.

Two concepts have emerged in terms of thinking about how we might design a mix for surround sound. There are two basic styles that accompany these concepts; let's call one *fantasy* and the other one *real space*.

Fantasy

A fantasy surround sound recording lives up to its name. Consider creating a sonic picture that paints an image that would be unlikely or even impossible in real life. We sometimes do this in stereo through odd, reverse-gated reverbs or sampling; in surround it becomes even easier. A good example of this might be recording an orchestra completely surrounding the listener, as if the listener were a player in the orchestra or otherwise situated right in the middle of the musicians. For the casual listener, this could be extremely distracting.

There are some phenomenal surround sound recordings that have been mixed and produced in this way; however, the location engineer is typically hired to document performances or events, not manipulate them beyond reality. Thus, creating a mix that seems jarring or out of context with a video signal your audience may be watching will be at best unhelpful and at worst unpleasant. As a result, we strongly suggest that if you are going to do a surround recording of something on location, particularly with orchestral recording, you should try to keep the recording as natural and faithful to the real experience as possible. An exception to this rule obviously exists if a client requests a different approach to the engineering of the location recording, such as if the client asks you to make it sound as if the recording is in a larger or more reflective hall. The client may not always be right, but the client is always correct.

Real Space

Most surround sound projects that location recording engineers typically will be called to will be event projects, such as sporting events, news events, or concerts performed live. All of these events have a single common element, which is an audience. When you are actually sitting in the concert hall witnessing a concert, you are presented with a frame of reference. Your seat is facing a general direction, typically toward a very large stage and sound system.

As the engineer recording the event in surround sound, you should not lose sight of the fact that the concert is being performed in a space, in front of an audience. The majority of the sonic source listeners will be conscious of will be in front of them. We tend to be directional animals with omnidirectional perception. In other words, although we hear in all directions, our focus is typically toward the front. As a result, the concept of a real space re-created in surround is based upon recording the sound of the room with detail in the front of the mix and a certain ambience behind, unless something happens behind the audience in real life during the event.

Basic Setups

Most home theater systems use this theory of front-weighting as well. This is particularly true of lower-end systems that employ band-limited smaller rear speakers in their system design. Modern surround systems have arrived in homes, primarily as a result of the popularity of DVDs and movies. The 5.1 surround sound setup takes advantage of the knowledge of which direction the listener will be facing; we anticipate that the viewer/listener will face the giant video screen. As such, the 5.1 specifications have a "stage" already set up for us. According to the NARAS Producers and Engineers Wing's handbook on surround sound recording, the basic setup for a 5.1 surround mixing and playback system should be as follows:

- All speakers should be full range and equally powered.

- Create an imaginary circle that has a diameter of 6.5 to 7 feet.

- Place your forward left and right monitors as you normally would at 30 degrees, with the center channel in the middle.

- Under the center channel place your subwoofer.

- Your rear speakers should be placed in a range between 110 degrees and 150 degrees, with 135 degrees being the ideal placement point.

Now that you have an idea of how the sound should be played back by the end user, you can begin to design a setup to capture the event. Remember that even though a surround system is designed with the setup as described, the truth is that most systems in the home are not set up to the manufacturer's specifications. Claiming domestic space in a common area is quite a balancing act and can often lead to domestic disputes, with issues of wires strung across the room as well as space taken up in the back of the room and a couch smack in the middle instead of against a wall. Thus, the rear speakers are often relegated to the third shelf on the bookcase six feet to the left and under the geranium, pointing up at the ceiling, on the floor, two feet to the right.

Obviously, this will be detrimental to the general imaging of the surround recording; nonetheless, you always need to mix for the end user with the ideal setup. The inherent problems we have discussed, coupled with the preponderance of limited-range rear speakers and delivery codecs that band-limit the rear channels, create an atmosphere that is deadly to fantasy mixes. A bass coming out of a speaker sending from 200 Hz to 12 kHz will sound thin. A drum kit panned to the rear speakers will become light and tinny as well. In the event that you use the rear channels to capture and reproduce the reflections of a concert hall or stadium, with crowd noise and healthy reflections, the rear channels will give a sense of space and presence that doesn't exist in a similarly priced stereo system. Even with the rear right speaker on the floor firing up into a geranium, it will sound better than if there were no rear speaker.

If the rear channel is fairly diffuse and noncritical in directionality, localization, and frequency, you can create a basic sense of space that will be enjoyed by anyone using their setup even somewhat correctly. Is this dumbing down for the masses? Possibly, but there are two things to remember. First, mixing is all about concessions. Second, in location recording, part of the point is to re-create the live experience. When you are recording and mixing live classical music, the interaction of the hall with the instruments is critical. With surround, an element of the hall is introduced in a more natural and subtle manner. As with all types of recording and mixing, you should plan and record for the full-range system, but remember the little guy when you do.

As surround sound continues to grow in popularity, the need to record in surround also increases. If you are doing some quick down-and-dirty newsgathering or you are just looking for simplicity, there are surround microphones available. I typically like to think of the playback system as attempting to re-create the space in which you were recording. You have five speaker elements in which to create this surround bubble. Typically, I like to capture the reflections of the walls of the space as they come back toward the stage. If there are actual direct performance elements that should come from the rear channels, then a stereo technique for the rear channels is appropriate—perhaps even some spot miking is required.

A simpler way to capture surround sound is to purchase a ready-made surround microphone. Much in the same way that there are specifically designed microphones that can record in stereo, such as the Fritz Head (Neumann KU 100 dummy binaural head), there are microphone designs, such as the SoundField microphone and the Holophone H2-PRO, that can record in surround from a single microphone, allowing manipulation between the six channels at a later time (see Figure 13.5).

Figure 13.5 A SoundField microphone.

This give you a wonderful opportunity to record now and image later, because you can remix the listener into an alternate position in the house by varying the audio information sent to different channels.

These microphones allow you to record the sound source with its natural ambience in 5.1 with a minimum of fuss. These microphones are all designed featuring a pickup pattern based on the basic setup for a 5.1 speaker system. This collection setup makes a lot of sense if you are attempting to accurately re-create a sonic space based on five speaker positions, because it offers a collection point for each speaker. This may be the most effective method for collecting and re-creating a 5.1 space.

Often, a truly accurate re-creation of what was going on does not match our audio memory, real or imagined, of the original event. This could be due to psychoacoustics, or it could be as simple as the fact that anyone who has created sound effects knows that gently shaking a sheet of metal sounds more like thunder than a recording of real thunder does. Here in the business of illusion, presentation, audience impression, and aesthetics, you sometimes need to sweeten this effect or at least focus the sonic cues. This is why you use spot microphones and sweeten the mix later, readjusting it to your impressions and aesthetics and away from accuracy. This is done commonly in the studio for stereo recording and is also useful when you are mixing live recordings in surround.

When you are thinking about placing microphones in surround sound with an eye and an ear toward the mix, the aspects of the playback system should be your first priority. Consider where the sound sources are located and how they may be played back. The next layer of thought regards the specific recording, so now it is time to make some specific aesthetic decisions—ones that you are not accustomed to in the stereo realm.

It will be helpful to look at two hypothetical examples of surround sound recordings on location. First, let's look at a classical recital of a concert for pipe organ, tympani, and trumpet, and then we can compare it to the challenge of recording a rock band in the local pub.

Space as Part of the Instrument

Surround sound is at its most effective on location, where the location itself is integral to the recording that is being created. As we have discussed in previous chapters, often a particular concert hall is chosen because in classical music the location is integral to the music that is being performed and its sonority. Surround sound is therefore a natural fit for classical work. An installed pipe organ by definition must be recorded on location. This instrument, more than most others, is defined by the space in which it is located. In many European cathedrals, installed pipe organs are growing entities, often with the installations gradually modified over the centuries, constantly being added to and changed. As when you place microphones on any instrument, you need to place the microphone in a place that will accurately capture the intended sound for that particular instrument. With a pipe organ, the intended sound is that heard by the congregation in the cathedral or church, so to properly capture the sound, you need to capture and balance the sound of the hall.

The first job of the engineer for a 5.1 recording is deciding how to "face" the listener. Keeping in mind the fact that the resurgence of 5.1 is largely due to the 5.1 systems set up for DVD home theaters, you need to select the locations for the three front channels. The obvious choice would be to face the listeners toward the altar and pulpit, as they typically would face for a service. This could sound fine, and this approach is a distinct possibility for strictly solo organ work, although you should consider the location of the ranks of pipes. While we are trying to capture the sound of the space, artistically the listener will be expecting most of the direct sound to come from the forward speakers. If the main ranks of the organ are behind the congregation, it might be wise to face the other direction. Most organs have effects ranks that often are placed in locations away from the main ranks, which may be the 15th-century version of 5.1 (see Figure 13.6).

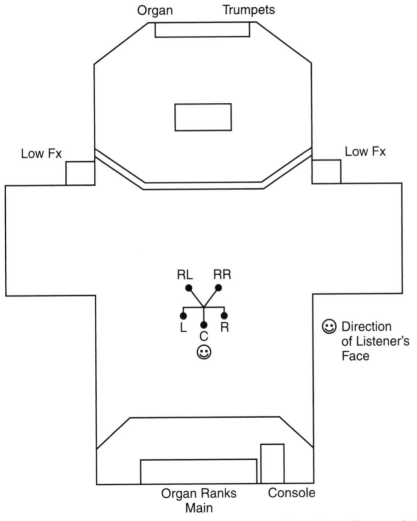

Figure 13.6 A sketch of a cathedral with pipe rank location, effects, and 5.1 "face."

If, in addition to the pipe organ, you are doing works with tympani and trumpet, this arrangement can change significantly. In most cases the trumpet and tympani will be in the same plane—in other words, on the floor in front of the altar or possibly up in the choir loft, near the ranks. If they are placed near the main section of ranks, the location of the face is fairly easy to figure out (see Figure 13.7).

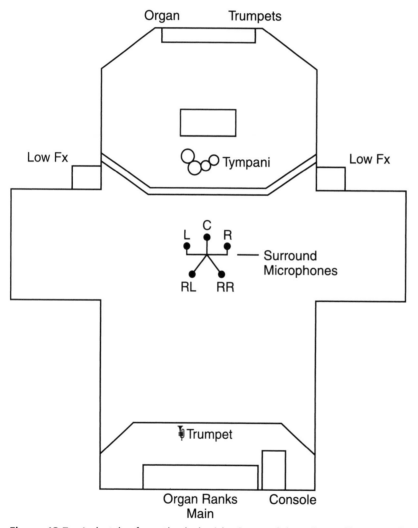

Figure 13.7 A sketch of a cathedral with pipe rank location, effects, 5.1 face, and the tympani and trumpet.

For a more interesting surround recording, if all components meet the NARAS specifications, are set up correctly, and pass muster all around, the trumpet and tympani can be split around the room. This setup will allow the listener a full, rich, dynamic 5.1

experience when played on the aforementioned 5.1 system. The question now becomes where to face. Sometimes it depends on the score and music. Typically, you will choose to have the audience face toward the most prominent instrument in the score (see Figure 13.8).

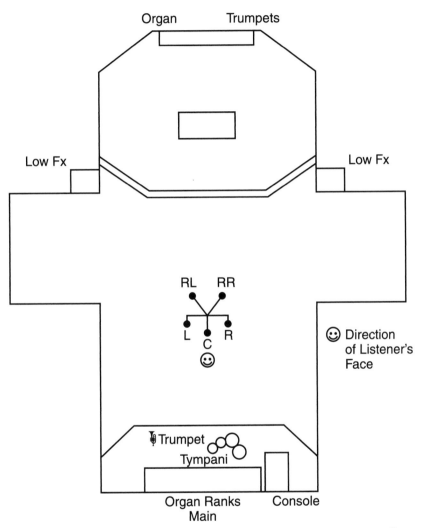

Figure 13.8 The same sketch of a cathedral with pipe rank location, effects, and 5.1 face, but with the tympani and trumpet located around the cathedral.

Figure 13.8 shows a very common setup. It might be tempting to place the trumpet toward the rear of the cathedral to get a "call and response" effect, also called the *ping-pong effect*. Ping-pong might be an enjoyable game for participants; however, it can get old to the observer after half an hour or so, and the same holds true when one is listening to the ping-pong effect.

A better approach is the envelopment, or transportation, of the audience to the actual space of the recording. Having some ranks of the organ around in space is a good thing, but the ultimate effect of the well-engineered 5.1 location recording is to re-create the sound of the space. The reflections and decays of the organ and instruments as the sound bounces off and around the stone walls, wooden rafters, and flying buttresses comprise the ideal composite sound. These reflections allow the sound to fill the listener's room in 360 degrees, with the same time elements as the original performance. Although it can be very engaging, full of depth and image, a stereo recording of the same work simply cannot extend the back wall of your living room to match that of the Gothic stone cathedral! It should be noted that to get this effect, the rear channels must be set up somewhere behind the listener, and not left in the original packaging.

Space as Part of the Experience: Check Please!

In other recordings, the space might be less sonically important to the event. Sometimes the space can even be sonically distracting. Much like working in stereo, you will need to craft the audio to bring out the best of the space. Suppose you are hired to record a rock band in a local club. In this case it is a small room, say 50 feet by 60 feet, with a stage at the front, with all sorts of stuff (such as tables, drunks, and waitresses) in the middle of the room (see Figure 13.9).

Figure 13.9 Club room BISTRO in St. Louis.

The room pictured sounds nasty, as this type of club typically will. There is a bad slap from the back wall due to the PA system. Street noise bleeds in through the front windows, though with the volume of a rock band, street noise may not be a big concern. Getting the true sound of the space is secondary for two reasons: The space is not integral to the music as it is in classical music, and we already are accustomed to audio trickery in rock. Width and dimension within the room are not your focus because you can create these later. Your focus in this space is the reaction to the music by the crowd. You want to maximize the crowd reaction, minimize the room, and energize the recording in the process.

Finding your forward-face position is easy in a room like this—it's the band on the stage. The more important question will be where to place the listener. Obviously, unless you are doing a documentary about the horrors of bar chatter, the back of the club is not a good choice. Too much extraneous environmental noise will distract from the event at hand—the band. The environmental noise can be everything from the crowd in the small club to the cavernous sound of an arena at a Bonnie Raitt concert. This is an easy trap to fall into—it's not a good idea to place your listener too far into the ambience of the space for no reason other than it is in "surround." As the engineer you need to get a balance between the live performance and the environment, without falling so in love with the effect that it takes over everything.

The elements and information you need from the recording are not just that this is a small club of a particular shape and size, but the way the audience is into the music and the manner in which the band and the audience are interacting. You do need to hear the excited scream when the first chord sounds and the audience recognizes the hit. You need to hear the audience response to "Hello SPRINGFIELD!," "Y'all having a good time tonight?," or even "Does anyone know how much of their hearing they are going to lose tonight?" Basic generic whole-crowd events, behind the listener and maybe a little in front, will place your listeners in the audience of the concert. They don't need to hear the band's groupies singing along with all the words in the rear left channel, the waiter asking whether they need another brew, or the brawl starting in the right channel over the color of another man's shoes.

You want to create a surround soundtrack that is fairly dispersive, without much in the mix that needs true stereo accuracy. Blended sound from left to right and nonspecific audio information generally work well. If the club's acoustics are unusable, then avoid them by mixing in some fake ambience along with the real crowd (see Figure 13.10).

So as you record in surround sound with an eye toward your mix, your criteria remain consistent. You still observe good basics of capturing sound, only now you pay more attention to the reflections and slap from the back wall. You also pay more attention to

Figure 13.10 Club room with some microphone positions.

the random noise in the room, but ultimately your goal is the same—to capture the event accurately and with good aesthetics.

To accomplish this goal, you must harness the raw and often uncontrollable power of sound waves as they reflect, refract, and absorb their way through a variety of rooms, clubs, studios, sets, and so on.

14 Harnessing Sound

Sometimes we walk into a space to do our site survey before recording, and we are amazed. The source of that amazement could be the warmth and beauty of the reflections in the room. It could be the aesthetics of the room. It could be how nicely everything is laid out, with good, clean power and microphone drops leading to the exact place where you want to set up. Then there's reality. That gives us the other kind of amazement, which usually runs more toward the bad reflections in the room; poor construction; parallel walls; hard, flat ceilings of varying heights; or any of a number of other factors that will make your job more difficult. Let's see whether we can control some of these factors.

Controlling the Uncontrollable

First off, fuhgeddaboutit. You aren't really going to be able to control the acoustics on a grand scale. You cannot fix architectural flaws or major acoustical anomalies any more than you can make a band that sucks sound good. The best you can hope for is to be able to control some minor aspects. You can accomplish this through good microphone choices and placement, some baffling, and effective use of microphone rejection. Perhaps this would also be a good time to remind yourself that the location is part of the reason you are there and part of the reason you were hired. Always try to acknowledge the space and use the space to your advantage. Although you might focus first on the deficiencies in a space, make sure you listen for characteristics and features that will ultimately help your sound and help you to create the best possible recording (see Figure 14.1).

If you are in a concert hall with a phenomenal sound, obviously you will incorporate this in a jazz or classical recording (see Figure 14.2).

Also think about trying to add the ambience to the rock or blues space. As recordists and mixers, we need to be thoughtful of the end user and the space he will perceive. As funky as some spaces may be, they could also be appropriate to the style of music you are recording. Equally important, you do need to get the eleventh man in the band into the mix—the audience. I have had great success recording ambience and hall returned by placing a microphone directly below a house sound system reinforcement cabinet, with the cabinet in the null area of the microphone; however, this is effective only if you

Figure 14.1 Multiple architectural features make this a difficult room for live recording.

Figure 14.2 Powell Symphony Hall in St. Louis, a wonderful room for live recording.

have a responsible front-of-house engineer who keeps the sound pressure level of the sound reinforcement system at a reasonable level.

Alternatively, try to find a good-sounding place in the room, a spot that accentuates the aspect you want to capture. Try to move your microphones toward the rear of the house, where the SPL is lower. Remember, the effect you are trying to get is that of a wash. Picture it as the wide crowd shot for a film. This is the same basic use in the mix—more of the big picture and a little less definition. Add a bit in for texture, warmth, and color. If things are wildly out of control or if the room just sounds bad, you can make some adjustments or scrap the true ambience entirely.

In most situations, asking the owner of the concert hall or nightclub to modify his space to make your recording better is impractical or impossible, although it will be a useful request if the owner needs a good laugh. Just remember that a good engineer will listen to the hall, examine its quirks, and offer suggestions for how to minimize the adverse effects and maximize the positives.

Analyzing the Space

The first task is to analyze the space. Use your ears and listen for reverb time. The easiest and most common trick is to clap and count until you can't hear the reflections. Not exactly a SpectraFoo reading, but good enough to give you an idea of the nature and length of the reverberation in the space. This will help you as you determine microphone positions. We tend to cheat closer to a sound source in more reverberant halls and move further back in non-reverberant spaces. The same can be stated for good versus bad sounds. If the church in which you happen to be recording has a horrible 1970s drywall sound that is thin and has a slappy reverb, then it is time to break out the Lexicon and create a better room (see Figure 14.3).

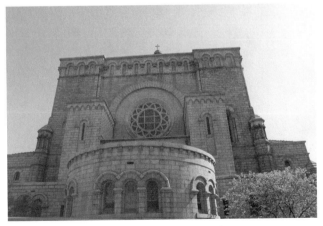

Figure 14.3   A church with poor sound.

As we discussed in earlier chapters, microphone placement is the first step when trying to get a clean sound. The same can be said for the position of the instruments onstage. If the bass amplifier is placed too close to the drum kit, the snares on the kit can rattle when the bass booms. A drum kit too close to a piano means heavy snare and drum bleed into the piano's soundboard and therefore into the piano microphones. Basically, think about loud sounds versus softer sounds and conflicting sounds of the different instruments onstage, particularly from the point of view of how the microphone will hear the instruments.

Now that we have talked about rooms and instruments that can cause problems, remember your number one enemy—the monitor wedge. Although in-ear monitoring is becoming more popular all the time, the lowly club typically does not have such a beast. If you are lucky, you will have to deal with a nice set of well-equalized, low-volume monitors firing directly into your microphones. If you are not so lucky you will have badly equalized, howling feedback firing directly into your microphones.

The solution still goes back to the basis—the microphone. As we pointed out earlier, make sure your microphone's null point has the monitor wedge squarely in the middle. If you can, get the monitor to go away from your microphone signal. That is your first task. If that is not possible, your next task is to make it sound acceptable or get it placed in a position that least affects your microphone—the null.

Remember that the best-sounding recording will always be the one where the artist was comfortable and happy and therefore performed better. Err on the side of making the artist comfortable. A great-sounding recording of a flat note that is out of time or rhythm with the rest of the band is a useless recording. A little distortion or interference in a perfectly hit note, perfect harmony, or amazing rhythm can be overlooked (see Figure 14.4).

Figure 14.4 A happy musician.

Now that you have analyzed the space and figured out what you like, what you dislike, and how you will deal with it, it's time to figure out where you want to set up your gear to make the most of the advantages and minimize the problems.

15 Finding Your Perch

A fter the assessment of the stage, the space, and the basic performer setup, the next most critical aspect of the location recording is a quiet space that is great for listening, which is where you will set up your gear. Ideally, this is the spot that is right on top of the performance area, adjacent to the loading dock, with great access; plenty of good, clean power; short microphone line runs; and a latte machine. I can hear you laughing from here. Stop laughing. There are many remote trucks that are available for rent, and they can offer you most of this.

Here's why you need to stop laughing: All of the aforementioned criteria are key to creating a good recording. Except maybe the latte machine. Having said that, sometimes pointing out the location of the coffee machine to a member of the band or showing up and handing the band's manager a cup of coffee at the right time can ensure your future with that band. Never underestimate the power of coffee; it is the grease on the wheels of this business.

A Quiet Place

You need a quiet space for listening. Seriously, a very quiet place. This is important because you need to be able to identify recording problems as you track the recording, especially if it is a multitrack. If it is for a broadcast, you must mix a product that is going to be consumed in real time, so your listening becomes absolutely critical (see Figure 15.1).

Listening can mean any number of things. Do you need to listen on headphones or on loud speakers? Obviously, as in the studio, you need to do a little of both. Headphones will give you a clearer reference that is more consistent from location to location, particularly with closed earphones because they are not colored by room acoustics. Any consistency you can add into your regular rig will allow you to better judge what is happening to the sound in the house and assess what you are recording. It is worth the extra money to get a high-end A-to-D converter headphone preamp, such as the Benchmark DAC 1 or the Grace m902 (see Figure 15.2).

Figure 15.1 A good perch.

Figure 15.2 The Benchmark DAC 1.

These take your monitoring source back to the digital-to-analog conversion stage, so you are not relying on the $20 DAC and headphone amp of your computer—or even worse, the all-in-one computer interface. Taking the digital output of your computer or digital board preserves the integrity of the signal flow of the monitor chain, as the digital-to-analog converter and the analog path and amplifier are contained in the boxes and therefore are consistent from place to place. The Grace will also allow for an analog signal input, providing consistency for analog gear as well. A high-end headphone pre-amplifier, without DAC, can also be an improvement over the standard headphone jack because it can be set to provide the correct impedance and deliver adequate power to the headset drivers.

Some prefer to monitor via speakers. We all have a producer friend who cannot truly grasp the sound of a recording until he is back in his own room and he listens to the recording on his own system. In the event that you need to monitor on speakers, you will have a much harder time finding the consistency between spaces. If your speakers happen to be mounted in the mobile recording truck's control room, then you have your room that travels with you, and consistency is maintained.

For churches, you can often find an anteroom or vespers chamber just to the left or right of the altar, behind the sanctuary. Typically, these spaces have at least some power and are relatively close to the performance area (see Figure 15.3).

Figure 15.3 An anteroom or vespers chamber in a church.

If you are working in a modern church or cathedral, built in the last 25 years or so, there might be a sound both or media center that has lines built into the building. Although these can be useful and sometimes are well equipped, make sure that you are really in the best spot.

Right on Top of the Performance

To get the best recording, you must ensure that access to the performance area is relatively simple and that the cable runs are relatively short and clean. In many cases, the cable runs are more than 200 feet. In these situations, it might be better to find a less quiet room closer to the action. This would allow for quicker access to the microphones and a shorter run of cable to improve the sound.

The impedance added to the microphone over a longer cable run can wreak havoc with the clarity and coloration. Most microphones and preamplifiers are designed with a specific electrical load in mind for operation, so the variable in the microphone-to-preamplifier circuit becomes the cable run between the two. The longer the cable run is, the more impedance is created in the circuit. Runs longer than 200 feet begin to show noticeable high frequency loss. Placing the microphone preamplifiers close to the performance and running line-level (or preferably digital) signals back to the control room greatly improves the overall sound.

Access to Clean, Plentiful Power Is a Must

Typically, a single, clean 20-amp circuit should power a basic computer and microphone setup. When you are interfacing with the front-of-house amplification system, make sure that the cable providing your power is at least 14 gauge, preferably 12 gauge or even 10 gauge. (Remember, small is the new big in electricity.) Having your power on the same leg and phase as the FOH power prevents all sorts of ground loops, hums, and buzzes, as we discussed earlier. The other important factor that shows up in picking a location is the latte machine (see Figure 15.4).

Figure 15.4 A latte machine.

Again, if you have the recording truck, this is not an issue. You may not be a latte type of guy or gal, but in all seriousness, make sure you have provisions, such as water, snacks, and a restroom, readily available. Also remember to keep the liquids away from the gear. It seems like a no-brainer, but be aware of patrons' drinks and migration paths.

This is very relevant in most clubs and bars. Also, beware of waiters' serving patterns. If you are near said latte machine, you will be hearing a lot of hissing throughout the performance. Particularly pay close attention to cable runs to your position and make sure they avoid marked fire paths. Remember to tape and mark all cables that have to cross egresses.

The final note about finding a perch is being able to see what you are recording. Line of sight is often an afterthought and, honestly, the last thing on your list of priorities. A cheap 900-MHz video baby monitor can often be enough to get through the show, particularly if you are multitracking the recording. And of course, baby monitors have awesome preamps (see Figure 15.5).

Figure 15.5   Video baby monitors are known for their full frequency response and high pixel rate. Not really, but they are darned convenient.

As in all situations, remember that you are a guest. Be respectful of the space and test paint, concrete, and carpet for the effect that your tape will have on it. Duct tape should never, *ever* be a part of your pack. Spend the extra money and buy gaffer's tape. The cloth backing (as opposed to plastic) and the higher-quality adhesive result in a less painful experience for the space. It is also available in many wonderful colors, such as black, that look better than the glossy gray that duct tape comes in.

Now that you understand where you want to be and what you want to do, let's take a look at interfacing, both with equipment and with people.

16 Work and Play Well with Others: Interfacing with the Live Sound System

When you are recording on location, working well with the "other" sound guy, or the person doing the reinforcement or live sound, is absolutely critical to a great recording. Your final product will be dependent in part on the quality of his work. A good sound in the house will ultimately impact the sound on the recording you create in many ways, ranging from a more confident, comfortable performance to something as simple as the lack of ringing, raging feedback. Interfacing with the reinforcement system and crew is imperative and should never be underestimated or downplayed. It is also imperative that, just like with every other group of folks at the venue, you make their lives easier and happier, and you do your best to leave them smiling.

The first of many reasons to befriend the live sound engineer: Often it is desirable to take a split from the reinforcement microphones or to send your microphone signals to the house mixer and the PA system. This improves the aesthetics of the stage, which pleases the non-audio folk and makes set or stage changes much easier to accomplish. Unfortunately, it can also have some drawbacks.

Sometimes the ideal microphone choice and position for the live system will not be the same as for the recording. Although good sound is always critical for both applications, the live engineer is positioning his microphones looking at gain before feedback—feedback not only from the main house system, but also from the monitor speakers onstage. His choice of microphones might also be different.

Microphone Choices

Among microphones, every engineer has his set of personal favorites and a specific level of comfort with different microphone types in different situations for different applications. When agreeing to split microphones with the live engineer, the conversation about what will be split, as well as which microphones will be used and how the microphones will be placed on the instruments, is critical to both of you. This discussion should occur early enough for both parties to consider all ramifications and to figure out how to integrate these decisions. It may be unreasonable to expect a live sound engineer—particularly a monitor engineer—to accept a change in the type of vocal microphone he is using on the lead vocal. This is particularly true if the engineer has already completed a number of shows or even has done his first sound check. His system has been tuned with those microphone selections in mind and in place.

Remember that in live reinforcement, you "fix it in the mix" in real time, in front of the client. (The monitor engineer has it worse because not only does he have to fix it in real time if he screws up, sometimes he has to fix it even if he doesn't screw up!)

If you were to swap out the live sound engineer's microphones, you would create real havoc in the system. EQs, compression, and balance would all need to be readjusted. You don't want to shake things up that much. It is much easier to EQ a less-than-stellar choice for a microphone than it is to deal with bad feedback or a bad performance. In the event that a microphone choice or placement is so useless for your purposes that you would rather have the rolling meter popping feedback, then the option of a secondary microphone is probably your best bet.

If you *do* require a different microphone but the position of the existing stand and the other microphone is more or less in the correct placement for your purposes, then a drum claw or stereo bar attached to the live stand can often yield a great result while keeping stage clutter to a minimum (see Figure 16.1).

Figure 16.1 A stereo bar holding two microphones—one for live use and one for recording.

Remember to make sure the stand is sturdy enough to hold both microphones. It might be quite acceptable to place a Neumann KM 84 alongside a Shure SM57 on a stereo bar, but adding a TLM 149 might be a different story altogether; it might just be more than the stand or the stereo bar can handle. Sandbags can be quite useful in stabilizing the base, but remember to check the boom arm as well. Often these are simple, friction-based adjustments, with a washer and a bolt, which can wear out quickly. In a well-loved live sound rig, these stands often do the slow fade into the sunset, drooping slowly while attempting to hold a larger microphone. Over the course of the gig, or even within the first few songs, as the vibrations of the sound waves start mounting, the boom arm will slowly drop under the weight of the microphone. Remember to use your Newtonian physics and geometry, just as you do every day. To combat the dreaded droop, make sure that you counter-weight the boom or that the stand is near the fulcrum point of the boom arm—in other words, with the vertical component of the microphone stand relatively centered under the boom arm (see Figures 16.2 and 16.3).

Figure 16.2   A poorly balanced microphone stand.

Figure 16.3   A well balanced microphone stand.

Splitting the Signal

When it becomes necessary to actually split the microphone signal, there are a few different ways to accomplish this, and each has merit. Due to convenience and low cost, your first choice is often a splitter box, which is designed specifically for this application. There are two basic flavors of boxes—direct splitting boxes and parallel splitting boxes. The parallel splitters are the same as an old-fashioned Y cable. Each input pin has two wires coming off of it, and they run directly to the outputs of the box. In other words, the signal is simply split in half, in parallel. This can be a problem due to increased impedance and load on the microphone. It is important to note in a situation such as this that only one board or microphone preamp should be designated as the provider of phantom power. While most modern console manufactures take steps to protect equipment from reverse phantom power, the system is not foolproof. If both preamps were sending phantom power, tremendous problems could be created for power supplies and could be particularly grave for vintage microphones.

Keep in mind that as soon as you connect your system to the splitter, you have connected to the electrical system of the house. Your grounding now connects to their grounding. If you are not on the same power, or at least the same phase leg, you are now in a situation that will typically create hums and buzzes. If you do get a hum, chances are it is due to a grounding issue. It is tempting to take the easy route and solve the hum issue by lifting the ground, but this is not recommended. Although it might resolve your hum problem, it removes most of your safety measures. In addition to your safety, it removes the grounding safety measures for the people using the equipment onstage, who are connected through guitars, keyboards, and handheld microphones.

Maybe you do not view this as a serious issue. However, in 2005, in Waco, Texas, a pastor was electrocuted when he stepped into the baptismal pool, then reached out and grabbed a microphone that was connected to a system with faulty ground. Do not mess with ground (see Figure 16.4).

Figure 16.4 Many have cheated ground; few have returned to tell the tale.

The ground in a circuit acts as a safety exit for electricity in a circuit. Usually the electricity flows through the hot and the neutral in a predictable and reliable manner. The ground wire is your safety net—it is the safety exit if the designed circuit fails to operate properly. The ground allows the circuit to be complete without exiting through the person using the equipment by providing an alternate path. Electricity wants to go to the earth, and it will do it any way it can, without malice or intent, but swiftly and certainly.

Okay, so you can't break the ground or lift the ground without creating great risk for yourself and those who trust you. How do you correct the buzz? Typically, the issue is the difference in ground between the two systems. To break that connection, one side needs to be physically detached from the other, but signal still needs to flow. The best and only way to do this is by utilizing a transformer.

An isolated transformed splitter will physically break the connection between the two consoles and still allow signal from the microphone to pass to each console (see Figure 16.5).

Figure 16.5 An isolated transformer.

If you cannot find or get access to a parallel splitter box or an isolated transformer, another less desirable option is to get a direct output from the front-of-house console (see Figure 16.6).

It is important to get the most direct signal possible from the console. This often can be difficult, but if you are in this situation, the direct output of the channel is your best option. If at all possible, you want the direct output to be pre-fader and before all processing, including EQ and dynamics. What you want on your recording will probably be significantly different than what the house engineer believes he needs in the PA system. If a direct out is not available, see whether there is an open aux send or group

Figure 16.6 The back of a console tapped for direct outputs.

bus, or even a matrix output. Any bus with a discrete output control will serve your purposes.

Although a large number of tracks cannot be taken from the FOH in this manner, it may be possible to get a few critical tracks cleanly to your recorder. Consider the use of stereo stems in this situation. For example, a stereo mix of a drum kit might be useful if time permits for a nice balance from the FOH, or a stem of the backing microphones, or perhaps even the lead vocals. In some cases, a mono or single track could contain things you would normally want to break across tracks, particularly if they are not being used at the same time for the most part. This happens frequently at concerts with a large number of solo microphones that are set up more for convenience than for efficient track count. Something is always better than nothing, and a relatively clean something can often be cleaned up to be usable in post-production.

The Digital Split

No, we are not talking about the ongoing argument about the superiority of digital versus analog—for once. The final possible split solution would be a digital split. Some of the newer live digital boards have microphone preamplifiers with A-to-D converters located onstage or backstage, with a digital snake feeding the FOH console. In this situation, it might be possible to take a digital split from these units, as long as you have a rig that can take an AES/EBU digital input. Digital splits avoid many issues that stem from line runs, impedance, ground loops, and more. This is due in part to the gain structure of the digital system; it is also due to the simple reality of sending an algorithm down a wire instead of an electrical analog of the original signal (see Figures 16.7 and 16.8).

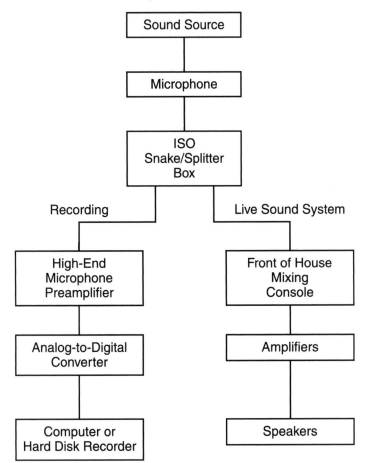

Figure 16.7 Analog signal flow.

In an analog live sound system, a microphone is connected to a preamplifier that is usually embedded in the mixing console's architecture, which then connects to a mix bus that sends the signal to a track to be recorded. In a digital system, the microphone is connected to an analog preamplifier, which is then connected to an analog-to-digital converter. Then the digital signal is sent to the board, where the signal is manipulated digitally, as in your DAW. The main difference here is that your DAW runs on your trusty computer, and the live digital board is part of the trusty computer, which just happens to be optimized to deal with audio, with a user interface that resembles an analog board. The digital board will have the same operational issues as any digital device—specifically, the system will need a reliable clock source.

Digital Snake/Split Flow

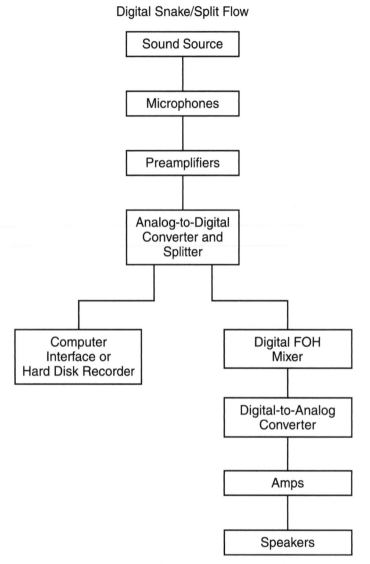

Figure 16.8 Digital signal flow.

One very important aspect to discuss when taking a digital split is the clocking information; it is important that all clocks agree and that there is a reliable master clock. It also is important to point out that many live systems, although capable of operating at a sample rate of 96 kHz and a bit depth of 24 bits, are run at lower levels to increase track count and processing power. The sample rate is directly controlled by the master clock, which you will be sharing if you take the split. Remember, there can be only one clock—one clock to unite them all. You need to assign your clock source either to a master clock for the whole system or to the clocking device that is closest in the chain to the analog source.

Always double-check to ensure that you and the FOH are on the same sample rate and bit depth. If you cannot strike an agreement—he wants 44.1 for the track count, and you want 88.2 for the quality—the final solution may be a sample rate converter (see Figure 16.9).

Figure 16.9   The RME ADI 192 real-time-format sample rate converter.

The side of the split that requires the lower sample rate must take the converted signal. A low–sample rate signal that is "upsampled" to a high-sample signal will not gain any benefits from the process, since it is limited to the information available at the original, lower rate. If the signal is upscaled or otherwise enhanced in the chain, you might see some benefit, but generally as you are working with direct analog signals, the highest sample rate should start the digital chain, with the lower source taking an SRC split. Remember the feed from master clock when you are taking the split. The two systems' clocks will need to be tied together at some point—directly if the sample rates are identical for recording and reinforcement, and indirectly at the sample rate converting box when it varies, as the master clock for the sample rate converter will use the highest resolution clock as its master clock and generate the lower sample rate signals.

This pretty much takes care of the gig, but what happens the next day? Let's explore some of the important things you need to know on the day after the gig.

The Day After

17 What Have We Got? Can We Fix It in the Mix?

I 'll bet you thought that once the gig was over, you would have a little breakfast, fix yourself a nice, stiff drink, and try not to think about it for a little while. Guess again.

The Night and Day After

The gig is finished. You've packed the last cable and done your idiot walk. (The idiot walk is where you walk around the location to see what you—the idiot—have left behind that is irreplaceable, such as a Neumann FET47 or your car keys.) See Figure 17.1.

Now what? You head home to unpack, and you begin to make the first of many safety backup copies of the audio and your paperwork. This may also be when you give the client a copy of the rough mix you've been running as a safety, as you begin the next phases of the recording process. But, wait a minute…you just gave the client a mix. Depending on your agreement, a live-to-two-track stereo mix may be all they are requesting. And they may even be thrilled with the mix. Most of the time, however, you will want to go back and really work on the mix in the controlled environment you have been craving through the whole book—I mean, through the whole gig.

First of all, how rough is that rough, live-to-two-track mix you just handed the client? If you did your job well, it shouldn't really be all that rough. Keep in mind that while creating a live-to-two-track mix for the location recording, you don't have as much freedom as you would normally have in a standard studio recording. It is much harder to "fix it in the mix." After all, your mixing process began back when you answered the phone call from the client. For every step of the recording process that followed, you should have had the mix in mind as you made choices. Microphone choices and their positions were early mix decisions, as were the location of your perch and the gear you chose for tracking. The mix itself is the combination of all these decisions—some simple, some complex.

Remember all that time you spent choosing microphones and finding the best positions for them? Remember all those diagrams that you drew and redrew with distances?

Figure 17.1 Don't let this happen to you—do the idiot walk to make sure you don't leave this microphone behind after everything else is cleaned up.

Remember that early decision you made regarding how much bleed would be acceptable, and how that informed your microphone decisions—both selection and placement? That last question determined many of your microphone choices and influenced you toward a tight pattern or a wide pattern.

Let It Bleed

The microphones you selected—and, more specifically, the placement of those microphones and the amount of bleed from other sound sources—will help you determine the amount of studio placement you can do with your mix after the fact. You will never be able to "fix it in the mix" the way you can in a studio recording, but we will do what we can. The biggest issue when dealing with a live recording is often phasing; if your sound sources are out of phase, you will have tremendous difficulty in attaining a quality mix. Unless you can use direct boxes or contact microphones on all elements of the recording, bleed will be a factor, and phase will therefore be a potential issue in your mix.

If you have a bass amp right next to the grand piano, the bleed from the amp into the piano microphones will be apparent (see Figure 17.2).

Soundboards in pianos are built to pick up vibrations from the piano strings, then amplify and project them. The soundboard will be equally efficient at amplifying and projecting vibrations from the bass amp. Depending on your piano microphone selections and placement, this could end up reducing and limiting your mix options by affecting the position of the bass in the mix.

Let's take an example. If you want to have your bass as a center image in your mix, you pan the microphone, DI, or a mixture of both for the bass to the center. It sounds fine;

Figure 17.2 When the bass amp and the piano are too close onstage, you have a potential problem trying to use the large-diaphragm condenser microphones placed outside the piano (in the lower-right section of the photo).

all is hunky dory in the world because the sound is warm and rich. Now you decide that because this is a jazz group with a phenomenal 14-year-old piano player who played some killer piano fills and answers, you want your piano image to go from hard left to hard right. You pan your XY pair (which was 6 to 10 inches off the strings in the center) hard left and hard right and bring up the tracks. You now have a great image of the piano. Then you add your center-panned bass back in, and the image of the bass pulls to the right and loses something. What has happened is that you now have the bleed in the piano pulling the bass to the right, with a phase shift due to time of arrival difference between the microphone placements and a phase shift based on panning position. Your phasing issues clean up quite a bit if you shift the position of the bass in your mix to match the position of the bass bleed in the piano, and even more if you time-align the piano microphones with that of the bass. The problem with this is that the bass would end up panned hard right, along with most other elements of the recording, because the piano was located farthest to the left of all the instruments.

Obviously, if you do a closer microphone placement technique, then the location of the bass won't be predetermined and will be less of an issue (see Figure 17.3).

Figure 17.3 When other instruments are nearby, you need to use close microphone placement in a piano, placing your microphones right inside the box, above the soundboard.

The other solution is to re-create your mix based on the locations of the instruments, much the way that recordist Rudy Van Gelder created so many classic jazz mixes in the '50s and '60s. His theory was that wherever the instrument was in the studio, that's where it should be placed in the recording. If the piano is hard left on the stage, then it needs to go on the left in the mix. Drum kits on the right side? Then the entire kit needs to go on the right. Although Van Gelder's reasons for this type of placement were based on honestly representing the original experience, we have a happy byproduct by following his lead. By placing the instruments in their natural positions, the number of phasing issues you will encounter will be decreased.

Of course, this means that throughout the whole process, you need to have the image of the final mix tucked in the back of your mind so that you can nudge the setup to match your intended image. If you want the drum kit to be centered, then you might want to consider having a discussion to see whether it can be moved to the center. Obviously, the necessity of this varies based on the amount of isolation you can achieve through microphone techniques or stage isolation.

Is It Live Reverb or Canned?

Even if you are extremely careful with your microphone placement and effectively eliminate all bleed, you must take the setup into consideration. If you have set up room microphones, they will reflect the band's physical location and the mix in the PA system. It is possible to ignore these microphones and use completely canned reverb, either conventional or impulse response–based. Using this method, you carefully place your microphones in positions to reject as much bleed as possible and take pickups off the basses, guitars, synthesizers, and anything else you can.

Remember to make sure you have microphones to capture the audience's response to what happens onstage. The audience is such a large part of the location experience that they simple cannot be left out. Cardioid microphones placed directly under or even above the PA stacks can give wonderful rejection of the PA and get a great stereo image of the groupies who have no hearing left due to standing under the PA stacks. This can be extremely effective for a rock, blues, or jazz band.

In most situations, the microphone placement is extremely similar to that of the placement for the live sound engineer and even a studio engineer. Rejection, rejection, rejection. As careful as you are, you still need to keep an ear out for the occasional bleed. Typically, the more electric the group or event—in other words, the more directly you can take the sound sources—the more flexibility you will have in the mix.

When you mix for video, you create a mix that represents what is onstage. However, beware of following the camera, particularly if you are mixing live. As the director chooses his shots, you need to stay focused on keeping the audience rooted in their seats. Consider when you go to a concert. While you are looking at everything—the band, the lights, the crowd, your date, the next guy's date—the music stays constant, with no significant change in the mix or panning (unless it is a Flaming Lips concert, in which case all bets are off and you are on your own). When you mix for a video, you should project the same idea—your audience is sitting at the concert. This concept holds true for stereo, as well as the even more tempting surround sound.

Bleed in your headphones can also be an issue if you are not in a controlled location that is quiet. Often you are forced to set up your control point in the same room or too close to the room in which the concert is being performed. If you hear a significant amount of bleed or direct audio from the live performance, it will affect the audio you hear in the cans. Often if your control room is set up in a room adjacent to the main performance space, the low end will bleed into that space, because those larger, stronger wavelengths that accompany low frequencies retain their energy as they transition through walls. The low end will also bleed into your perception of what you are mixing in your cans. Upon return to the mother ship (or the studio, as the case may be), you will have a mix that is so lacking in bass due to bleed (or overpowering in bass due to the inherent deficiencies in all headphones) that neither your mother nor Bootsy Collins will be proud of you.

Headphones versus Speakers

Although your trusty headphones are your constant companion, best friend, and source for consistency from room to room, console to console, and studio to location, they will still lie to you in a live setup as just described. Don't blame them; they are just headphones. Even though you gave them a cute name, they're not even alive, and they are certainly not vindictive (see Figure 17.4).

In most cases, you should probably assume that at some point, someone somewhere will play the mix back on speakers. So you need to at least check all your mixes on speakers. If your tracking setup is one in which you have an isolated room, it is a great idea to set up a pair of monitors to provide you with an immediate speaker-based reference. Headphones tend to lack the ability to reproduce low frequencies accurately, and they also do not accurately reflect a good sense of space. Actually, they seem to represent a phenomenal space. Because they are piping direct sound to your eardrum, your head is taken out of the listening experience. Your left ear is hearing the left track. The right is hearing the

Figure 17.4 Trusty headphones.

right. This is fine if you are only going to have the recording played back on headphones, but it creates a world of problems when you switch on the speakers.

When you listen to speakers, each of your ears hears part of the sound that is emitted from each speaker. Sitting in the sweet spot, exactly between left and right, gives you a very nice picture. Listening at this point, the sound from the left speaker directly hits your left ear, and slightly later your right ear. Then the sound continues on to hit the wall, the ceiling, the rug, your highly reflective dog, and then maybe back into your right ear. The same thing happens for the left ear. The sound is not contained to one audio path. Sound from a speaker gets reproduced at the speaker, as it did in the headphones, but then standard acoustics take over. Typically, mixes that are done strictly on headphones tend to become extremely wide, to get the instruments out of your head.

Some hi-fi external headphone preamplifiers have circuits in which an attempt is made to mimic space. When mixing in headphones, a good rule of thumb is to make sure you create an image that is full and wide but does not have a hole in the center. This is usually an issue mostly with stereo recordings or stereo microphone techniques, such as an ORTF or a spaced AB technique. Typically, if you have a hole in the center, the microphone's capsules are too far apart relative to the sound source. When you are back at the studio, you will have the luxury to mix on phones or speakers.

Mixing

Let's explore some of the criteria for mixing. Mixing is a hands-on endeavor, and one that can only be truly learned by an aspiring audio professional turning the knobs, pushing the faders, and hearing the results. Nonetheless, mixing offers some universal guidelines, which we will explore.

One of the inherent problems with learning to mix from both a hands-on and a text-book perspective is that there are few absolute truths. Ten engineers will produce ten different mixes from the same elements, which are all acceptable; they are all "good" mixes. One mix's superiority over another is often a matter of personal taste, assuming certain basic technical aspects have been fulfilled. In a heavy metal mix, the guitars will usually appear to be placed way up front, or loud, and will sound very full, sometimes partially masking the vocals. In other forms of rock, this would be unacceptable. While mixing a soundtrack for a film in which guns and explosions are featured, extra loud-ness on these elements would be appropriate because we perceive gunfire and explosions as louder elements within a soundscape. In all forms of audio production, the mixer attempts to balance the elements, effects, or instruments such that they can all be heard and are at appropriate levels in relation to each other. In some film mixes and radio production, certain elements will be heavily favored over others, just as in some forms of music, such as heavy metal, pop, and country, where our expectations of this form of music can supersede issues such as masking. While understanding conventions is useful, it is helpful to begin by understanding what constitutes a good mix.

A Good Mix

What constitutes a good mix? Some engineers will answer that question with a list of subjective or quantitative qualities, including descriptions of relative timbre, loudness, and placement. Audio professionals will all agree that a mix needs to be free of noise and distortion. There will be general agreement that the end users or observers should be able to hear all elements. When we get to the part about just how clearly all these elements need to be heard, their opinions will depend on both their personal taste and their work history. Someone who loves country music may be predisposed to like a tune with fiddles way up front, just as an engineer who has been specializing in dance remixes for the last 10 years will probably appreciate a strong backbeat, a kick drum that makes your chest thump, and a powerful bass sound. Are any of these audio pro-fessionals wrong? Not if their mix is appropriate for the style they are attempting to create or imitate. There is a lot of leeway in creating the relationships within a mix from a purely aesthetic standpoint.

Other engineers may answer that the best mix is the one that sells the most, whether it's records or tickets at the box office. Both answers—"sounds good" and "sells a lot"—are correct. The first type of answer is correct because taste is personal. The entire expe-rience of listening to music or watching a movie is subjective; therefore, whatever anyone likes cannot be considered wrong. Never be a snob about a style of music you don't like; if someone else appreciates it and if it fits their personal aesthetic, it is valid. The second answer is also correct because, as a famous record executive once said, "We are in the business of selling records, not making records." Successful projects result in greater opportunities for those who were a part of the team responsible for its success. When you engineer a hit record, your name gets out there, and more producers will be interested in working with you. Also, producers will often want to match the sounds of a successful record or production, so they may come looking for you to get that "[*Fill in a name here*] sound." Furthermore, historically, there have been some musicians and engineers who have been thought of as "lucky"—a producer believes that by using his lucky engineer or his lucky drummer (the one with whom he had his last hit), he will have another hit. It might seem a bit silly, but there are some very superstitious people in the music business, and if they believe you are a hot engineer, then you will be a hot engineer, regardless of the platform in which you work (see Figure 17.5).

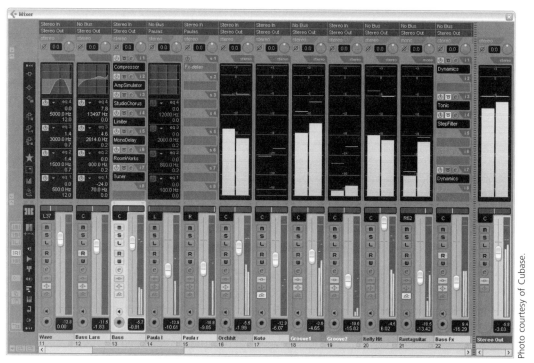

Figure 17.5 The Cubase 4 Mixer.

Photo courtesy of Cubase.

If you are now wondering which of the two answers weighs more heavily, consider this: It is necessary for an engineer to be able to deliver whatever type of mix the client wants. Being able to please a client will ultimately determine the success of an audio professional. To do this, it is necessary to know the mixing techniques involved in many types of music and production. Be open to other types of music and film than what you usually listen to or watch. Listen to all types of music, and listen to them closely. Keep in mind that there is no bad music and no bad taste. Never consider yourself to be above certain types of music; if you've heard of a particular form of music, it's because people have bought it, and if people have bought it, then people have made money from it. Similarly, it is easy to poke fun at commercial feature films or commercials on the radio, but there is a good living to be made by audio professionals in these areas.

To capitalize on the opportunities that become available to you, you should be ready for anything. Being at the beginning of your career and having little control over the type of client, venue, studio, station, or film house that will offer you an opportunity, you should develop the skills needed to make the most of whatever type of entertainment is being created in the facility where you find yourself—and beyond. To accomplish this, it will be necessary to study different styles of music and different genres of film, listening as an engineer does. This means listening for the techniques used to shape the character of the sound. Although you may object on some level to music that you think you dislike or a film that you believe to be in some way inferior to what you normally watch, you now have another reason to pay attention. Aside from personal enjoyment, you are now listening to become aware of the stylistic and idiomatic trends employed by engineers and producers. In other words, you are listening professionally and critically, not merely for your own enjoyment. When you go home, you can pop any CD you want into the player, and you can listen to or watch whatever you want. At work you will need to develop the ability to operate in a successful and nonjudgmental manner with any form of music, no matter how superfluous you might think this genre is when you are not at work.

Using myself as an example, I have never favored heavy metal. The first time I was asked to mix a heavy metal album, I listened to a great deal of heavy metal the night before. I asked questions such as, "What does the vocal sound like? The guitars? What is the balance between the bass and the drums?" When I mixed the album, the band loved it. They had no idea that it was the first heavy metal album I had mixed; based on the product they believed I was experienced, and they had no idea that I held heavy metal in anything other than the highest regard. Of course, I did not tell them my personal opinions about heavy metal. There was no point in giving them a reason to dislike my mix. If they thought I didn't respect them as artists or the genre in which they work, it might have colored their opinion of the mix. I did not see any reason to give them that opportunity, and the fact is those mixes came out good. They were appropriate for the style, and the client loved them. Keeping a poker face is important in these situations. As an engineer, you are constantly dealing with huge, fragile egos. There is no excuse for insulting their music. After all, they have fans who buy their albums—that makes it a

Figure 17.6 The Nuendo Mixer.

Photo courtesy of Nuendo.

valid form of music, and you have no basis to judge them negatively, especially if their check clears the bank.

I ran into the same situation a short time later, when I was booked to overdub vocals and mix an opera album. I had a neighbor who frequently had the sound of opera discs leaking out of her apartment. I knocked on her door and asked her to play me some opera the night before the gig. She thought it was all very amusing. I knew what opera sounded like, but not as an engineer. Once again, I listened in detail to the vocal quality, the relationship between the vocal and the orchestra, and the internal balances of the orchestra. The producer enjoyed my mixes so much that he booked me for three more opera projects over the next few years. As a freelancer, this was a wonderful opportunity to fatten my bank account while learning about a style of music I had previously gone out of my way to ignore. And never once in all that time did the producer or artists think that I held opera in anything but the highest esteem. Stay open to different styles of music—they are all potential income streams for the audio professional—and keep that poker face on at work!

As a sound designer I have also found myself in similar situations. No surprise here; I do not like operettas, yet I have been sound designer for two plays by Gilbert and Sullivan. I may personally think they are the pits, but I did not tell the directors, actors, or anyone else of my personal dislike of that genre. Instead, I did my job and did it well. I must have done it well because they hired me to do a second one. There is a theory that audio professionals may do better work in genres we like less, since we can be more objective about a genre that we marginally understand than we can be with our favorite artist's next album. The sad truth is that, as an engineer or sound designer, you do not have the opportunity to work with your favorite band or on your favorite play every day, and the rent still has to be paid. Besides, it builds character and expands your repertoire to work in forms of music that are beyond your comfort zone.

Using Monitors

The difference between the sound of music in a dance club, in a concert hall, on a clock radio, or on a car stereo is obvious. As previously discussed, the difference in the quality of the sound as the monitor system changes is something of which engineers must have an acute awareness. Let's examine in more detail how this sound difference impacts the audio engineer.

Most engineers, early in their training, have experienced being pleased with the quality of the sound of a project while in the studio and then, when listening to their mix elsewhere, being very disappointed in the quality of the sound. The reason for this is often a lack of insight into the character of the control room's acoustics and of the monitor speakers being used for the mixdown. All aspiring engineers, therefore, must learn how to understand the character of any of the many monitor speakers they may encounter while creating their mixes.

When mixing, the engineer must have an understanding of the character of the speaker system that is being used. If the engineer does not, he may disproportionately compensate, especially with equalization, for some quality inherent to the speaker system. If the speaker system is inherently boomy, an engineer, unaware of this characteristic, might feel that there is enough low end on a recording when this is not the case. This could result in a recording that sounds thin when played back on other speaker systems. Conversely, if the inherent characteristic of a speaker system is to be overly bright or have a shallow low end, a well-balanced recording might sound in the studio, to the unaware engineer, as if it is lacking in low frequencies. This can cause an engineer to compensate by increasing the volume of the lower frequencies on a number of instruments. The result of this could be a recording that sounds muddy when played back on another speaker system or a production that sounds boomy in a theatre. Each monitor system has its own inherent character; therefore, the sound of a mix played on different monitor speakers will change. The monitor system is the only component in the studio system that gives the engineer an audible insight into the character of the sound being recorded. If the inherent character of the monitor system is not known, the engineer is only guessing about the nature of the sound that is being recorded onto tape, and he may be setting himself and his clients up for some unanticipated additional remix time.

Photo courtesy of Neve.

Figure 17.7   A Neve 8078 is a much sought-after classic mixing console.

As stated earlier, some engineers feel that the best mix is the one that sells the most records. If a mix does not sound good in every environment in which a consumer may listen, potential sales are lost. There is a wide variety of systems and speaker types that consumers use when listening to music. The first time that someone hears a record, he might be listening to the sound system of a nightclub, a car, or a home stereo. Many people listen to personal stereo systems or boom boxes. Each of these systems has dramatically different sound qualities. It is the engineer's job to ensure that the sound of the recordings works well in all of these types of systems. Each of these system types represents millions of listeners or viewers and millions of potential sales. If the production team has done their job properly, a consumer should want to buy a record the first time that he or she hears it, regardless of the type of system on which it is heard.

When mixing, engineers use several speaker types. Using studio monitors, home-quality bookshelf speakers, and sound cubes, the engineer can have a good idea of how the sound of a mix will translate on almost every type of commonly used system. Some studios, including the former Sigma Sound Studios in New York, went so far as to wire a clock radio to the console. In other studios, an engineer and producer will run a rough mix off onto a CD, listen in the manager's office on his computer, then run down to the car and listen to see what it sounds like on a different system (one that is commonly used). An audio professional should listen to a mix on as many sets of speakers as he can before calling it a good mix; otherwise, he cannot be assured that the end user's experience will be a positive one.

Through the process of switching between speaker types, then compensating for incongruities, then switching and compensating again, the engineer will come upon a blend that works well in all of the speaker types, and therefore all possible environments. In each case, however, the engineer must be intimately aware of the special character of the speaker being used in order to avoid the pitfalls described earlier.

To learn the characteristics of a set of speakers that an audio professional will be using for the first time, it is helpful to always carry around three pieces of music. The source of the music should be of the highest possible quality. Each of the three selections should be very familiar to the engineer; the engineer should have a clear idea of what he or she expects to hear. The greater the number of systems on which the music has been heard, the better it will serve. Choosing a recording that the audio professional has heard at home, in a car, in a club, in other studios, and in the homes of one or more friends will ensure that he is as aware as possible of how this recording will sound under different listening situations. To save time, it is not necessary to use the entire composition; the object is to listen to sound quality, not musical composition. The engineer should bring along a pair of headphones he trusts for reference and then listen to the three selections on all speakers available at the new facility. On each of the monitors, the engineer should compare the sound in the speakers to the sound in the headphones, comparing back and forth several times.

Note the differences between your expectations of the sound, based on your knowledge of the mixes, and the reality of what is output from the speakers. Are the low frequencies, mid frequencies, and high frequencies consistent with your expectations based on your familiarity with these mixes? Is the character of the music different from what you expected? Is it different from the sound you are referencing in the headphones? If you were to mix on these speakers, can you identify frequency bulges or deficiencies for which you may need to compensate? Comparing different systems, from headphones, to car audio, to cheap bookshelf speakers, to audiophile speakers, is the beginning of developing your ears to listen critically, the key to mixing.

Methodology

Now that you have a basic idea of what to look for, let's discuss how you actually put a mix together. If this is a project that you have been working on, you will already have ideas that you tried during tracking and overdubbing. You would have already tried several reverbs and other effects, and you will already have an idea as to the relationships of the elements and the producer's and artist's opinions about different approaches. Starting a mix like this is easy; you simply begin blending the tracks as you have heard them blended before.

An audio professional who comes in as a remixer faces a different challenge. Sometimes the engineer will receive a copy of monitor mixes or other mixes; other times, the engineer will hear the song for the first time when he pushes up the faders. In this second situation, the best approach for the audio professional is to push up the faders and listen through a couple of passes of the song. The engineer will think up ideas at this point, consider some approaches, identify the genre and consider how to make this song fit the genre, consider subgroups and effects, and consider different approaches to the mix. It is best to resist the urge to dive right in and start EQing something at this point; the mix will benefit greatly from a few minutes of contemplation and evaluation of the tracks.

Once you have settled on an approach, you can begin the mix in earnest. Beginning with some fairly standard instrumentation for rock, pop, dance, and country, and starting with the mechanics, most engineers (though not all) build a mix from the bottom up—in other words, they start with the drums. Experimental mixes and unconventional music styles aside, the kick drum (or bass drum) and snare drum should always be centered. A mix with the kick and snare anywhere but center can be somewhat disorienting; most listeners will seek the kick and snare in the center as an anchor for the mix—something to hold everything else together.

Assuming the rest of the drums have been miked in stereo, follow the audience's view of the drums with the pan pots. In other words, place the cymbal that appears on the left as you stand in front of the kit on the left side of the mix. The cymbal on the right goes on the right side of the mix; the hi-hat also goes on the right (while it is on the drummer's left, it is on the audience's right). The tom toms can go right to left for high to low, which is how you see them. Or, for something different, try going hard right for the high one, hard left mid tom, and hard right low tom. It gives a different sense of movement, and this hard-panning method works even better if the drum kit has four toms. Drums are a good place to experiment with panning as well as with reverb, since reverb establishes the character of the room in which the mix is taking place, and placing the drums in the room gives you the foundation around which the rest of the room is built— around which the other instruments are placed, as we previously discussed in great detail. Let's place some more instruments in this room.

Continuing to build from the bottom up, let's add the bass next. Like the kick and the snare, the bass should be dead center unless heavily effected or used experimentally. Use some of the tips on EQing we've already discussed to blend the timbres of the bass, kick, and snare. Pay attention to the style: Are you mixing pop or dance, where the bass' high end tends to be exaggerated, or are you mixing jazz or bluegrass, where the bass tends to

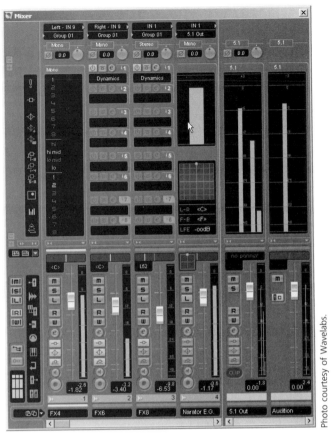

Figure 17.8   The WaveLab Mixer with mix bus and Nuendo audition bus.

be darker, fuller, and rounder? Remember to stay focused on the style you are mixing and keep the information entering your ears consistent with your understanding of this particular sound.

Let's put in some guitars and keyboards next. If there is more than one guitar, or if a guitar part is doubled, it can be very effective to split them using the pan pots. Should they be split slightly, extremely, or somewhere in between? That depends on the song, the style, and the mix. Listen to the guitar in many locations as you sweep it from one side to the other and ask yourself, "Where does it sound best?" Wherever it sounds best is exactly where it should be. Splitting a doubled guitar part slightly out from the center can be an effective way to thicken the sound while separating the guitar sounds and making them more distinct, but you do not need to have two of something to pan it. Anything can be placed anywhere if that is where it sounds best, and there doesn't have to be something panned against it on the other side.

Keep in mind that hard panning is not necessary, and in this situation it is often not desirable; often a slight split is most effective. Experiment with a doubled guitar split to varying degrees off center; see what sounds good to you. A lead guitar part can also be split against a keyboard line that is full of fills or answers; any two parts can be juxtaposed, or a part can be panned off by itself. Once again, it is a process of experimentation, especially at the outset of a career. Stay open to what your ears are telling you. Does this keyboard part sound better against this guitar part? Is there another part that would sound better against it? Does this part sound good panned to one side without anything balancing it on the other side? Anything is possible in a mix, and every piece of music is unique; use your ears and start to really listen to them.

The other sweetening is added next. This could include more keyboard parts, horns, strings, woodwinds, or some light percussion. Keep in mind that sweetening is frequently relegated toward the back of the mix or is low in volume, and often more reverb or delay is added to increase the idea in the listener's mind that the sweetening is at the back of the stage, rather than up front, the way a lead guitar or a lead singer would be.

Next come the vocals. Vocals can be extremely tricky because the frequency range of a vocal falls in a similar range to guitars, many keyboard parts, and even the high end of the snare drum. To make the vocal shine out in front of the mix without making it so loud that it sounds like the singer is in a different room, try equalizing the vocal to dovetail into the other sounds. Try boosting the high end of the vocal while pulling some of those same frequencies out of other instruments, such as the guitars, which are also occurring in this range. Also, since vocals tend to be centered at 1 kHz, try pulling some 1k out of any instruments that will potentially mask the vocals. Vocals often sound better with a certain amount of signal processing. Try a different reverb on the vocal than you have on the drums, guitar, or keyboards. Vocals often sound better with a short pre-delay (indicating that the singer is in front of the band) and a medium decay time (indicating again that the singer is closer to the audience than the rest of the band—in other words, in front of the band). Like everything else in mixing, finding the right balance between the instruments, then the balance between the instruments and the vocals and the balance between each instrument and its reverb or effect, requires experimentation.

Having said all this, there are many extremely successful mixers who take a very different approach. They may start with the vocals, considering that to be the most important element in the mix, and build everything around the voice. They may consider the guitars to be critical to this style of music and start with a smoking-hot guitar mix, and then ease everything else into that blend. There is no wrong place to start if the result is a good mix. Personally, I tend to start with drums, but if I reach a point where I am unhappy with my mix, I will pull all the faders down and start over, usually starting with a different element—the guitars, the vocals, even the horns if they are prominent. Audio professionals should never be afraid to pull down the faders and start over, keeping the EQ settings and effects. The balancing of levels in the mix is probably the easiest part, so never be afraid to pull the faders down.

While we are on the subject of EQ, it is worth mentioning that it is usually better to subtract than to add. This is a gross generalization, but there is a tendency among beginning engineers to add EQ to everything, when taking away certain regions of timbre can be far more effective at helping everything in the mix sound clear and cut through. If a particular instrument is too thin, try EQing out some high end before you add bottom. If you try to cure a boomy sound by adding high end, the boominess may be less apparent, but it is still there. If you can cure timbral problems by subtracting EQ rather than by adding EQ, you have less of a chance of creating a nasty frequency bulge.

Something related to the idea of subtracting EQ rather than adding it is that some sounds get bigger in the mix when you make them smaller with EQ. Heavy-metal guitars are a great example. If we followed our inclination to make heavy-metal guitars big and fat with effects and EQ, then make them loud in the mix (appropriate for the style), we would never be able to hear the vocals because the big guitars would completely mask the vocals. Instead, do the opposite and use your EQ to make the guitars tiny from an EQ standpoint. Guess what? When you make them loud in the mix, they still sound really loud, but you can hear the vocals just fine because they are no longer masking in the 1-kHz to 3-kHz range. This leads me to something I learned a long time ago about mixing. If what you thought should work didn't, then try what shouldn't work. Oddly enough, things that shouldn't work sometimes do, and usually it's when the things that should work don't. Go figure.

Now suppose for a moment that there is no drum kit. If you have the opportunity to mix a string quartet, a full 60-piece orchestra, or a folk singer with just a guitar, the aforementioned principles still hold; either start from the bottom and build your way up or find your focal point in the instrumentation and build the mix around that sound. If you have nothing but strings, start with the double bass. Add the cello. Seat the viola into the mix, and then add the violin. If you like building from the bottom up, then establish it as your convention and try to always start by building from the bottom up. In the case of an orchestra, begin with the percussion section, building it within itself—in other words, start with the tympanis, add congas or other low- to middle-frequency instruments, then work your way up to the high-frequency sounds, such as cymbals and bells. Now work on the horn section unto itself from the bottom up—the tubas, baritone horns, bass trombones, trombones, and finally trumpets. Seat the entire horn sub-mix into the percussion sub-mix. Next, balance the woodwinds, bass clarinet, baritone sax, tenor sax, clarinet, oboe, soprano sax, flute, and piccolo, bottom to top. Once again seat this entire sub-mix into the existing percussion and horn mix. Finally, sub-mix the strings, bottom to top as earlier, and seat this sub-mix into the existing mix. If you listened to classical music among other forms, as suggested earlier, you would have an idea of what the end result should sound like, and mixing is often the process of filling in those gaps and mimicking those sounds. Of course, if you feel that the bassoon drives this whole 60-piece orchestra, try getting a really nice sound on the bassoon and building everything else around it.

Mixing in a Sphere

Having dealt with the nuts and bolts of the technical end of the mix, let's discuss an aesthetic approach to mixing. Ask a dozen engineers about their aesthetic approach, and you will get a dozen different answers. There is no simple right or wrong, because two engineers can mix the same piece of music, take radically different approaches, end up with radically different mixes, and both could be right. I have heard engineers describe their aesthetic approach in many different terms. Some audio professionals will think of their mixes in terms of construction (building a foundation and building on it brick by brick), while some view it like a pyramid (still construction, but with a stronger base and a narrower top). I've heard it described as opening a window into a piece of music (with each element filling in part of the aural view), and I've heard it described as filling in a circle. If any of these visualizations work for you, then they are right for you.

My personal approach involves visualizing a sphere and filling it in. The advantage in my mind to a sphere is that it has three dimensions, as do all the best mixes. It allows for movement on three axes, which ultimately produces a mix with more depth in more directions. To break down the three axes, let us consider the side-to-side axis as controlled by panning; the top-to-bottom axis as controlled by pitch and timbre, effected by equalization; and the front-to-back axis as controlled by the relationship between loudness, delay, and reverb.

Aside from the mechanics of placing sounds where you want them using panning, equalization, and reverb, there is an aesthetic associated with where they belong or seem to belong. Part of the idea is that if everything is bunched up in the center, the result will be a flat, lifeless mix. Think of it as two-dimensional—the kind of mix that, if you tried to touch it, would reject your hand like a pane of glass. This bunching may occur on only one axis; for instance, suppose you have spread out all the elements well through panning and equalization, but everything is at the same loudness level with the same amount of reverb. The resulting mix will be flat and two-dimensional. The listener

Photo courtesy of Neve.

Figure 17.9   A Neve Libra mixing console.

will perceive the musicians to be standing crowded together or right on top of each other, and the individual elements will be indistinct, lacking depth, and masking each other.

Similarly, if the panning is effective, and different reverbs are used on elements presented at different levels, but the frequencies are bunching up due to lack of effective equalization, masking will occur. These frequency bulges are very common, especially in mixes executed by neophyte engineers, since the ear must be developed through experience and critical listening to pinpoint and correct the bulges. Most frequently, these bulges will occur either around the drums and bass in the 80- to 200-Hz area or in the vocal range, around 1 kHz to 3 kHz. As mentioned earlier, masking and the ways to cure it were discussed previously at greater length.

Now suppose we were to spread out our elements, or create the perception that they were spread out, on all three axes. We have placed different elements left to right—some centered, some a little out from center, some further out, all complementing each other. We have EQed where it was necessary to avoid masking, and the result is that, top to bottom, there's a lot happening, but not too much in any one place. And front to back? There is good depth; the relationship between the elements, their delays, and reverbs places them in the same room but with a little space between them, giving the illusion that there is good movement front to back. The result is more than just an aesthetically pleasing mix; it is a mix that you can reach right into, perhaps even stand in the middle of.

The ultimate goal in visualizing a sphere and adding to it as the mix progresses is that no part of the sphere should remain empty when the mix is complete. Perhaps one spot up and off to the right doesn't have much happening in it, but suddenly in the bridge, a glistening sound appears. That can be a wonderful spatial surprise. The entire sphere does not have to be full throughout the piece, but ultimately every part of the sphere should have some activity, preferably at just the right time. As with any aesthetic

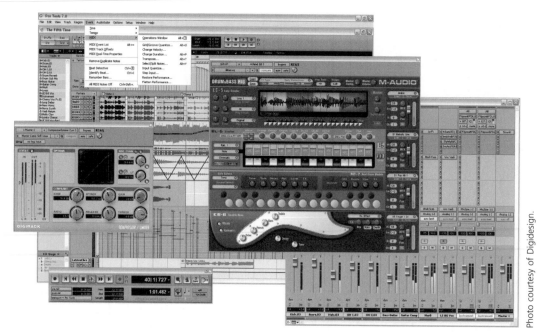

Photo courtesy of Digidesign.

Figure 17.10   A Pro Tools M-Powered 7.

decision, there is no clear-cut right or wrong; there is only experimentation leading to the development of skills upon which you will eventually, through experience, develop your own aesthetic sense.

So what do you do once you are back in the studio? You use all of these tricks and more to make it sound as good as you possibly can. How do you do this? Through more than just mixing; through editing and sweetening. Let's take a look at the methods at our disposal.

18 Editing and Sweetening

S o the client listened to the CD you gave him, your rough mix, and likes the shows. He calls and thinks it is great—he loves the mix. Fantastic! You're the best, and he promises to hire you to record him live every time because you are magic. A genius. You understand his music like no one ever has, and what you do with it is exactly what he wanted, almost as if you two were communicating telepathically. Soul mates, maybe. He does have one question, though: "Um, I sang the third song a little flat. Can we fix that? And, oh, the drummer forgot to hit the snare on the third bar of the fourth tune in the second set. Can we fix that? Oh also, we forgot to hire the backup singers that night, so we want to add them in, okay?" Now what? As they say in Jamaica, "No problem, mon."

Editing

The primary element of editing that differentiates a live recording from a studio recording is that there is generally more elemental noise in the tracks from a live recording. Ultimately, a studio recording will have other issues (some similar), with the difference being that in a studio, the elemental issues have (hopefully) been addressed earlier on, from construction (making the air-handling system as quiet as possible) up to the session itself (throwing up gobos between instruments and throwing the loud drunk out before the group starts to record). The basics of editing, nonetheless, remain consistent.

Back in the analog days, when clients sat around on bearskin rugs while we cut tape with stone knives, editing was done pretty much by hand. We cut and taped back together (see Figure 18.1).

When we made a mistake—and yes, mistakes were made—we needed to reconstruct the original or reprint the tape—because we almost never worked with the original master tracks (always a safety)—and try again. No one had come up with the Undo button yet. But edit we did, and for good reason.

The basic idea behind the edit is to fool the turkey—er, the listener—into thinking that the event actually happened the way he is hearing it. If there is to be any pop, fade,

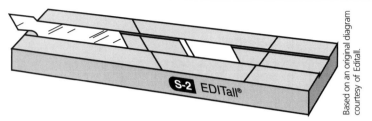

Figure 18.1 The industry-standard EDITall splicing block, showing the 45-degree angle (center), which is recommended for all 1/4-inch and 1/2-inch splicing.

abrupt stopping of a sound, change in level or ambience, or unnatural change in the sound, the listener will become aware that an edit has occurred and may therefore realize that they have been deceived in some way. The editor thus needs to pay attention to all the sonic details in the recording when making an edit.

Details that need to be monitored at an edit point are the primary sounds, the rhythm of primary and other sounds, the basic image (if you are working with a stereo mix), the sound of the space in which the primary sound is taking place, and the general context in which all elements exist. A mistake with any one of these elements will be a clue to the listener that the performance has been changed!

For example, suppose we need to replace a bad "lamb" in a stirring rendition of "Mary Had a Little Lamb" by Sally in Mrs. Smith's first-grade class. She nailed it at the early assembly for the school, but nerves overcame her in front of the parents. If it is on multitrack, we'll find the performance from the afternoon, grab a copy of the good "lamb," and paste it over the offending "lamb" from the evening. If there is no bleed and the tempos are relatively close, as are other elements of the sound, we should have a good track for Sally and Mrs. Smith. If we have only the stereo (mixed) masters to work with, we now have to examine the bass, organ, horns, and drum kit that were also in performance at the same time as Sally.

Usually this does not lead to issues, but all of the elements in the section you are splicing in need to match seamlessly, or the edit will fail. If you get Sally's "lamb" edited in correctly, it flows with her melody line, and things sound great for her, but the drummer was slightly off tempo from concert to concert, you could end up with a noticeable jump in the rhythm section, which could be more distracting than a slight warble in the original vocal.

In general, the worst issues that are missed are usually background noise changes. For example, a bus could pull up for the concert on the first night's recording, but be gone on the same tune the next night, making a rumble magically disappear in the middle of the sax solo. When you record a large group, such as an orchestra or a chorale, it is possible that the musicians will be placed differently each night and will therefore be slightly out of place in the stereo image from one night to the next. This could result in a marching-band effect from one night to the next.

The way to fix these issues here in the world of modern digital edits is through careful selection of your cross-fades in conjunction with selection of the position and point of the edit in the recording (see Figure 18.2).

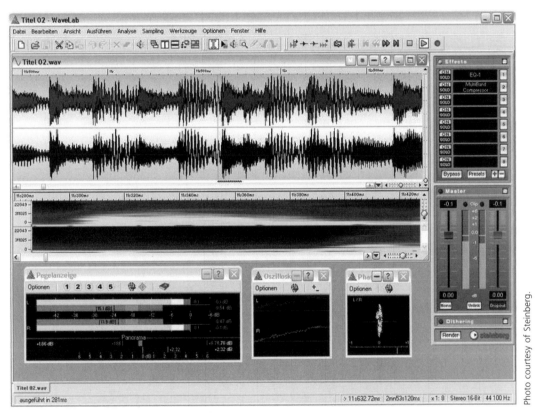

Figure 18.2   WaveLab 6 audio editing and mastering software by Steinberg Media Technologies.

The best place to make an edit is usually at an expected point of change. Whenever possible, try to place your edits in spots where the music or recording makes a natural sonic change. Some good, typical spots are the beginning of a musical phrase, the beginning of a chorus, or after a loud note hit has faded. These are all good places to look for an edit point. We often hide our edits in natural transient points. Be aware that sometimes more is more—although you might be seeking to correct only one note, it is sometimes less obtrusive to remove the whole phrase, rather than to risk a bad edit on one side or the other of the single offensive note.

If you only need one measure corrected but there is that darned bus in the good take, you could try a short surgical cut, taking out the bad measure and putting in the good with a short bit of the bus. Another option, if the bus isn't too offensive and the other solo was good except for the bus, would be to use the take with the bus. With a good fade-in, the bus's entrance should be less noticeable because the attention should be grabbed by the smokin' sax solo anyway. When performing a fade like this one, you need to pay attention to how the background noise is acting. A long, slow fade (one to three seconds) allows the ear to become accustomed to the noise behind the primary sound.

The issue of the background noise becomes less apparent if you attempt to insert or replace the audio on the multitrack, only on the single problem track. In this situation, the bus is now only on the sax track and is most likely soft enough that it won't be noticed.

Another common problem is that the bleed and reflections from the original track might be an issue. This is something to listen for, and it often prevents certain elements from being "fixed" with a studio overdub. If you do plan to attempt studio overdubs, then you might not be able to use a room-based mix or a mix that relies heavily on the room microphones of the location to provide ambience or reverb for the performance—the bleed from the original track will be noticeable to the listener. Although these original tracks will not give you the ambience you need, they are still useful to provide a good reference point for creating the reverb program and, more importantly, as audience microphones to add the live crowd's energy back to the concert.

Cleaning Up the Mess

So what do you do about that bus, and while we are at it, how about that horrible hum, not to mention the jerk yelling expletives at the violin recital?

It is a live recording, and audiences can be unpredictable. That's what you wanted, right? It's what the client hired you for. If that doesn't seem to placate your client, there are a few tricks and technologies available that could help. Technology exists to help the engineer overcome many obstacles created by the ambience of the field.

The first step is to do everything you can to resolve the noise issue, first by editing or adjusting the basic mix. Save the more drastic measures for last, because as soon as you start reaching for the noise-removal software, you are reaching out to affect the phase and EQ. It's like the physicians' code—the Hippocratic Oath. First do no harm. You'll often find that a little goes a long, long way in reducing noise. Remember, the trick is not to completely eliminate the offending noise, though that is nice if possible. If all you can do is reduce it from the sonic consciousness, that will be fine. Let's look at possible ways of reducing noise.

- Track muting—it's time-tested and mother-approved in the studio and on the road. It's the muting of unneeded tracks on the multitrack mix, keeping them down when not in use. Always be aware of the large mix or image shifts this can create, particularly on tracks that have a lot of bleed. This method is most effective on tracks that have relatively small amounts of information, such as backing vocals or some horn microphones.

- Pick the most offending track—the one with the most noise—and apply EQ to eliminate that noise. A more high-tech version of this is to use any type of noise-elimination software, which is effectively a dynamic EQ.

- Edit the offending section, substituting a different take from another performance in the same space.

- Overdub the offending track in the studio (or most of the offending tracks if the sound is pervasive), replacing the original, uncontrollable sound with one created in the controlled studio environment.

Studio Overdubs

The first issue when you bring live tracks to the studio is compatibility. If you recorded in Broadcast Wave format (BWAV), you will be fine in virtually any major production facilities (see Figure 18.3).

Photo courtesy of AMS Neve.

Figure 18.3 Consoles such as the Neve 88R at Skywalker Sound can handle almost any format you can throw at them.

BWAV is the industry-standard format at the moment. In the event that the studio you like (or that your client insists upon) does not have a compatible system, you can bring your box to their place.

Ensure that you track consistently to the original live recordings. Beware of bleed of the original tracks if you are overdubbing vocals. Think of it like a scratch vocal track in a studio, although you might have more bleed due to monitors, PA, and general stage volume. Sometimes you'll want or need to process your overdubbed tracks to better fit with the location recording. We'll talk about some strategies to do this in the next chapter.

As with any other part of this process, what you do often depends on what you are comfortable doing. These days, two-track editing is primarily the domain of the final stages of production, performed during the mastering process, but it is still done frequently during sweetening, especially with classical recording. Two-track editing can be more difficult than multitrack editing, due to the necessity of making all of the fades at the same point. The big advantage of the multitrack edit is that not all of the cuts need to be at the exact same point in time, which allows for a more gradual sonic shift.

Producers Mess It All Up

Well, hopefully not. With any luck, your producer has been with you from the inception, but often the producer will make his appearance after the initial project has been recorded and mixing is nearly complete. This is a particular problem on the "last minute" or "I have a friend" gigs. Often these folks are not really producers, but well-meaning people—friends of the band or the client, friends with an artistic vision. The producer role varies from project to project, but typically these folks are the ones who outline what they want to happen with the raw recording. They determine how they want the final product ultimately to sound; they pick the takes and the tracks and decide whether they want to overdub the horn section. The producer often has the unenviable task of deciding when the budget won't allow for more intonation correction for the lead singer.

In many ways, the live-recording process is just like doing a studio recording, only without the ability (usually) to call the group back in to do another take. Another problem producers make worse deals with their growing dependence on artificial tuning. Nowadays, Auto-Tune, Melodyne, and time correction are ever-present. Often, it is expected that these programs will be used. Unfortunately, as recordists and engineers, we must be conscious of the difficulties of using programs such as these with all due subtlety, just as all effects need to be done in a manner that will be unnoticeable to the consumer. What's worse than hearing apparent pitch correction on a studio album? Hearing pitch correction on a live album.

During a remix of live tracks, we are commonly asked to add additional reverberation. A bad location can be made good by dropping the room microphones and adding the well-loved Lexicon, Yamaha, EMT, or any of a variety of different rooms through the IR Reverb, which we will discuss in more detail next chapter (see Figures 18.4 and 18.5).

Photo courtesy of EMT.

Figure 18.4 An EMT 140 analog plate reverb, with the front of the case removed.

Figure 18.5 The Yamaha SPX 90II digital multi-effects processor.

Using this type of after-the-fact reverb tends to cut down on the ambient crowd noise, trucks, buses, and so on, and it is therefore a good choice, particularly for a noisy venue. Remember to bring the audience back for their cameo appearances in applause or woot for a good passage. After all, the listener needs to believe it was live.

We just mentioned IR response reverbs. What else can you do in the box? What about noise reduction, track cleanup, and other DAW considerations? In the next chapter, we'll take a look at the software at our disposal.

19 Software and Such

In the old days (or if you like working in Retro World), you would return home after a gig with a pile of 24-track 2-inch masters and start the tedious task of editing and mixing. In today's digital world, things are far simpler—most of us come back to the studio and fire up our computers, grab the mouse or the HUI, and start mixing. Digital audio workstations (DAWs) are extremely powerful and can deliver extraordinary results. Quality that was only available from a topnotch studio in the past now can be created at home or in Starbucks, all done with the computer (see Figure 19.1).

The DAW also allows for tweaking and sweetening that simply isn't available in the analog realm. For example, with the convolution reverb, it is possible to take your favorite room with you. You can delay every single channel to time-align phase and increase depth. Not to mention all the wondrous things you can do with multiband compressors, FFT, EQs, noise reduction, and so on. So the $64,000 question becomes, "Which DAW should I get?"

The answer is … what do you want to get? What environment is most comfortable for you, and which one sounds best to you? Just like a musician who delivers the best possible performance when he is comfortable, you will perform your best work in an environment in which you are comfortable. This means it will sound good, and isn't that the whole point—making things sound good? You need to find a DAW that is a comfortable fit.

All DAWs are not created equal, but they are pretty close. I am not going to say that Nuendo is better than Pro Tools, or that Pro Tools is better than Digital Performer, or that Digital Performer is better than Logic, or … you get the picture. I *will* say that any of these is more functional than GarageBand or any relatively low-end, consumer-level software package. There are differences between the systems, and we think some sound better than others, but that determination is personal. Ultimately, it is up to the user—you.

Native Processing

Most DAWs are currently designed around native processing. *Native processing* is when the CPU of a computer is used by the DAW to process the audio—in other words, the processes are internal and direct. While this is the prevalent way of designing software

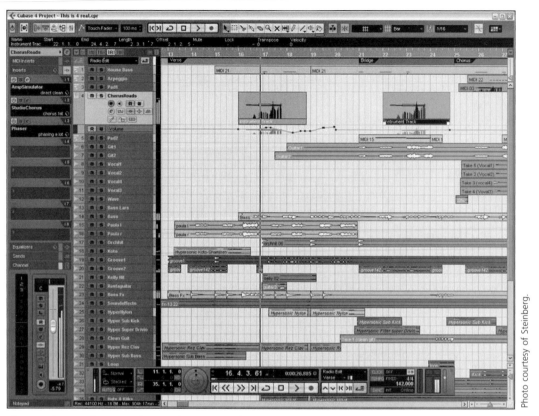

Figure 19.1 Cubase 4 advanced music production system.

at present, in the past most DAWs were card-based systems with processing chips on separate design cards. Pro Tools|HD systems are card-based, whereas the Pro Tools LE, Digital Performer, Nuendo, and Tracktion systems are all native-based programs (see Figure 19.2).

The debate can and will rage over card-based versus native for audio quality. The processor that is dedicated to running the audio engine can be more efficiently built and may handle data better, but ultimately it is the code that crunches the numbers and creates your audio. As processors and processing power have grown more available to the end user, the DAW has migrated from dedicated card systems to native-based systems running the digital audio engines.

The bigger and more significant debate seems to be in terms of the size of processing digital word length, with options such as 48-bit fixed, 32-bit floating point, 64-bit fixed, or 96 gazillion–bit floating point. There are differences, and each has its champions, but that is a very long story for a different book—one all about digital audio. For the most

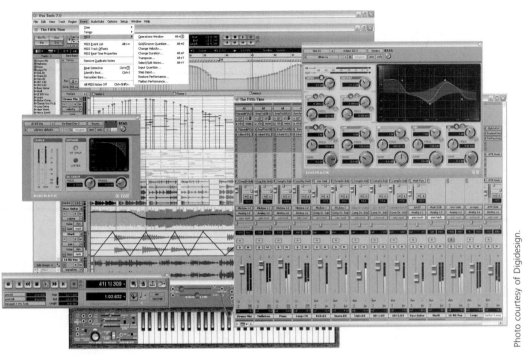

Figure 19.2 Pro Tools LE 7.

part, the salient question is, does the software do what *you* want it to do? Does it run the plug-ins you want? Above all, does it sound the way you want it to? See Figure 19.3.

For tracking, the program you use really doesn't make that much difference as long as it can take the digital stream and write it reliably to the hard disk in the format, bit depth, and sample rate that you want for your mix. Bit depth and sample rate are not small issues, because they determine the fundamentals of your recording—the frequency response, dynamic range, and resolution. Digital bit depth determines the length of the digital word and therefore the overall dynamic range of your recording and in how many steps the dynamic range is stored. A 16-bit recording can have a theoretical dynamic range of 96 dB, while a 24-bit recording can have a theoretical dynamic range of 144 dB. Real-world converters are limited by the current technology of analog-to-digital converters to about 115 dB. The real difference between a 24-bit stream and a 16-bit stream in the audio realm is the resolution. A 16-bit file contains 65,536 possible levels, or "boxes of sound to fill," on every sample. A 24-bit file or stream contains 16,777,216 boxes to fill with audio.

Sample rate controls the number of bit samples taken in a given time period and is usually expressed per second. A sample rate of 44.1 kHz means that 44,100 samples are taken each second. The number of samples determines the upper frequency that can be

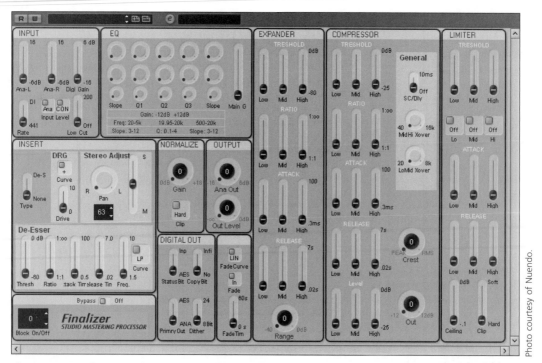

Figure 19.3 The Nuendo Finalizer offers signal processing, including expanding, compressing, limiting, and more.

recorded. In a typical pulse code modulation convertor, the anti-aliasing filter, also known as the Nyquist filter, is set at one half of the sample rate. The Red Book (normal, everyday) compact disc has a sample rate and bit depth of 44.1k samples per second at a bit depth of 16 bits. So it can reproduce frequencies up to 22.05 kHz with a dynamic range of 96 dB and a resolution of 65,536 steps in the 96 dB. Got it?

So what should you record in? That depends. We generally would recommend 24 bits at 88.2 if your hardware can support the number of tracks you require. When in doubt, drop the sample rate first, because you can double the number of tracks. Only reduce the bit depth as a last resort. When you drop the bit rate, you only gain a third of the space back while reducing your dynamic resolution greatly. Above all else, make sure you can record all the tracks you need. The track count always beats the sample rate. You have so little control on location with so many factors to take into account that you need all the help you can get.

When you are choosing a DAW, the studio you work out of is often the ultimate factor. It is easier to mix later if the recorded program's EDL can be opened in the studio in which you want to work; however, it is possible to transfer the recording from one brand of DAW to another when necessary.

Transferring Data

There are many popular ways to transfer a recording from one DAW to another. The most basic and relatively straightforward method is to import all your raw files, one by one, into the DAW in which you would like to work. This can be quite time-consuming and troublesome if you have not recorded the original tracks in a file type that contains original time stamps, such as a Broadcast Wave file. This is why BWAV is the preferred method of recording—because of all the data it carries. Another advantage to BWAV is its almost universal compatibility on all DAWs. The biggest obstacle is getting all of your tracks to line up, but that's about the only major potential problem, and the time stamp information in the BWAV makes that a breeze. Of course, if you want to transfer edits, cross-fades, and such, you will have to look to a more sophisticated format interchange protocol.

OMF (*Open Media Framework*) and AAF (*Advanced Authoring Format*) are both file format exchange protocols, allowing sessions to be opened on other DAWs. For example, if you track or record a concert on Nuendo, and you need to mix it at a studio equipped with a Pro Tools|HD rig with the additional Digi-Translator plug-in, you would need to export the Nuendo Edit Decision List to an exchange format that Pro Tools (outfitted with the Digi-Translator) can understand and open, such as OMF or AAF (see Figure 19.4).

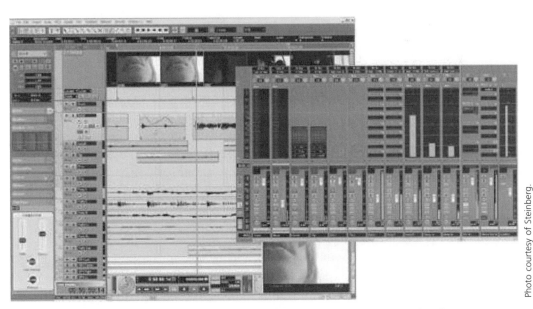

Photo courtesy of Steinberg.

Figure 19.4 A Nuendo 3 media production system by Steinberg Media Technologies.

Both OMF and AAF allow for easy exchange of basic file EDL data. Remember, though, that they will not transfer plug-ins or built-in EQ. If you need to take your effects with you, remember to embed, render, bounce, or do whatever your brand of DAW calls processing the track of audio with your settings and plug-ins. Then render a new track. That is the only easy way to take work on tracks from one station to another. Remember that you cannot adjust the plug-in after it is a rendered track, because it is not a process on an audio track any longer.

Impulse Response (IR) Reverbs

One of the more useful developments in digital audio, particularly for location recording, is the affordability of the convolution-based reverb. These are more commonly known as *impulse response reverbs*. There are currently many versions on the market, ranging from the free, open-source SIR to the very flexible IR-1 by Waves. All of these reverb units allow for an accurate re-creation of an actual space's reverb. Sort of—as much as can be hoped for, anyway.

In the past, digital reverbs used basic algorithms to simulate spaces; by applying that algorithm to the audio signal, they modified the signal to simulate it in a chosen space. These algorithms are generally broken down into standard response patterns, such as plate, hall, coffin, doghouse, and so on. The algorithms can be adjusted to modify size, early reflections, and the like, and they are successful at achieving a similarity to the space intended. Some quite good sounds can come from the "box." But as every ADR engineer can attest, you can get really close with these algorithms, but you can never get the exact sound you seek. Until now—at least in theory.

Unlike the algorithm-based model, the impulse response reverb takes a sample of an impulse that is created in the space and then uses a convolution operation to create a reverberation algorithm based on the impulse. This allows you to re-create the reverb of a real space far more closely. Another great thing about these software packages is that they allow for user creation—in other words, you can sample or impulse any space you need. If you love the sound of a particular concert hall or club, you can sample it and bring it along to remix tracks recorded in any other space that may lack good ambience.

How to Capture Impulses

Most convolution reverbs have suggestions for collecting impulses; however, the basics are always the same. As much as possible, an impulse should be a loud, instantaneous bang of equal power on all frequencies. It might sound complex, but it really isn't. You need a loud snap or crack. Typically, a starter pistol is recommended because it has a loud bang on most frequencies that can activate the room. However, we found that most security personnel get testy if they are not informed of the impulse capture or they discover that you have brought your favorite starter pistol into the building. They tend not to understand that it is a valuable tool for capturing the beauty of the reverberation of the space they are guarding—they see it as a gun!

Even if you are not planning to take your impulse response with a starter pistol or other explosive, it is wise to contact the personnel in charge of security and inform them that you will be making a loud, sharp noise on stage that will sound like a gunshot. Not telling them could potentially lead to a lot of sirens, whistles, and police shouting, which raises the ambient noise floor of the recording to a point that often makes it unusable (see Figure 19.5).

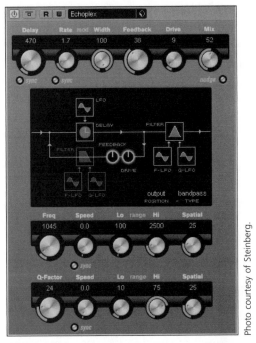

Photo courtesy of Steinberg.

Figure 19.5   An Echoplex plug-in, signal processing in Cubase.

Although starter pistols can attract unwanted attention, scare people, and often jam, they are relatively easy to use and they *do* create a fantastic impulse. Remember, if you do use a starter pistol, *wear ear protection*. That being said, in this day and age, many halls will not allow them in their spaces. Alternatives can be anything that makes a loud bang. You need something that will activate many frequencies as evenly as possible. We have found that a 12" or bigger balloon fully inflated is a good substitute. You will notice that attempting to get the balloon to pop the same way twice is quite difficult. You will want to pop a few balloons and pick the best, fullest-sounding one.

Remember that a loud bang will generate a tremendous peak, so watch for—or, more aptly, listen for—distortion. The transient can be so quick that a clip might not register on your recorder. We suggest that the digital PPM meter does not peak beyond about –6 dB to a maximum of –3 dB. This will ensure that the transient is not clipped and will help lower the chance of distortion. In other words, bring a lot of balloons.

Use the Best Microphone Here, Too!

To do the best possible capture of the impulse response, you will need to set up the best stereo full-range, natural-sounding microphone set you can get your hands on, preferably one that has a flat frequency response from 20 Hz to at least 20 kHz. You are attempting to capture the sound of the reverberation of a space, so you need to capture the basic sound of the space. Have your assistant stand onstage, preferably in the area from which most of the sound will emanate, and clap. Then walk around the hall listening to the reflections or reverb. When you find the sweet spot, set up your stereo pair there. More often than not, this sweet spot will be somewhere near the center of the room, but this is not always the case.

Next, make sure the room is as quiet as it can be. Shut off all HVAC systems or anything else that can make background noise. Because the convolution algorithm will make use of the impulse recording to model the reverb on, you want the recording to be of just the impulse and its decay tail as far down in dB SPL as possible. This means that you need to lower the ambient dB SPL as much as you can. A lot of samples have a wildly strong low-end reflection around the frequency of the HVAC system in the space in which it was recorded.

We often capture multiple positions so we can re-create different listening positions in our mix. Make sure to take notes on where each impulse is created and all the details of the microphones that were used while recording it. You should take notes regarding the microphone type, the technique used, and the location(s) of the stand(s). We have found that the best convolution-capturing microphone techniques tend to be those that mix well to mono, such as an XY, ORTF, or NOS pair. Spaced omnis do a great job for stereo work but can create phase issues when used to capture reverb for a mono or mono-compatible process.

Another way to create a convolution for the impulse response reverbs is to use a frequency sweep generator and a fantastically expensive, completely flat speaker. The speaker needs to be able to reproduce all frequencies of the sweep at even power throughout the sweep. The sweep is run and recorded in the same way as the impulse, then fed into the convolution reverb's sweep response algorithm. Although this often produces the best capture of the space, it is more difficult to do because it requires so much equipment and a more complicated setup. On the other hand, this method is quite well suited for taking IR samples from your favorite outboard gear, such as an EMT 140 plate or a delicious old Fender Twin Spring Reverb.

With the impulse response reverb, you truly *can* take it with you. So the mix is done, as are our eggs and our Bloody Marys. Yet we still have one or two more crucial questions to answer. Will we master our mix or not? What about pressing and encoding? Any other final touches we should consider? Read on ...

20 The Final Frontier

Yuo've recorded it, you've mixed it. If you are lucky, you hand it off to the client, they love it, you collect a large paycheck, and you head to Nimmo Bay for some extreme fishing. More likely, you hand the final mix to the client and are greeted by, "So, what's the next step?" Put the waders and the suitcase back in the closet. There is still more work to do.

Ultimately, the client wants to get the product to someone—an end user or consumer. The question is, how do you get your mix there, and in what format? These are questions that a mastering engineer will ask. But you ask, "Do I need to send this to a mastering engineer?" Technically, no. There is no law or mythos that requires you to send the recording to a shaman of audio or a voodoo king known as a mastering engineer. But it might be helpful. Maybe you need to know a little bit about what mastering is.

Why Master?

Mastering originated with the record. The mastering legends of old had to match head alignments, balance EQ for vinyl cutting, and make sure the sound was still outstanding. Vinyl had specific sonic requirements, such as the RIAA EQ curve, that were set up to ensure the playability of the record. A few super-loud, very percussive hits, and your needle could go flying. Too much high-frequency information, and the wiggling of the needle would prevent it from tracking properly (see Figure 20.1).

The mastering engineer's job now entails getting your final master into the format the end user is requesting—an MP3, a CD, or even a surround sound DVD or SACD. These are the areas the mastering engineer works in, aligning and quantizing PQ codes on CDs and choosing the right codecs to crush your audio data down to an MP3.

Although the tools have changed, the skill, ears, and artistry of old are still required to create a fantastic recording. Mastering is all about the final artistic vision that unifies and creates the overall sound of an album. Through the proper use of compression, limiting, EQ, and other very simple processes, the sound of the album as a whole is unified (see Figure 20.2).

Figure 20.1 Vinyl had some specific criteria that required mastering.

Figure 20.2 Another look at Nuendo Finalizer, a mastering program that offers signal processing, including expanding, compressing, limiting, and more.

It is sometimes worth the money just to have a fresh set of ears listen to the overall project and tell you that yes, Virginia, that bass is way too loud, and the banjo is too far in front of the ukulele and the didgeridoo, or the accordion isn't popping because it's being masked by the bagpipe. It often is easier for a fresh set of ears to hear the sonic difference from one track to another and apply correction to the 40 hours of work you have done.

Individual tracks should be listened to carefully for sonic errors, imbalances, and frequencies that are out of place. A mastering engineer can do this without the baggage you may have accumulated during recording, reevaluating the mix and the process, and he can really dissect each track. This can unify the whole album. In a format such as CD or LP—anything that is intended to be listened to as a whole—aspects of both how the tracks sound individually and how they come together as an album are important.

After the individual tracks are reviewed and adjusted, sequencing and layout follow. Close attention is paid to the negative space between the tracks. The in and outs of the tracks can leave almost as big an impression on the audience as the track itself can. An abrupt fade out can be as obtrusive as a drop out in the middle of a track. In a location setting, this can be devastating to the feeling of being there.

When the client is happy with the layout and sound of the project, the next step is preparation for duplication if the end result will be a CD. If you are releasing your recording for download only, then you can jump to distribution.

Duplication

You or your mastering engineer gets everything set and ready to go, you listen to and love the edit proof (a CD of the final copy), and the client is ecstatic. It is time to find a duplication company. What do you send them? The CD-R edit proof? Maybe. At the duplication house, a *glass master* is created, from which your pressed CDs are made. Are you comfortable with the fact that a master can be made from your 41-cent CD-R (see Figure 20.3)?

Thousands of copies of your work will be pressed from this disc. It is critical that your data be pristine at this point. Error correction in CD-Rs has come a long way in the last 10 years, and they can produce some great-sounding recordings, but can you trust them completely?

The unknown with CD-Rs in today's industry is the type of error correction the pressing plant or CD broker will use in the creation of your CD's glass master. The Red Book CD format does not have a built-in error-checking protocol. Thus, a master will be an exact duplicate of the CD-R that was sent, bad bits and all. A professional mastering engineer can create a DDP (*disc description protocol*) master, which allows the engineer to error-check the data that will be stamped to the glass master before it is sent to the plant. The

Figure 20.3 Do you trust me? I cost a dime and claim to hold your mixes, your days and days of work. Really baby, you can trust me.

DDP has an error-checking protocol, as does the DATA CD or DVD, making them preferred protocols.

Web Distribution

If you are creating a file just for download, the process is somewhat simpler. Just find out what type of file is required by the online store, encode it, and send it to them. Here is the potential rub: Each store, each website, will have its own preferred protocols and formats. Often it is easier to just hire a company such as IODA (*Independent Online Distribution Alliance*) to handle the distribution. Like any distribution company, they are in business of making money, so costs are involved. However, the requirements for delivery are streamlined (a CD or CD-R), and they will distribute to many different digital outlets on your behalf with a minimum of work on your part.

Mechanicals

So you have your product, you've shipped it off to be dubbed or downloaded, you've collected that fat paycheck and fired up the helicopter, ready to make your getaway... but wait, there's still more. Has everyone else been paid? I don't mean did the producer or client pay everyone who worked the gig, but rather have all of the mechanical licenses been obtained? Although this is not typically the responsibly of the engineer, your help to your client might keep them out of jail long enough to do another project. Also, when the subpoenas start flying, one could get thrown in your direction. Unless you are recording music or other content that is either in the public domain or a completely original work, someone will want his fair share.

Most pressing houses will ask whether you have secured the rights for duplication. To get these rights, you need to contact the music publisher. If your client is a band that specializes in cover tunes or a jazz combo doing standards, the composer still needs to get paid. The artist needs to contact all of the publishers of all of the songs on your record and negotiate the amount owed. Typically, this is based on the number of CDs being pressed. There is a theory, hopefully valid, that you might actually sell all of them.

Online rights are much stickier at the moment. There isn't any consensus on what someone should charge. Costs and use fees are varied, and things are a bit murky, as they always are with new technology. MTV started in 1981, and it took them 25 years to figure out how to pay royalties for music videos. At the moment it looks like mechanicals are owed after the point of sale, or when someone actually downloads and pays for the track, if the product downloaded is expected to have less than 2,500 downloads per day. It is the artist's responsibility to send a report and a check to the publishers. As in all situations where things are confusing, a company has been formed that can help you through the minefield. Originally formed to collect royalties for sheet music, then for synchronization rights, the Harry Fox Agency, or HFA, is a great place to start looking for those hard-to-find copyright holders (see Figure 20.4).

As with everything in life, there is a cost for the all-in-one convenience that HFA offers. To get the best deal, it might be worth the search time and negotiation, especially if you have a little downtime between gigs. Otherwise, spend the money and go with the easy route of HFA.

So that's about it. You now know enough to make a quality recording. Remember that you can never know it all; there is always more to learn. We hope this book helps you in your location recording projects, but just so you know, even the most experienced among us learn new things every day. It is important to keep yourself open to new ideas and new methods, and to always strive to improve your craft.

Now, listen to what your mother tells you. We should have.

hfa. The Harry Fox Agency, Inc., 601 West 26th Street, 5th Floor, New York, NY 10001

Mechanical License Request
(First Time Licensees Need to Complete New Account Form)

Anticipated Quantity of Units ___ Over 2500 ___ 2500 or Under
Failure to check one will delay processing

HFA USE ONLY

TRX#_____

Record Company/Licensee Name

Date ___/___/___

Address

Contact Name   **Fax**

City   **State**   **Zip**   **Telephone**

Title (One Per Form):   **Writers:**

Publisher(s) *(one per line)*	Percentage
	%
	%
	%
	%
	%

For Manufactures of Over 2500 Units

Song #

M				

Catalog Number-Album

CD_____ Cass_____ Midi_____ LP_____ Digital Comp Cass_____

Minidisk_____ MiniCass_____ DAT_____

Catalog Number-Single

CD single_____ Cassingle_____ Minidisk_____ 12" Single_____ Midi_____

DAT_____ MaxiCass_____ MiniCass_____ 17" Single_____

Rate: Statutory ___ Other _____   **Label:** _____

Playing Time   **Release Date** ___/___/___   **UPC**

Artist   **ISRC**

Album Title

Explanation

Publishers Approval _____

****PLEASE BE SURE TO COMPLETE ALL APPLICABLE FIELDS****

Figure 20.4 The Harry Fox Agency Mechanical License Request.

Appendix A: Popular Microphones and Their Placement

Figure A.1 You can get a beautiful sound on a flute with a Neumann TLM 170, a large-diaphragm condenser microphone (left), or a Red Bottle Type A with an R6 capsule (right).

Figure A.2 Another very popular choice for flute would be the small-diaphragm condenser Neumann KM 140 (left), and an interesting sound can be obtained with a large-diaphragm condenser like the Heil PR 40.

Figure A.3 An extremely accurate microphone, the Bruel & Kjaer (DPA) 4007 condenser microphone (left) may pick up too much for some, while the large-diaphragm dynamic Heil PR 30 (right) has a nice round tone.

Figure A.4 The small-diaphragm AKG 451 (left) is a popular choice, as is the extremely accurate Earthworks SR77 (right).

Figure A.5 Moving on to the piano, a pair of Neumann TLM 193s, large-diaphragm condenser microphones, can really bring out the rich tones of the instrument, although we do not always have the opportunity to record pianos at full stick, as this one is pictured.

Figure A.6 Another excellent choice to bring out the character of the piano is a pair of Schoeps CMC6s with the MK 4 capsules.

Figure A.7 Here is a pair of Neumann KM 140 small-diaphragm condenser microphones in a piano.

Figure A.8 A classic choice for the piano is a pair of Sanken CU-44X condenser microphones.

Figure A.9 The Red Bottle Type A with an R4 capsule is another good choice in a piano. Red microphones are made by Blue microphones, if only to ensure your confusion.

Figure A.10 In the category of "don't try this at home," these Bruel & Kjaer (DPA) 4006 condenser microphones would sound very clean on a piano if they were placed correctly, instead of pointing at the hammers.

Figure A.11 At the top of the "you can't go wrong with this choice" category, a Neumann U 87 is a top choice for a trombone or pretty much any brass instrument. Beware of placing condenser microphones like the U 87 too close to the instrument—brass has high SPL output that can damage a condenser microphone if placed too close.

Figure A.12   This Sanken CU-44X condenser microphone sounds as good as it looks.

Figure A.13   A Shure SM7 dynamic microphone might seem like an odd choice, but it has a nice, full sound on brass.

Figure A.14   Many consider a Beyer M88 dynamic microphone as their last choice, while others love its round tone.

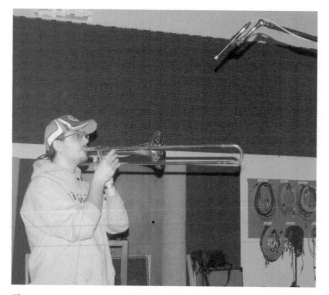

Figure A.15 Another fine choice among the condenser microphones is the Bruel & Kjaer (DPA) 4006.

Figure A.16 Although relatively new to the market, many engineers love the rich tones of the Heil PR 40 on a bass.

Figure A.17 A popular technique when recording double bass begins with a small-diaphragm condenser microphone like this Neumann KM 130, wrapped in foam and inserted up the bridge. Always ask the bass player before you insert a microphone up his bridge. Also, because this KM 130 is an omnidirectional microphone it doesn't matter, but be aware that if you are using a directional microphone and you cover the side ports with foam, you are changing the directionality and character of the microphone.

Figure A.18 Another small condenser that sounds excellent up the bridge of the bass is the Schoeps CMC6 with the MK-2 capsule.

Figure A.19 The Earthworks SR-77 is designed to pick up sound the same way the ear does, and it is an excellent choice on bass.

Figure A.20 The highly accurate Bruel & Kjaer (DPA) 4006 will accentuate the higher tones of the bass while reducing the woofy bottom tones.

Figure A.21 Some recordists like the depth of the EV PL20 on bass, or its sister microphones, the RE20 and PL27.

Figure A.22 Most of us drool when we see a classic like this Neumann M 147.

Figure A.23 Another classic, the Apex 460 vacuum condenser microphone.

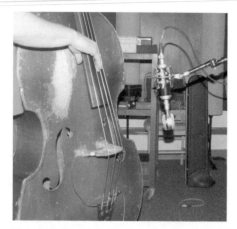

Figure A.24   Just for fun, do what we did. Compare the Red Bottle Type A with the R6 capsule against the...

Figure A.25   ...Red Bottle Type A with the R7 capsule.

Figure A.26   Another classic choice—you know this tune. You can't go wrong with a Neumann U 87, although few recordists end up using it on a bass.

Figure A.27 A more common choice on the bass among Neumanns is the Neumann TLM 170, a large-diaphragm condenser microphone.

Figure A.28 In the interest of trying everything, a Sennheiser 421 would more typically be found on a guitar amp or a high tom, but it might be exactly the sound you are looking for.

Figure A.29 An AKG 451 with CK1 capsule, a small-diaphragm condenser microphone, sounds great on a guitar amp.

Figure A.30   A newer AKG 451 boasts the same characteristics as the classic CK1.

Figure A.31   Time to drool again, a beautifully rebuilt Telefunken U 47 condenser microphone sounds great on everything. This one is truly a classic.

Figure A.32   And this classic Neumann M 147 condenser microphone is nothing to complain about either.

Figure A.33   The Red Bottle Type A with the R7 capsule is another good approach for a guitar amp.

Figure A.34   And you can never go wrong with the old stand-by Neumann U 87.

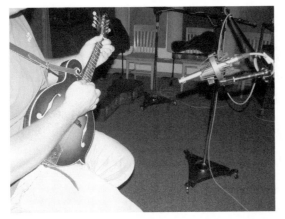

Figure A.35   An AKG 451 is a prime choice for a mandolin.

Figure A.36 Another popular choice for stringed instruments like the mandolin is the small-diaphragm condenser Neumann KM 140.

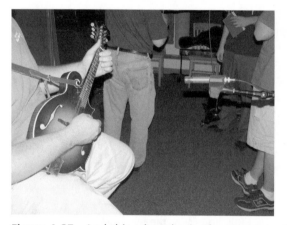

Figure A.37 And this other classic, the Neumann KM 54.

Figure A.38 Getting into the good stuff here, this is a Microtech Geffel UM 92.1 tube microphone on the mandolin.

Figure A.39   A Korby KAT 47 cardioid pressure-gradient microphone gives us an interesting sound on the mandolin.

Figure A.40   Back to the basics, a Neumann U 87 offers a consistent sound on an acoustic guitar.

Figure A.41   I would expect a sweeter, warmer sound from this Neumann M 147 condenser microphone.

Figure A.42   And even sweeter still from this classic Neumann M 49 condenser microphone.

Figure A.43   Another view of the exceptional Neumann M 49.

Figure A.44   More modern but equally yummy, the Neumann M 149 sounds great on a guitar.

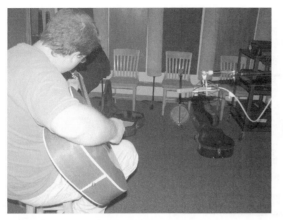

Figure A.45 It may look like the sound would be a bit thinner than some others, but the Schoeps CMC6 with the MK-4 capsule has a big sound on a guitar.

Figure A.46 Some people just love the sound of the AKG C24 stereo vacuum tube microphone.

Figure A.47 Once again, the Red Bottle Type A with the R6 capsule, a solid sound on a guitar.

Figure A.48   The Microtech Geffel UM 92.1 tube microphone that sounded great on the mandolin sounds great here, too. No surprise there.

Figure A.49   This Microtech Geffel UM 70 sounds amazing on a guitar.

Figure A.50   Another view of the Microtech Geffel UM 70.

Appendix B: Glossary

5.1 surround sound. Standard five-channel surround sound setup that is typical for most HD TV and DVD soundtracks.

absorption coefficient. A ratio that compares the amount of energy that is absorbed to the amount of energy that is reflected by a given surface.

ADSR. Attack, decay, sustain, release—the components of the envelope, or duration of a sound event.

amplitude. The quantitative size of a sound wave, which affects the perception of loudness.

antinodes. Fixed high-pressure locations within an enclosure or room that, along with nodes, form a stationary waveform called a *standing wave*.

attack. How a sound event begins; a component of envelope, or duration.

audible bandwidth. The range of the frequency spectrum that humans can hear, approximately 20 Hz to 20 kHz.

auto panner. A signal-processing device that varies the output signal between the left and right sides of the stereo bus.

aux sends. *See* auxiliary sends.

aux send master. A master trim that controls the overall level output by the summing network of a specific auxiliary send.

auxiliary sends. Additional feeds from each module that allow for simultaneous multiple mixes. Commonly referred to as *aux sends* or simply *sends*, they are commonly used for monitor or cue mixes and effects sends.

bandpass filter. A signal processor that eliminates all frequency components of a sound above and below selected frequencies.

bias head. The first head in the tape path, the bias head, or erase head; erases tape by returning magnetic fields to a neutral or random position. This also places the molecules in an excited state, providing superior signal-to-noise ratio when recording.

bidirectional. A polar pattern for microphones in which they are most sensitive directly in front of and behind a microphone and least sensitive to the sides.

binaural hearing. Hearing through two ears, which allows us to perceive and localize sounds by hearing in three dimensions. Binaural hearing has three components—interaural intensity, interaural arrival time, and physiology.

bit depth. The number of bits described or recorded for each sample.

bookshelf speakers. Monitors used in the studio that mimic common household speakers; used by engineers while mixing to ensure that their mix will be effective in the consumer market.

boundary microphones. Flat, metal-plate microphones are usually attached to stiff sound-reflecting surfaces, such as walls, floors, or desktops. Also known as *floor mics* or *pressure-zone microphones,* they are commonly used in theatre or for ambient sound gathering.

bus. A send of any type that contains a summing network on a console. The most common types are the multitrack buses, aux sends, and the stereo bus.

bus faders. A master trim that controls the overall output of a specific bus.

busing. The process of sending a signal into a bus; usually associated with multi-track busing.

cannon plug. *See* XLR.

capacitance. The ability of a condenser to store a charge and release it at predetermined intervals. This is the electronic theory behind condenser microphones.

capstan. The capstan, along with the pinch roller, initiates and maintains the motion of the tape transport during play and record functions, controlling the tape speed.

capstan motor. The motor that controls the capstan and therefore the tape speed.

carbon microphones. The oldest of microphones, carbon microphones were used in telephones.

cardioid. A heart-shaped polar pattern for microphones that is most sensitive at the front, least sensitive in the rear, and gradually less sensitive down the sides as one moves toward the rear.

channel assignment switching matrix. A combination of push buttons and pan pots that determines where a signal in the channel fader will be routed, usually onto a track of the multitrack recorder or into the stereo bus. Also known as *multitrack buses*.

channel faders. A separate gain control for each I/O module of the console that commonly leads to the multitrack recorder, the stereo bus, or the speakers in the theatre.

chorusing. A combination of pitch shifting and short delays used to make an individual voice or other input signal sound doubled, as if more than one instrument is present.

clip-on microphones. Microphones typically used where an invisible microphone is needed. Also known as *lavalieres;* applications include television newscasters and body microphones on theatrical performers.

clipping. *See* distortion.

close-miking. When a microphone is placed close to a sound source, the acoustic phenomena caused by the surrounding environment have little or no effect on the signal captured. Close-miked signals lack the natural ambience of an environment, and as a result they can sound unnatural and one-dimensional. To a great extent, the development of signal-processing equipment is a result of close-miking technique and multitrack recording—something of an effort to re-create an environment.

complex wave. A wave containing harmonics and overtones, which can be viewed through Fourier analysis as a combination of sine waves.

compression. When molecules move toward each other within a medium after the force of a sound event has momentarily displaced them.

compressor. A device that decreases the dynamic range of program material.

condenser microphones. Microphones that work on the principle of variable capacitance; generally accepted as the highest quality and most expensive microphone type.

console. The heart of the control room, the device through which all signals pass and are routed.

constructive interference. Constructive interference occurs when two sound waves combine and the result, referred to as the *sum wave,* is an increase in amplitude of the sound waves.

contact microphone. A small, clip-on microphone, somewhere in design between a lavaliere and a guitar pickup.

control room. The heart of the production facility. Along with housing the console, tape recorders, signal-processing gear, and monitor system, it is the location where signal routing is determined.

cross talk. Information from a track playing back on an adjacent head.

crossover frequency. The dividing point between frequency bands, determined by the frequency dividing network, or crossover, in a speaker.

crossovers. A frequency dividing network, directing frequencies to specific speakers within a monitor.

cue mix. A mix used by musicians to monitor themselves, other musicians, and/or sounds already on tape; often a separate mix.

cue sheet. In recording, a running list of the beginning and end of each take, or attempt to record a piece, including spaces for start and end times, title, take number, code (such as CT for complete take, FS for false start, or PB for playback), and comments. In theatre, a numbered list of all cues used in a production.

cycle. One oscillation of a waveform, comprised of one complete compression and one complete rarefaction. One cycle per second equals one Hertz.

DAW. Digital audio workstation. A device used to record playback and manipulate audio in the digital realm.

de-esser. A combination effect made up of an equalizer and a compressor.

decay. The decrease in volume of a sound after the stimulus has been removed; a component of envelope.

decibel. A ratio describing the difference between one power and another or one sound pressure level and another.

delay. A single, discrete reflection of a sound; the ear's first clue about the size and shape of a room.

destructive interference. Occurs when two sound waves combine and the result is a decrease in the amplitude of the sound wave.

DI. *See* direct box.

diaphragm. A thin, flexible membrane under tension in microphones, similar to a drum skin or the paper in a kazoo, which vibrates in response to the changes in atmospheric pressure caused by the compression and rarefaction of molecules of a sound wave.

diffraction. The property of low-frequency sound waves that allows them to bend around corners more readily than high frequencies.

diffusion. The spreading out of a sound. Due to the physical properties of lower frequencies having larger wavelengths, low frequencies diffuse, while high frequencies are directional.

digital-to-analog conversion. The process of converting a signal from digital to analog.

direct box. A step-down transformer used to change line-level, high-impedance signals to mic-level, low-impedance signals.

directionality. *See* polar patterns.

distortion. The equivalent in equipment of the threshold of pain in humans; unpleasant or unwanted sound caused by excessive amplitude.

dropouts. In editing, when the level literally drops out momentarily at the edit point. In tape, when the magnetic particles held into place by the binder fall or drop off of the tape, which leaves an area that cannot hold any audio information.

dub. (n.) A tape copy. (v.) To make a tape copy.

dump mode. A method used in editing to eliminate large sections of tape.

duration. Or envelope. The volume shape of a sound over time, or the lengths of time of the components of any sound; how much time passes as the sound begins, continues, and ends.

dynamic microphones. Microphones that work on the principle of inductance, in which electric current is created, or induced, by a wire or any conductor as it senses movement within a magnetic field. There are two types of dynamic microphones: moving-coil and ribbon.

dynamic range. The span of volume that the human ear can perceive, ranging from the threshold of hearing—the softest sound the ear can hear or the minimum energy required for the average person to experience the sensation of sound—to the threshold of pain—the point at which sound intensity causes pain in the average listener.

early reflection. The first few reflections to arrive at the listener's ears just after the direct sound, which can often be discerned as discrete from the reverberation.

echo. A discrete individual reflection, indicating a large space.

edit mode. *See* dump mode.

editing. The removal of unwanted noise and reordering of recorded material.

effect loop. Used when a signal needs to be split into a processed and unprocessed signal. The processor is inserted at the end of an auxiliary send, allowing signals from any I/O module to be processed. The output of the processor is recombined with the dry signal at the master fader by using either an effects return or an available line input.

envelope. Or duration. The volume shape of a sound over time, or the lengths of time of the components of any sound; how much time passes as the sound begins, continues, and ends.

equalization. Frequency-selective amplification.

erase head. *See* bias head.

expander. An amplifier whose output level decreases by a preprogrammed amount when an input signal falls below a user-defined threshold.

expansion ratio. In an expander or noise gate, a comparison between the input and output signals once the input signal falls below the threshold.

external triggering. Dropping the level of a track being modified in an expander or gate when the keying or triggering signal is not occurring.

fader. A sliding control over a potentiometer or voltage-controlled amplifier; commonly found in audio consoles.

FFT. Fast Fourier transform

flanger. A signal-processing device that splits an input signal and then recombines it with a dynamically changing phase relationship, causing a sweeping sound.

floor microphones. *See* boundary microphones.

FOH (front of house). The engineer who executes the mix for the audience.

Fourier analysis. A graph that plots amplitude versus frequency of the component frequencies. Fourier analysis is a concept in which complex waveforms are viewed as a combination of many sine waves.

frequencies. The measurement of the speed at which a periodic or repeating waveform oscillates. Responsible for the pitch of a sound.

frequency dividing network. *See* crossovers.

frequency-selective amplifiers. *See* equalizers.

full normal. Connected to the input side of a patch bay, full normals disconnect the bridging wire when a patch cord is inserted. This is necessary because input signals cannot be combined without a summing network.

full track. A mono tape format in which the entire tape is used as one track.

fundamental frequency. The frequency within a complex wave that is most responsible for the sound's pitch. Usually the lowest and loudest frequency in a complex waveform.

glitch. A pop or an electronic jolt. In razorblade editing, usually the result of a blade containing a magnetic charge, or an old blade that results in a jagged cut.

graphic equalizer. A processor that changes the harmonic content of a sound, giving a graphic representation of the change.

guard band. The space between tracks and on the edges of magnetic tape. Reduces crosstalk and edge damage.

half normal. The patch point for the output side of equipment, allows the signal to flow through the bridging wire regardless of whether a patch cord is inserted.

half track. *See* two track.

harmonic content. Whole-number multiples of a fundamental frequency. The timbre of a sound is a direct result of its harmonic content.

harmonics. Simple waves of varying frequencies and amplitudes, each representing one component of a complex waveform.

harmonizer. Extreme pitch shifters that are also used where pitch shifting will create a very unusual and mechanical sound.

head lifters. A component of tape machines that engages during fast wind, moving the tape back off the heads.

Hertz. A measure of frequency; one Hertz (Hz) equals one cycle per second.

high impedance. A line-level signal, generally between –30 dB and 0 dB.

high-pass filter. A filter that affects only low frequencies, allowing high frequencies to pass unaffected.

hypercardioid. A polar pattern for microphones used to describe the directionality of shotguns.

I/O module. *See* input/output module.

icon. In the language of semiotics, a sign that is exactly what it appears to be.

index. In the language of semiotics, a sign that points to something else.

inductance. The theory by which dynamic microphones work, in which electric current is created, or induced, by a wire or any conductor as it senses movement within a magnetic field.

input mode. A console mode in which microphone pre-amps feed channel faders and line pre-amps feed monitors. Used commonly for recording.

input/output module. A console module capable of handling both input and output signals simultaneously and discretely.

interaural arrival time. Perceiving the location of a sound by the difference in time of arrival at each ear.

interaural intensity. Perceiving the location of a sound by the difference in loudness at arrival at each ear.

isolation. Separating sounds from each other in different rooms or within one room.

keying. Triggering a noise gate or expander to allow signal to pass unaffected.

lavalieres. Clip-on microphones commonly used in theatre and television.

leader tape. White or yellow tape that cannot be recorded upon; used to mark locations within a reel of audio tape.

leveling amplifier. *See* compressor.

limiter. A device that decreases the dynamic range of program material by a greater than 10:1 compression ratio.

line input. A console input designed to accommodate line-level signals.

line level. The typical level of signals from electronic instruments and recorder outputs, −30 dB to 0 dB.

line pre-amps. A passive attenuator designed to boost a line-level signal to the console's standard operating level.

line trim. A potentiometer that controls the level of a line input.

location. One of the five perceptions of sound establishing distance and direction.

longitudinal compression waves. When waves propagate in the same direction as the displacement of the molecules in the medium. Sound waves are always longitudinal compression waves.

loop insertion. When a processor is inserted at the end of an auxiliary send, allowing signals from any I/O module to be processed. The output of the processor is recombined with the dry signal at the master fader by using either an effects return or an available line input.

loudness. One of the five perceptions of sound; the perception of amplitude.

low impedance. A mic-level signal, generally between −65 dB and −30 dB.

low-pass filters. A filter that affects only high frequencies, allowing low frequencies to pass unaffected.

magnetic tape. Commonly used with analog recording devices and sometimes with digital recorders. Stores the audio information converted at the record heads to magnetic information.

masking. One sound blocking another through loudness, pitch, timbre, or location.

master fader. A fader that controls the overall output of the console.

master section. The part of the console that contains the master fader, monitor source selection switch, monitor pot, aux send masters, and aux returns, among other specialized features, depending on the console.

master. A passive attenuator or voltage-controlled amplifier that controls the output of any bus.

medium. A space with molecules in sufficient quantities for sound waves to propagate, such as air or water. One of the three minimum requirements for a sound event.

mic level. The typical level of signals from microphones, −65 dB to −30 dB.

mic pre-amps. An amplifier connected to the mic trim, a passive attenuator, designed to boost a mic-level signal to the console's standard operating level.

mic trim. A potentiometer that controls the output of a mic preamp.

microphone. A transducer that converts acoustic energy to electricity.

mid-range driver. A speaker that is responsible for middle frequencies.

mixing console. A device responsible for the processing and routing of many signals; the center of any production room. The console is the link between all devices in the facility.

monitor. (n.) A speaker or group of speakers in one cabinet. (v.) To listen.

monitor fader. A fader that feeds the monitor bus. Depending on the console's mode, this bus either can feed the stereo bus or can be routed elsewhere.

monitor modes. The various modes of a console, including input, mix, and mixdown/overdub.

monitor pot. A passive attenuator that adjusts the control-room monitor volume.

monitor source selector switch. Part of the console's master section; allows the engineer to select which of the buses or machines will be monitored.

mono. A format requiring only one track.

moving-coil microphones. Microphones, such as dynamic microphones, that work on the principle of inductance.

mult. A patch-bay option that allows one output signal to be sent to many locations.

multitrack. A recording device that allows recording on more than one track, either simultaneously or subsequently.

multitrack buses. Sends used to access individual tracks on a multitrack recorder; also used in mixing as additional aux sends.

nodes. Fixed low-pressure locations within an enclosure, or room, that, along with anti-nodes, form a stationary waveform called a *standing wave*.

noise. Undesirable sound.

noise floor. The ambient noise present in all devices.

noise gate. An amplifier whose output level decreases by a greater than 10:1 expansion ratio when an input signal falls below a user-defined threshold.

non-harmonically related overtones. Overtones that are not whole-number multiples of the fundamental frequency. Non-harmonic overtones are responsible for white noise.

nondirectional. A description of microphones with an omnidirectional polar pattern, equally sensitive in all directions.

normalling. The process of returning all console controls and other equipment to their null points.

normals. *See* full normal.

NOS pair. (Nederlandse Omroep Stichting.) A stereo microphone technique consisting of two cardioid microphones, preferably identical models, pointed at a 90-degree angle to each other and spaced approximately 30 cm apart.

observer. One of the three minimum requirements for a sound event to occur.

octaves. A tonal relationship between sounds with a 2:1 frequency ratio.

omnidirectional. A polar pattern for microphones in which they are equally sensitive in all directions.

ORTF. (Office de Radiodiffusion Télévision Française.) A stereo microphone technique consisting of two cardioid microphones, preferably identical models, pointed at a 110-degree angle to each other and spaced approximately 17 cm apart.

outboard gear. Signal-processing equipment that is not located within the console.

overdub. Adding new tracks to existing tracks on a multitrack recorder.

overtones. Whole-number multiples of a fundamental frequency. The timbre of a sound is a direct result of its overtones, also known as its *harmonic content.*

pan pot. *See* panoramic potentiometer.

panning. The process of placing a sound from left to right in the stereo bus. Also used in multitrack busing to place a sound between two tracks.

panoramic potentiometer. A dual passive attenuator that continuously varies a single signal between two or more output buses. Used when placing a sound from left to right in the stereo bus and when including a signal in two tracks on a multitrack.

parametric equalizers. A frequency-selective amplifier that allows control over the bandwidth of the frequencies.

passive attenuators. Resistors controlled by a potentiometer. When set for maximum level, generally turned all the way to the right, the trim control is adding minimum resistance to a circuit, allowing the maximum signal to pass. When set to the left, the trim control is reducing the level of the signal.

patch bay. Access points that interrupt the normal signal flow through a module and give access to the inputs and outputs of every device in a production facility. A patch bay will provide access to signal flow between normally interconnected devices. The purpose of the patch bay is to allow for the rerouting of the normal signal flow and the insertion of additional devices.

peak meter. Used to monitor the amount of electricity passing through equipment. Specially calibrated volt meters are inserted in the signal flow within the recorder or console. Peak meters are calibrated to respond faster than the human ear does, showing transients.

peaking equalizer. A frequency-selective amplifier featuring a fixed bandwidth.

period. The inverse of frequency, seconds per cycle.

peripheral. The second zone in semiotics, when the senses are aware of a sign but not focused on it.

phantom power. The electrical charge (+48vdc) held by the capacitor within the condenser microphone's diaphragm supplied directly from the audio console. Phantom power has no effect on the audio signal passing through.

phase. The phase relationship between two sound waves is determined by a comparison between the point of compression or rarefaction each waveform is at in its period when they meet.

phase shifters. A signal processor that splits an input signal and then recombines it with a dynamically changing phase relationship, causing a sweeping or swishing sound.

phase-shifting network. Creates a cardioid polar pattern in moving-coil microphones by causing sound waves approaching the microphone from the rear to impact on both sides of the diaphragm. These sound waves will have their phase reversed on either side of the diaphragm and will therefore be greatly reduced in intensity.

pickup pattern. *See* polar pattern.

pinch roller. Initiates and maintains the motion of the tape during play and record functions, controlling the tape speed, along with the capstan. When Play is pressed, the pinch roller presses against the capstan, causing the tape that is in between the capstan and the pinch roller to be pulled along.

pitch. One of the five perceptions of sound; our perception of frequency.

plate reverb. A form of classic analog signal processing where a thin metal sheet is mounted under tension in a box. When signal is fed to the plate, the waves travel through the plate, bouncing back from the sides, simulating the way that the waves bounce through a room. By mounting a pickup on the far end of the plate, the resulting signal will be analogous to the same wave traveling through a room.

playback head. A transducer found in recording devices that converts magnetic information previously stored on tape into electricity.

polar pattern. A map of a microphone's directional sensitivity, graphically depicting the way a microphone will respond depending upon the position of the sound source relative to the microphone's position.

post-fader send. A send into an auxiliary summing network whose level will be unaffected by movement of the corresponding fader.

potentiometer. *See* passive attenuator.

pre-delay. Used in signal processing as an emulation of early reflections.

pre-amp. *See* mic pre-amp *or* line pre-amp.

print through. When audio information passes through the backing of the tape, creating a faint imprint on the next ring.

production room. A space designed to capture, route, process, and store audio information.

pulse waves. Complex waves that are very rich in harmonics, with all harmonics equal in amplitude to the fundamental frequency.

Q control. In parametric equalization, the control that modifies the bandwidth of frequencies affected.

quarter track. A consumer format featuring quarter-inch tape with four tracks, two in each direction.

range. The amount of level reduction, in decibels, that will be applied to the output signal once the input signal falls below the threshold on an expander.

rarefaction. When molecules move away from each other within a medium after the force of a sound event has momentarily displaced them.

record head. A transducer that converts electricity to magnetic energy, to be stored on tape or disc.

redundancy. A feature of I/O modules in consoles where if one module is understood, they can all be understood.

reflections. *See* early reflection.

release. A component of envelope, release is the eventual cessation of a sound.

reverberation. A series of random, indistinguishable reflections, growing denser and diminishing over time.

ribbon microphones. A type of dynamic microphone with a thin, metallic ribbon for a diaphragm.

rocking. A technique used in editing to move the tape back and forth across the heads.

route. To send or bus a signal.

RT-60. Reverb time minus 60, or the time required for reverberation to reduce by 60 dB.

saturation. Excessive level on tape.

sample rate/frequency. The number of samples per unit of time as taken from an analog signal.

sawtooth wave. A complex wave that contains all harmonics at relatively high amplitudes relative to the fundamental frequency.

security guard. Your new best friend.

semiotics. A system of codifying signs received from various media.

send. A bus; a method of routing signal.

send master. A passive attenuator that controls the overall output of a send.

shelving equalizer. A frequency-selective amplifier that affects all frequencies above or below a user-selected or preset frequency by an equal amount.

shotgun microphones. Microphones with tight polar patterns, commonly used in theatre, film, sporting events, and surveillance.

signal flow. The chosen path for a signal to follow.

signal processing. Effecting a signal.

signal-to-noise ratio. The relationship between desirable signal and undesirable signal.

sine wave. A simple wave or pure tone, devoid of harmonics.

slope. A choice between a linear or exponential (logarithmic) rate applied in an expander; a choice between expansion proceeding at a constant or accelerating pace.

speed of sound. The speed of sound is 343 m/s (1,235 km/h or 770 mph or 1,129 ft/s).

speaker. A transducer that converts electricity to acoustic energy.

SPL. Sound pressure level.

splicing. The removal of unwanted noise and reordering of recorded material.

square waves. A complex wave that contains only odd harmonics at high amplitudes in relation to the fundamental frequency.

standing wave. When some of the energy of a sound wave travels back along the same path as the direct energy, which happens between parallel surfaces, it will interfere with the incoming sound wave, causing increases and decreases in amplitude, depending on the phase relationship between the two waves. Frequencies with wavelengths that are whole-number multiples or subdivisions of the distance between the surfaces off which they are reflecting will interfere with each other in such a way as to cause a standing wave.

stereo. A format that requires two tracks, typically bused to a left speaker and a right speaker.

stereo bus. The sends from the console that feed the mix machines and studio monitors.

stereo master. A passive attenuator that controls the output of the stereo bus.

sub-faders. Also known as *bus faders,* they alter the level of a group of faders as they feed the stereo bus, but will not alter the level of a signal routed to a post-fader send.

sub-masters. Along with altering the level of a group of faders as they feed the stereo bus, they will alter the level of a signal routed to a post-fader send.

sub-woofer. A speaker that is responsible for reproducing the lowest frequencies.

subliminal. The third zone of reception in semiotics, in which the audience is cerebrally unaware of a sign that is subconsciously understood.

summing network. Located in every bus, individual signals are reduced by 3 dB, then combined. Because 3 dB represents an approximate halving of the signal, when they are combined, the end result is an output level consistent with the original input levels.

supercardioid. A tight polar pattern; one of the patterns used in shotgun microphones.

sustain. A component of envelope, sustain is the continuation of a sound.

sweetening. *See* overdubbing.

symbol. In semiotics, a symbol is a sign that represents something totally different than what it appears to be.

sync mode. A recorder mode in which some information is being played back while other information is being recorded; both tasks are performed by the record head.

tails out. A method of storing tape that protects the audio information and reduces print through.

take sheet. *See* cue sheet.

tape release form. A form commonly used in studios before a tape will be released. Used for tracking purposes.

tension idler. A multipurpose tape guide that acts as an on/off switch.

threshold. In a compressor or expander, the user-selected level measured in volts or decibels at which a change in level will begin.

threshold of hearing. The softest sound we can hear; the bottom of the dynamic range in humans.

threshold of pain. The loudest sound we can hear without pain; the top of the dynamic range in humans.

timbre. One of the five perceptions of sound, timbre is our perception of harmonic content.

track. A memory location on tape.

track sheet. A way of cataloguing the track locations on which instruments are recorded.

transducer. A device that converts one form of energy to another.

transients. Instantaneous peaks in amplitude.

transverse wave. A wave that propagates perpendicularly to the original displacement.

triangle waves. A complex wave that contains only odd harmonics at very low amplitudes relative to the fundamental frequency.

trim pot. *See* mic trim, line trim.

tweeter. A speaker that is responsible only for reproducing high frequencies.

two mix. *See* stereo bus.

ultracardioid. A tight polar pattern; one of the patterns used in shotgun microphones.

unidirectional. A polar pattern for microphones that are not equally sensitive in all directions.

volume control. *See* monitor pot.

V.U. meter. Used to monitor the amounts of electricity being passed through equipment. Specially calibrated volt meters are inserted in the signal flow within the recorder or console. V.U. meters are calibrated to respond in a similar fashion to the human ear.

wavelength. The physical distance required for one cycle of a sound wave to complete.

white noise. Any and all frequencies occurring randomly.

woofer. The speaker that is responsible for reproducing low frequencies.

work order. Studio paperwork that contains pertinent information, including the names of the client, producer, and artist; the time the session begins and ends; spaces for purchase order numbers and job numbers; setup information for the assistant, including the instrumentation and the types of mics requested by the engineer; along with billing information.

wow. A clearly audible and sudden dip in the frequency of the recorded material, usually the result of tape stretching.

XLR. A three-pin, barrel-shaped connector commonly used for microphones and balanced lines.

X-Y. A stereo microphone technique utilizing two identical cardioid microphones, placing the two microphone capsules as close as possible (coincident) or within 12 inches of each other (near-coincident) and spread at an angle of between 90 and 135 degrees.

Index